Heidegger's Philosophy of Religion

Heidegger's Philosophy of Religion

From God to the Gods

Ben Vedder

DUQUESNE UNIVERSITY PRESS
Pittsburgh, Pennsylvania

Copyright © 2007 Duquesne University Press
All rights reserved

Published in the United States of America by
DUQUESNE UNIVERSITY PRESS
600 Forbes Avenue
Pittsburgh, Pennsylvania 15282

Library of Congress Cataloging-in-Publication Data
Vedder, Ben, 1948–
    Heidegger's philosophy of religion : from God to the gods / Ben Vedder.
        p. cm.
    Includes bibliographical references (p.   ) and index.
    ISBN-13: 978-0-8207-0388-6 (cloth : alk. paper)
    ISBN-10: 0-8207-0388-5 (cloth : alk. paper)
    ISBN-13: 978-0-8207-0389-3 (pbk. : alk. paper)
    ISBN-10: 0-8207-0389-3 (pbk. : alk. paper)
    1. Heidegger, Martin, 1889–1976. 2. Religion. I. Title.
    B3279.H49V39 2006
    210.92—dc22

                                                        2006029023

∞ Printed on acid-free paper.

Contents

List of Abbreviations

Volumes from Heidegger's *Gesamtausgabe* (Collected Works) (Vittorio Klostermann, Frankfurt am Main), are cited in the text. English translations of Heidegger that are cited in the text, as well as a few non-*Gestamtausgabe* editions of his texts that I have used, are listed in the bibliography under "Works by Heidegger."

GA 1   *Frühe Schriften,* ed. Friedrich-Wilhelm von Herrmann (1978).

GA 4   *Erläuterungen zu Hölderlins Dichtung,* ed. Friedrich-Wilhelm von Herrmann (1981).

GA 12   *Unterwegs zur Sprache,* ed. Friedrich-Wilhelm von Herrmann (1985).

GA 13   *Aus der Erfahrung des Denkens,* ed. Hermann Heidegger (1983).

GA 16   *Reden und andere Zeugnisse eines Lebensweges,* ed. Hermann Heidegger (2000).

GA 21   *Logik. Die Frage nach der Wahrheit,* ed. Walter Biemel (1976).

GA 22   *Die Grundbegriffe der antiken Philosophie,* ed. Franz-Karl Blust (1993).

GA 29/30 *Die Grundbegriffe der Metaphysik. Welt — Endlichkeit — Einsamkeit,* ed. Friedrich-Wilhelm von Herrmann (1983).

GA 34   *Vom Wesen der Wahrheit. Zu Platons Höhlengleichnis und Theätet,* ed. Hermann Mörchen (1988).

GA 39   *Hölderlins Hymnen 'Germanien' und 'Der Rhein,'* ed. Susanne Ziegler (1980).

GA 41   *Die Frage nach dem Ding,* ed. Petra Jaeger (1984).

GA 43   *Nietzsche: Der Wille zur Macht als Kunst,* ed. Bernd Heimbüchel (1985).

GA 44   *Nietzsches metaphysische Grundstellung im abendländischen Denken: Die ewige Wiederkehr des Gleichen,* ed. Marion Heinz (1986).

GA 48   *Nietzsche: Der europaïsche Nihilismus,* ed. Petra Jaeger (1986).

GA 50   *Nietzsches Metaphysik,* ed. Petra Jaeger (1990).

GA 52   *Hölderlins Hymne "Andenken,"* ed. Curd Ochwadt (1982).

GA 53   *Hölderlins Hynme "Der Ister,"* ed. Walter Biemel (1982).

GA 56/57 *Zur Bestimmung der Philosophie,* ed. Bern Heimbüchel (1987).

GA 58   *Grundprobleme der Phänomenologie,* ed. Hans-Helmuth Gander (1992).

GA 60   *Phänomenologie des religiösen Lebens,* ed. Claudius Strube (1995).

GA 61   *Phänomenologische Interpretationen zu Aristoteles. Einführung in die phänomenologische Forschung,* ed. Walter Bröcker and Käte Bröcker-Oltmanns (1985).

GA 65   *Beiträge zur Philosophie (vom Ereignis),* ed. Friedrich-Wilhelm von Herrmann (1989).

GA 66   *Besinnung,* ed. Friedrich-Wilhelm von Herrmann (1997).

Introduction

*T*he relation between philosophy and religion has always been problematic. It finds its expression in Plato and Aristotle, on through the syntheses of the Middle Ages, to the rationalistic reductions (religion within the limits of reason alone), further through the concept of religion as representation, and beyond. We find in each epoch more than enough examples of religion in relation to philosophy. The status of religion in contemporary philosophy is a problem more than ever, a problem connected with truth claims. Religion presents itself as the one and only guardian of truth.

The presumption of this book is that in Heidegger's philosophy there is a concept of religion in which truth is a given that moderates religion's principal truth claims. From the beginning of Heidegger's studies and lectures (from 1919 onward), his relationship to religion was a point of contention. Most literature treating this theme approaches it from a purely theological standpoint, either by way of the Christian faith, a general theism, or an atheism.[1] It has not, however, been taken up from the perspective of the concept of religion, more specifically from the perspective of a philosophy of religion.

It is well known that Heidegger's personal relation to religion underwent a series of transformations. Out of the Roman

Catholic monotheistic faith, he developed ultimately into a poetic polytheistic thinker. In Heidegger's late work, a language of divinity — exemplified by terms such as 'a god,' 'the god,' 'the divine,' 'the last god,' and 'the gods' — plays a central role in his philosophy. This general development in his thinking implies a theory of religion and, furthermore, a framework from which he understands religion. Once we trace out this framework, we can also see its salience for formulating an actual philosophy of religion. The philosophy of religion qua philosophy already possesses its own specific framework for understanding religion. When this framework is characterized as ontotheological, then a predetermined, and therefore guiding, conception of religion is operative from the outset. Yet what use is this framework for understanding religion, especially when a thinker attempts to overcome the traditional, i.e., ontotheological, thinking of Western rationality? It is not my intention here either to prove or to test the truth of Heidegger's view of god, the gods, or theology; nor do I wish to discuss his claim that Christian philosophy is impossible. These are questions already treated at length in other texts. Instead, my aim is to unfold Heidegger's implicit thinking on religion from out of his own philosophy: first by working through Heidegger's writings in order to uncover his thinking on religion; second by asking what consequences such thinking has for constructing a philosophy of religion.[2]

Within the scope of this study, I will not take up the question of Heidegger's relation to religion from the perspective of his supposed commitment to one or another religion. Nor will I discuss his personal position with respect to Catholicism or Protestantism.[3] Whether he was a Catholic or a Protestant has no bearing upon this project, for Heidegger the philosopher maintained a personal distance from both standpoints, and this study is limited to his philosophical writing.[4] It is necessary, however, to mark out the different positions he took with respect to Christianity in his work. Late in his life, in a letter written to Karl Jaspers, he states that it was his intention to explicate the religious tradition in which he had been raised.[5] To this end, Heidegger not only approached the Catholic theology of the Middle Ages critically, but also addressed the theology of the Reformation in his interpretation of Nietzsche's proclamation that "God is Dead." He writes in this connection, "At the beginning of the modern age the question was newly raised as to how man, within the totality of what is, i.e., before that ground of everything in being which is itself most in being, (God), (*vor dem seiendsten Grund alles Seienden*) can become certain and remain certain of his own sure continuance, i.e., his salvation. This question of the certainty of salvation is the question of justification, that is, of justice (*iustitia*)."[6]

In deriving philosophical insights related to religion from Heidegger's work, I am myself working in the sphere of a philosophy of religion. However, one tendency of a philosophical understanding of religion is to make religion itself into a part of philosophy. This is particularly apparent where all forms of religion get absorbed into an ontotheological philosophy. In such cases religion is understood from a concept of god, which is, as a philosophical idea, the beginning and the end of philosophical rationality. Hegel's philosophy is perhaps the clearest example of this tendency. When ontotheology is taken up in this way, however, certain possibilities for understanding religion are foreclosed. Heidegger speaks as a philosopher about god and the gods. Yet what is the status of his speaking? It is not, I shall show, a description of religion. Is it a poetry of religion, then? Is it a metaphorization of religion? How is it that, as a philosopher, he can say, "Only a god can save us!"?

It is my view that Heidegger's thinking on religion occupies a tension between the forms of poetic and philosophical speaking. To understand the poetic aspect of Heidegger's language, one must turn to his interpretations of Hölderlin. And to give his philosophical expression its proper context one must refer his "Letter on 'Humanism,'" which locates religion in the neighborhood of the thinking of being. Yet religion maintains its own tension with regard to both sides: if we grasp religion completely from a philosophical point of view we tend to neutralize it; on the other hand, if we conceive it simply as poetic expression, we tend to be philosophically indifferent to it. It will turn out that Heidegger's thinking in this sense is, in the end, theological. His thinking of being tends toward a poetic theology of naming the gods, which is both a praising and an invocation of them. According to Heidegger the thinking of being is a movement no longer in accordance with the thinking of faith, of religion, or of divinity (*Gottheit*). Each of these is heterogeneous in relation to the other. The experience of the thinking of being manifests itself rather as a topological disposition, that is, as an indication of a place characterized by availability. It is a topological disposition for waiting for, though not expecting, the reception of being, as a place for the happening of being. Therefore Heidegger states that he does not know god; he can only describe god's absence. His philosophy is a means for maintaining an openness toward the possible reception of religious gods. But this reception remains always unconfirmed.

The question of transcendence for Heidegger is not an immediate question about god but must be understood from the perspective of temporality. Only from this perspective is it possible to determine the extent to which an understanding of transcendence and being can be grasped the supreme and holy. It is not, then, a question of proving the existence of an ontic god. Rather, it is a question of analyzing the origin of the understanding of being with respect to Dasein's temporal transcendence. Only from the essence of being and transcendence can one comprehend the idea of being as primary. And we should not mistake this for an explication of an absolute Thou, nor as a *bonum*, nor as a value or something eternal. Heidegger states in his early lecture courses that he did not discuss these questions about Christianity because he observed the extent to which dialectic thinking, bound to inauthentic piety, dominated the academy during that period. He was content to undergo facile critiques of atheism by his critics, which, if intended in an ontic sense, were not without justification. Heidegger's response came in the form of a question: is not ontic faith in god itself in the end godless? That is, would not the real metaphysician be more religious than everyday believers, the members of a church, or even the theologians of any given religion?[7]

In Heidegger's case, we do find a persistent concern for piety, yet not directed toward a god either in a theological or in a philosophical sense; it is found only in thinking. This concern runs throughout the entirety of his work. It is this concern that allows Heidegger to write in *Identity and Difference* that "the god-less thinking which must abandon the god of philosophy, god as *causa sui,* is thus perhaps closer to the divine God."[8] From this perspective, we can see how philosophy is for him atheistic in principle.

Christian theology is the point of departure from which Heidegger unfolds his history of origination. As he frees himself from this starting point, one may ask whether his movement away from it is primarily biographically motivated, which Hugo Ott claims.[9] Counter to Ott, historical biography is not my guiding interest, and my methodological procedure thus gives priority to the course of Heidegger's thought. Heidegger himself maintains in *On the Way to Language* in 1959: "Without this theological background I should never have come on the path of thinking. But origin always comes to meet us from the future."[10] Here Heidegger speaks bound to his hermeneutics and therefore to his philosophical insight; it should not be taken to mean that he is furthering his own theological insights. Indeed, in the first chapter I will show the way in which

Heidegger frees himself from the theological roots forming his early education. There I emphasize that in this period his later interest in historicality remains in embryo. For this reason, I've entitled the first section 'pre-historic.'

Once he begins his analysis of temporality in his early lecture courses he devotes his attention in part to Paul and Augustine. It is in this phase that Heidegger formulates a special approach to factical life, which in turn gives him an array of conceptual tools for investigating religion from a philosophical point of view as will be worked out in chapter 2.

In his early period Heidegger not only works out what would later be published as his principal work, *Being and Time,* but also his own particular vision of theology. During his time in Marburg (1923–1927) he was in touch with a number of theologians, most notably with Rudolf Bultmann. This nexus of contact informed his thinking on theology, specifically his task at that time of differentiating between philosophy and an understanding of theology as an explication of faith. In chapter 3 it will turn out that Heidegger describes this relation as a question of mortal enmity.

Heidegger did not limit his interest to explications of faith, but sought also to reveal the structure of metaphysics, especially Aristotle's metaphysics as both ontological and theological. He took Aristotle to be the father of ontotheology, a form of thinking that continues to dominate philosophical thinking up to the present. The specific ambiguities of Heidegger's interpretation of Aristotle I will present in chapter 4.

The idea of ontotheology was intensified in modern philosophy, where the human comes to be seen as the highest entity, the creator not only of reality, but of himself as well. This modern conception neglects, however, the finite and historical characteristics of human life, which Heidegger takes up in his vision of the human as Dasein. In chapter 5 I will contrast these concepts of the human as the highest being and as historical Dasein. History reaches the point where the ontotheological god and the human subject are both declared dead; we discover that gods, too, can die just as humans do. As a result of this declaration, gods are placed inside the realm of the historical as well. And in the end, the death of god means nothing other than the lack of god. In chapter 6 I show how the death of the ontotheological god and the human means an openness for the historicality of gods and Dasein.

In an attempt to think the historicality of Dasein even more radically than in terms of its mortality (as explicated in *Being and Time*), Heidegger unfolds the idea of a last, passing god. This idea reflects Heidegger's use of theological language as a means for bringing to light the essential characteristics of the historicality of the event of being. In chapter 7 I interpret the notion of the last god as a 'concept' with which Heidegger emphasizes the historicality of the event of being.

In his rejection of subjectivism and in searching for an idea of being as historical event, Heidegger seeks a new status for the human as Dasein. This new attempt leads to the question of what the consequences of a subjectivist approach to theology and the appreciation of religion actually are. In chapter 8 I will point out that an understanding of religion from a subjective point of view may seem modern but is just an intensification of the ontotheological approach.

In order to get a nonsubjective approach to religion, Heidegger introduces the notion of the holy. Heidegger marks out a proximity to the holy and to the historical event of being precisely where he refuses to employ an anthropological approach to religion. It is not the human who constitutes the holy; the holy is given by the poets in order to create a place for humans and gods to encounter one another. But is there such a thing as a phenomenology of the holy? I work out this question in chapter 9.

The historicality of being and the historical ground on which humanity poetically dwells implies a new meaning for the word 'theology.' Theology, as Heidegger understands it, is the poetic praising of the gods by which the poet creates a place for both humanity and gods. The poet is the one who acts not by his own power but rather is the one upon whom the gods call. It is by this conception of the poet that Heidegger distances himself from an anthropological understanding of religion. That is, religion can never be understood as something motivated by men; it is always motivated by the gods, as I argue in chapter 10. In this sense, Heidegger's understanding of being proceeds in line with a kind of theology — as is the case with all great Western thinkers.

By proceeding along the course outlined above, I wish to make clear how certain tensions or paradoxes have to be approached: on the one hand in the writings published by Heidegger during his lifetime we find silence with respect to the question of god as an ontotheological god. On the other hand, in his interview with *Der Spiegel* he states that only a god can save us. Heidegger expressly subscribes to the problematic of the death of an ontotheological god, as proclaimed by Nietzsche, but at the same time he seeks to prepare the arrival of a new god with the words of Hölderlin. If he is to overcome metaphysics, Heidegger must reject the notion of god as *causa sui*, as a god defined ontotheologically. However, he wants to issue a more divine god to whom one can pray and sacrifice.

What I wish to be clear about is that Heidegger is in no way mired in a theism, a deism, pantheism, or an atheism. Nor does he appeal to the Greek gods or to the Christian God. Rather, he sees his thinking as a godless thinking. Naming and invoking the holy, and, moreover, explicating its content, is the task of the poet, not of the thinker. The task of the thinker is to clarify and explicate the place of the holy. The question of god in relation to the question of being, and the question of the holy in its relation to the question of being, need to be strictly separated. According to traditional metaphysics, god is the highest entity; as an entity, he therefore stands in an ontological difference with respect to being. On the other hand, what is godlike is a cornerstone of the experience of the fourfold of earth and heaven, divinities and mortals. There, divinity and human come into a relation of mutual reliance and need. The question of god for Heidegger is taken up into the encompassing question of being, and this means that it is only to be answered to the extent that the question of being is solved. And yet the question of being has itself fallen into oblivion, and therefore must first be reawakened and newly formulated. The question must be raised now: where is the holy in Heidegger's thinking to be placed and what status does it occupy? In what perspective does the holy stand to being and how does it stand with respect to the gods and to god?

A wealth of literature has already been provided by theologians offering an overview of the relations between philosophy and theology within Heidegger's thinking, and also an overview of his general development.[11] The sheer number of titles alone attests to the consideration that Heidegger receives on this aspect of his work. Most of this literature discusses Heidegger and theology, a pairing that provides ongoing, fruitful discussion.[12] However, the present study maintains a decidedly different focus: understanding Heidegger with respect to what he has to say as a philosopher on religion.

Within the field of philosophy of religion, such an undertaking calls for us not only to move beyond the descriptive approach to religion but to step over the bounds set until now by the dogmatic determinations of religion within any given metaphysical or ontotheological system. This does not mean, however, that we are consequently committed to an anthropological reduction of religion, in which god is conceived merely as a human creation. This is an approach to and an understanding of religion in its multiform and historical manifestations. Now more than ever it is necessary to gain an understanding of the historicity and the pluriformity of religion. The insights afforded by this approach will be formulated with an eye toward making a postmetaphysical theory of religion visible.

ACKNOWLEDGMENTS

The problem of religion in Heidegger's work has attracted my attention for a long time. It was not until my sabbatical leave from the Theology Department of Tilburg University that I had time to work out this study on Heidegger. The sabbatical leave in 2001 was made possible by the Theology Department for which I am very grateful to its director Lex Oostrom, and by the Radboud Foundation, especially its director Stefan Waanders. Next to this my sabbatical leave was made possible with the collegial support of my former colleagues in Tilburg: Donald Loose, René Munnik, Rudi te Velde, Harald van Veghel, Marijke Verhoeven, and Koos Verhoof.

During my sabbatical stay at Penn State University in State College my wife Yolande and I were generously supported by Jerry and John Sallis, Susan Schoenbohm, and Charles Scott and by Monika Lozinska and Rick Lee.

After my move to the Philosophy Department of the Radboud University Nijmegen, I was able to finish my project on Heidegger with the help of the Department of Philosophy and the collegial discussions of Gerrit Steunebrink, Ad Vennix, and Gerrit-Jan van der Heiden.

For the editorial work I am grateful to Ryan Drake and especially to Karen Gover who has an excellent sense for language.

ONE

The Pre-Historical Heidegger

An ongoing relationship to theology, to faith, and the church runs like a thread throughout Heidegger's life. Heidegger was born, so to speak, in the church. His father was a sexton, who led both a vocational and a familial life under one roof, in a house situated next to the church. As a young child and schoolboy, Martin's playtime was ever carried out with the church as his backdrop. And later, as a young student, Heidegger's intellectual pursuits were inspired by his interest in theology. It is highly likely that the relationship that Heidegger maintained to faith, theology, and the church throughout the whole of his work can be traced back to this early influence. Whatever value this backdrop may have had for Heidegger at different points in his life, it is the environment out of which his thought began.

In this chapter, I will discuss the way in which Heidegger first attempted to conceptualize an ahistorical Catholicism, and how he later came to the historicity of religion through Friedrich Schleiermacher. Moreover, I will discuss Heidegger's

rejection of a theoretical approach to religion, while nevertheless endeavoring to preserve the piety of philosophy — including the piety of the philosophy of religion. The term 'pre-historical'
is to be taken here in reference to the timeless character of scholastic and neoscholastic Catholicism, the intellectual environment
out of which Heidegger emerged, and the period prior to his
adoption of a historical perspective. The ontological and temporal determination of the 'earlier' and 'prior' is to be understood as piety (*Frömmigkeit*).

THE EARLIEST PUBLICATIONS

Heidegger's earliest published work borrows from the language
of Catholicism conveyed by his teachers, and he clearly identifies himself with this language.[1] For example, in his first
review in 1910, "*Per mortem ad vitam,*" he rejects all tendencies toward personality cult and individualism.[2] Also, in a short
essay, "*Zur Philosophischen Orientierung für Akademiker,*"
written in 1911, Heidegger maintains that philosophy must be
a mirror of the eternal, as it is in scholastic philosophy. The
problem that he saw in the philosophical work of his contemporaries was that it served as a mirror for their subjective opinions, personal feelings, and wishes. He reproached particular
worldviews that were grounded in life, rather than in the
eternal.[3]

It is likely that his youthful aversion to modernism was borrowed from Carl Braig, his mentor in theology during this
period.[4] Despite having giving up his studies in theology in
1911, Heidegger continued to attend Braig's lecture course on
dogmatic theology, and he recalled much later conversations
that he and Braig shared on scholastic and idealistic-speculative
theology.[5] As a high school student, Heidegger had already
read Braig's book, *Vom Sein: Abriß der Ontologie*. In this
book, Braig includes a passage from St. Bonaventure, which

holds that just as the eye does not see light itself when it is directed toward a manifold of color, the mind's eye does not see being itself when directed to entities singly or as a whole.[6] And yet, it is only by way of being that we can encounter entities in the first place. The mind's eye receives, as it were, an objectless impression, much in the way that one who only sees light sees nothing per se. What later emerges in Heidegger's work as the ontological difference has its roots in this connection between transcendental philosophy and ontology. The former asks about the conditions for the possibility of knowledge, seeking not to bring new objects of knowledge forth, but rather what makes objects of knowledge as such possible. The latter, seen from Bonaventure's perspective, gives the transcendental question an ontological answer through that nonobjective condition which Bonaventure calls 'being' (and here, Bonaventure also differentiates himself from Plato, who sought such a condition in the idea of the good). Here we can see an opening up of the difference between being and entities, which served originally to prevent the mistake of identifying being with the highest entity or with the whole of entities. In the later chapters of this study, we shall see how this theme becomes more central in Heidegger's work.

Braig himself was a notorious opponent of modernism, and was credited with coining the term.[7] Braig saw in modernism both a theology and a philosophy, which in the wake of Schleiermacher's influence places the essence of religion in the impulses of feeling, where feeling mediates religious truth. Braig opposed accounts seeking to conceive all images of god as the result of the faculty of imagination. He saw in liberal theology the tendency to simplify the truth claims of religion — especially those of Christianity — as a means of satisfying our human desire for religion. Braig took a critical position toward such forms of psychologism, which Heidegger in turn adopted. As an outgrowth of his association with Braig, Heidegger went on to produce a dissertation entitled *Die Lehre vom Urteil im Psychologismus*.

What counts as Heidegger's first scientific work was *Das Realitätsproblem in der modernen Philosophie*, published in 1912. Here, Heidegger presents an overview of Kant's contemporary reception and poses the question of how the problem of reality could be overlooked by scholars writing on Kant's epistemology.[8] In Heidegger's own interpretation of this problem, he betrays his training in the scholastic tradition; yet at the same time, he saw promise in the more direct approach to reality characteristic of the natural sciences. His aim was to unite both of these moments.[9] He finds a tension between, on the one hand, philosophical theory, realized in its most mature form in neo-Kantianism, and on the other hand, the practice of science, which served to undercut the tenability of philosophical theory. Heidegger takes this tension to be the product of a misguided valuation of the problem of reality on the part of the neo-Kantians, where the existence of transsubjective objects is denied. At the time, Heidegger's aim was to defend Aristotelian-scholastic philosophy, which had always made the problem of the real central, and was therefore better equipped to form the basis of scientific thought.[10] Due to Heidegger's particular education, however, the realism that he sought to defend rested in the end upon a theological form of metaphysics.

As Heidegger's work branched out into the study of logic, he retained his commitment to the basis of faith and theological metaphysics, conceived as a timeless truth. In both his early reviews and in *Neuere Forschungen über Logik* (1912), he continues to reject the standpoints of modern psychologism and historicism. In this work Heidegger claims that psychologism's principal fault lies in its inability to distinguish between a psychic act and its logical content; in other words, there is a difference between the process of thinking as a temporal development, on the one hand, and the ideal meaning that corresponds to this act, on the other. In short, what psychologism overlooks is the distinction between what in fact happens and what counts as valid. Interestingly, Heidegger does not therefore classify Kant as a subjectivist or a psychologist, for Kant asks about the logical value of the validity of knowledge and not its psychological origin.[11] In his review of Charles Sentroel's book *Kant und Aristoteles*, Heidegger notes that contemporary work on Kant lacks an adequate study undertaken from a Catholic perspective. From these early contributions onward, Heidegger's closeness to this Kantian problematic, as well as to the problem of ontology, shapes his own intellectual development.

Heidegger continued to oppose psychologism as he composed his dissertation in 1913. As he characterized it, psychologistic investigation directs itself toward the conditions of the possibility of judgment. Yet in its commitment to objectivity, psychologism does not allow any subjective relation to judgment to play a role.[12] Heidegger avoids both the exclusively psychologist and the exclusively historicist alternatives, but takes up elements of both by asking after the conditions of the possibility of judgment where historicity is involved. He asks for the necessary and sufficient elements that allow judgment to be possible.[13] In this way, he wins a philosophical stance by allowing truth to play a role in his investigation. For Heidegger the question of truth is always a transcendental question; even when he conceptualizes history, he asks about the conditions of its possibility.[14]

The fact that truth is to be sought in the realm of the ideal arises not merely out of his approach to psychologism, but also as something that is self-evident. Judgment lies on the other side of change and development, as something that can be grasped by a human subject, though not changed.[15] The ideal is to be found, on he other hand, in the unit of meaning of an assertion. The real preparation for logic, according to Heidegger, must be found in the analysis of the meaning of a word.[16] Only

from this point can the full extent of being be properly investigated. What is to be revealed, then, lies not in the sphere of
scientific evidence, but in the sphere of indication.[17]

The question of truth is a guiding factor in Heidegger's early
work, primarily in questioning the logical validity of the truth
of a judgment. This line of thought was continued in his 1915
Habilitationsschrift, *Die Kategorien und Bedeutungslehre des
Duns Scotus*.[18] Ultimately, the book takes as its fundamental theme
what Heidegger calls 'the real truth'.[19] By this point, however,
the scholastic timelessness that he had earlier found so compelling was beginning to lose its influence. For, in line with the
question into truth, his book on Scotus begins with the religious experience of the truth of the Christian faith in the Middle
Ages. Since the primary structure of the medieval attitude
toward life lies in "the transcendental relation of the soul to
God," a phenomenological application, i.e., a means of freeing-
up the calcified tradition of scholasticism, becomes an exigent
task for the present.[20] From Heidegger's earliest reviews we
find that he regards the modern subjective way of life as
obscuring the proper place for a truth that transcends the subject. Out of this concern, Heidegger became fascinated by the
contrast represented in the medieval temperament; during that
age, individuals were capable of devoting themselves to the
object of their investigation with a particular passion. The
devotion to the transcendent object overshadowed the human
subject's commitment to his own perspective.[21]

Through his study of Scotus, Heidegger forges a fundamentally new relation to the concepts of reality and individuality.
For Scotus, what really exists is what is individual; it is the
irreducible, underlying given. Two apples in the same tree, for
example, do not have an identical status from the perspective
of the eternal; each is distinct from the other even if they are
completely equivalent in all spatial determinations.[22]

Heidegger saw that medieval thought demands an approach
fitted to its own specific character. The specific will toward life

and the spirit particular to that age call for a similar mode of understanding as well as their own adequate philosophical treatment. Heidegger understands these concepts as originating out of an expression of inner life, an inner life anchored to a transcendental, fundamental relation of the soul to god, a relation that took its own unique form during the Middle Ages. In this sense, a "true reality" or a true worldview remains distanced from a theoretical construction that exists in alienation from life. The spirit of an age is only comprehensible when the whole of its acts, its history, is brought into view. The living spirit as such is essentially the historic spirit in the broadest sense of the word.[23] At the end of his study of Scotus, Heidegger remarks that he sees his prospective task as elevating the Christian experience of piety into a philosophy of the living spirit, the active love of, and the relation of worship to, god. This task is to be situated against the background of the experienced transcendence of individuals in the Middle Ages, on the one hand, and of his own origin in faith, on the other. Furthermore, Heidegger seeks to carry out this task without at the same time nullifying this faith on a higher level of speculative knowledge, as Hegel's philosophy does.

On the basis of his conclusions in the Scotus study, Heidegger notes that any purely formal approach to the problem of categories is doomed to fail, since such formal approaches do not take into account the culture and human experience of the period in which said categories are discussed. In fact, an appropriate understanding of medieval category-theory also requires a study of medieval mysticism and theology (for example, a full appreciation of the human and religious or ontotheological commitments of a concept like 'analogy'), and vice-versa. Moreover, a complete account of category-theory must comprehend the entire range or cultural 'history' of the unfolding of the living spirit.[24]

From the beginning, it is clear that Heidegger was motivated by the question of truth, which he first formulates as the question after logical validity. This finds its full expression in the afterword of his study on Scotus. There, he states that the "real truth" is his focus. And the experience of religious Christian conviction in the Middle Ages is the original region in which Heidegger seeks such real truth.[25] In order to do this, Heidegger was led to emphasize the role of history in understanding the living spirit: in the last sentence of his study, he indicates that historicity must enter the scene.[26] On this basis, he called for an engagement with Hegel as a means of overcoming the one-sidedness of a theoretical mentality with the help of a concept of living spirit.

PIETY

Heidegger was drawn to the question of what kind of truth would be the most original, and furthermore where this origin lies. The material that he had at his disposal was primarily by the mystics of the Middle Ages; he asked after the "basic relation of the soul to God." Following Eckhart, Heidegger investigated the relation between god and time in the soul itself, the soul which he refers to as the castle and dwelling of god.[27] Even though god is understood here through classical metaphysics as the origin of the soul, the images derived from Eckhart's mysticism were nonetheless paradigms for the philosophy of the "innerness of God" (*Gottinnigkeit*). Mysticism thus helped Heidegger rise above classical metaphysics.

The perspective of Aristotle's first philosophy, also called theology, teaches that god and world exist. This idea was shared as much by the Romans as by the Greeks. In addition, this perspective set the scope of Christian thinking for the subsequent millennium. It was not until the need to find evidence of god emerged amidst the struggle on the part of the monastics against a secularization of faith, that Christian thinking began to change in this respect. Arguments like St. Anselm's, in which the divine being is that other than which nothing greater can be thought, were posed in an effort to retain what was first *as* first. This tendency, along with the withering of piety in European scholastic philosophy, furthered the misconception that the first philosophy would be a science of god, *scienta Dei* — as if a love for knowledge could ever reach the level of a science and somehow achieve thereby an omniscience of the divine (which was precisely Hegel's pretension).[28]

Heidegger's research in this regard was not a guiding force in his later thinking.[29] Yet this early work is emblematic of the parochial world — dedicated to eternal truths — from which he descended, and from which he wanted to free himself through thinking. He later provided a sketch of this world in the essay *"Vom Geheimnis des Glockenturms."*[30] Throughout Heidegger's life, he states, the peal of the clock tower of St. Martin's Church in Messkirch resounded. This ringing bears witness to the divine rhythm in which religious holy days interweave with the course of the hours of the day and year.[31] It is the practically eternal rhythm that orders one's life.

The notion of piety (*Frömmigkeit*) plays an essential role in my explication of Heidegger's thinking on religion, and in this respect, I follow the direction set by Manfred Riedel in his analysis *"Frömmigkeit im Denken."*[32] '*Frömmigkeit*' is etymologically related to the Greek word *promos,* and subsequently the Latin *primum*; the relation between piety and the concept of 'the primary' guides the present investigation of Heidegger and religion as a whole. This principle applies not only to Heidegger's thinking about religion and his determinations with respect to it, but first and foremost to the fact that his thinking is continually motivated to seek what is previous or earlier, in short, the a priori.

As Thomas Sheehan has shown, three letters written by Edmund Husserl also serve to shed light on Heidegger's religious interests.[33] When Husserl arrived in Freiburg in 1916 and met the young Heidegger, the latter had already presented his *Habilitationsschrift* to the department of philosophy. Husserl supported Heidegger in publishing his book, although, because Heidegger was drafted into military service at that time, there was little opportunity for the two to forge a significant acquaintance. When Paul Natorp wrote to Husserl asking for candidates for a chair in medieval philosophy in 1917, Husserl recommended Heidegger, noting the latter's personal religious convictions in his reply. Subsequently however, Heidegger was passed over for the position. In a letter to Rudolf Otto dated March of 1919, Husserl mentioned Heidegger in connection with Otto's work on the holy. Husserl writes that Heidegger inclined strongly toward problems of religion. However, as he puts it, "In Heidegger it is the theoretical-philosophical interest which predominates." And it was Husserl who discerned in his student a gradual transition toward Protestantism.[34] On the basis of Husserl's correspondences, Sheehan concludes that Heidegger underwent a radical religious transformation between 1916 and 1919, motivated primarily by his theoretical pursuits. Though I agree with Sheehan on this point, I will argue in the following that this change was actually a transition from theory over into piety. Finally, in a letter written to Natorp in February of 1920, Husserl comments on Heidegger's personal religious development, as well as on his development as an intellectual. He notes not only that Heidegger had distanced himself from Catholicism, but also that his devotion to teaching had already distinguished him as an outstanding lecturer, drawing one hundred or more students to his lectures. It was during this time that Heidegger presented his analysis of a hermeneutic of the facticity of existence in his lecture course, "Grundprobleme der Phänomenologie." It was around this same issue that Heidegger went on to structure his course in the following autumn and winter, entitled, "Einleitung in die Phänomenologie der Religion."

As another documented source for Heidegger's intellectual development, we can turn to Heinrich Ochsner, who states that

Heidegger began his studies of Schleiermacher in 1917.[35] In August of that year, Heidegger presented a lecture devoted to the second of Schleiermacher's essays from "On Religion, Essays to its Cultured Despisers."[36] From the point of view of Heidegger's earlier position, in which he typified Schleiermacher as a representative of modernism — and therefore as objectionable from a Catholic philosophical standpoint — it is somewhat surprising that he then returned to this thinker.

If we consider Heidegger's letter to Engelbert Krebs, his former professor and confidant, in early 1919, we get a clearer picture of Heidegger's path of thinking in this regard. In the letter, he addresses his own development over the previous two years, beginning with his study of Schleiermacher's second "Speech on Religion." It is precisely here where we can discern a significant tie between his thoughts on historicity and religion. Heidegger confesses that epistemological insights concerning historical knowledge made Catholicism problematic for him.[37] This letter bears witness to a decisive turning point for Heidegger, then 29, both philosophically and religiously. Yet most importantly, it marks the end of his career as an aspiring Catholic philosopher, the course he'd set for himself since his dissertation in 1913. At this point, Heidegger found himself struggling to develop his own perspective and to free himself from his earlier influences. He describes this struggle in terms strikingly similar to those of Descartes, in the latter's resolution to break with his own past. "It is difficult," Heidegger writes, "to live as a philosopher . . . [yet] I believe myself to possess the inner vocation for philosophy."[38]

It was not, however, in his efforts to abandon Catholic dogma that Heidegger turned to Schleiermacher, but in his effort to engender a philosophical understanding of religion. For Schleiermacher, the question of god takes its leave from philosophy. What Schleiermacher offers Heidegger, therefore, is a means of overcoming the philosophical framework within which he operated as a young student. In this respect, I do not agree with Otto Pöggler, who saw in Heidegger's study of Schleiermacher a testimony to his farewell to Catholicism.[39] Rather, it was the vocation of philosophy itself that alienated him from Catholicism. In his second "Speech on religion," Schleiermacher sets philosophical theology, the root of philosophy from Aristotle on through Hegel, aside in order to introduce what he sees as the real religious dimension of life. Those who wish to follow him in this undertaking must therefore abandon pre-given concepts of god and immortality; Schleiermacher no longer allows for a classical metaphysical concept of god.

According to Schleiermacher, the real essence of religion is obscure; what is most often given the name 'religion' ends up revealing itself as either philosophy, metaphysics, or morality. In contrast to Kant, Schleiermacher rejects a reduction of religion to morality. For him, philosophy and morality are limited to the finite; they deal with abstract considerations or daily practical concerns. Religion, on the other hand, is involved in the infinite, in the universe; it is not a matter of thinking and acting, but of the unity of 'intuition' (*Anschauung*) and 'feeling' (*Gefühl*). Contact with the universe or infinity, Schleiermacher argues, is achieved through intuition. In a sudden moment, one experiences all discrete things as an infinite totality, in which one knows oneself to be included as well. Everything, that is, is experienced as a unity, in which the separation between subject and object is nullified. One simply abides in the experienced unity, without being able to represent it conceptually. Schleiermacher describes the union of intuition and feeling in the experience of unification with the whole of infinity in famous passage that is called the 'love scene.' Since Schleiermacher's theory provides an entrance point to religion because of this unification with the whole of infinity, he was consequently likened to Spinoza and accused of pantheism by his opponents.

Schleiermacher carefully avoids focusing upon separate elements of life or individuals in isolation, but rather aims at the totality of humankind and its 'eternal' history. Ultimately, he portrays the subject of religion as something that transcends humankind, giving it different names: the one, infinity, the universe, the world soul, or world spirit. It transcends not only humankind, but nature as well, though we can see it manifested through both. In the final sections of his speech, Schleiermacher attends to several themes that were then, as now, considered to be essential to religion. Dogmas, miracles, inspiration, revelation, and grace are reinterpreted in these passages from the new perspective on religion that he has worked out.

Furthermore, and perhaps most shocking to his contemporaries, Schleiermacher assigned new meaning to the ideas of immortality and divinity. For him, neither god nor immortality are "the hinge and the chief articles of religion."[40] The idea of religion put forward, then, is not based upon the idea of a supreme being. "To have religion means to intuit the universe, and the value of your religion depends upon the manner in which you intuit it, on the principle that you find in its actions. Now if you cannot deny that the idea of God adapts itself to each intuition of the universe, you must also admit that one religion without God can be better than another with God."[41]

It is to this world of theoretical knowledge of god that Heidegger wishes to bid farewell; he had to renounce it precisely because he identified himself with it both as a student of theology and in his early writings. And this distance from the timeless is also his farewell to the pre-historical.

For Heidegger, the primary importance of this point was to explicate the specific character of religion over and against the modern misunderstanding of it as an origin of a moral and metaphysical worldview. Through Schleiermacher, this possibility was opened up for him: "Most often, and also now, one appreciated the expressions, the documents of religion according to the profit they yielded for morals and metaphysics. So the cutting opposition of faith to morals and metaphysics, of piety against morality, is first to be shown."[42] The origin and end of religion is the infinite being, where god must necessarily be presupposed. Though god is not explicitly identified with it, god is nonetheless presupposed in it.[43] According to Schleiermacher, what is most important is "to get down into the innermost holiness of life" to explore therein the original unity of contemplation and feeling.[44] This unity is to be found in the human being itself; Schleiermacher writes therefore: "But I must refer you to yourselves, to the grasp of a living moment. You must understand, likewise, for your consciousness to, as it were, eavesdrop on, or at least to reconstitute this state out of the living moment for yourselves. You should notice here the becoming of your consciousness, rather than somehow reflecting on a consciousness that has already become."[45]

According to Heidegger, the task here is to uncover an original dimension of living and acting grounded in feeling, in which only religion is actualized as a particular form of experience. In this experience, the elements of religion are not determined by teleological coherence and corresponding noetic structures.[46] Rejecting metaphysical speculation, Heidegger utilizes instead Husserl's *epoché,* the method of phenomenological reduction.[47]

Because the phenomenological *epoché* eliminates all metaphysical or ontological claims and identification, the perceptions of faith and the world of religious experience are placed into a neutral domain. From the perspective of its content, no particular religion is given precedence above any other. Religions are here distinguished primarily by the way in which their content is experienced and how they are lived in the actualization of faith.

For Heidegger, religious experience is never theoretical; he therefore resists taking dogmas as truth as Catholicism, in his view, does.[48] He takes the immediate relation to religious concepts as analogous to the immediacy of philosophical understanding. "The 'concepts' of understanding, and all understanding in the genuinely philosophical sense, have not the slightest to do with rationalization."[49] It is this immediate understanding of the prior, signified by the term piety, which determines the religious for Heidegger. Through thinking the 'first,' the primary, one marks out the space of the religious, and this marking out must be itself undertaken piously. Thus, Heidegger brings himself into conflict with the traditional concept of the philosophy of religion as such: philosophy as metaphysical theory and religion as immediate understanding of the prior do not cohere with one another, as Schleiermacher maintained.

Alongside his study of Schleiermacher, Heidegger continued his research in medieval mysticism. Mystics maintained that their practice of taking the divine as an absolute object was not irrational, precisely because they rejected the opposition between rationality and irrationality from the outset. Mysticism moves outward beyond rationality because its object demands this. "Not the not-yet-determinable and not-yet-determined — rather, that which is essentially without determination in general is the primordial object, the absolute."[50] Taking this insight — that only equality recognizes equality — as its basis, mysticism explicates a theory of consciousness. Heidegger saw that an empty consciousness paired with an object that is likewise empty is the specific "seclusion" (*Abgeschiedenheit*) that lies at the center of mysticism.[51]

It was this involvement in mysticism that led Heidegger to Schleiermacher's concept of religion, taking over the latter's dictum that "The measure of knowledge is not the measure of piety."[52] God, thought from within the domain of knowledge as the ground of knowing and the known, is not the same as a pious relation to god, where 'knowledge' arises out of this piety.

Schleiermacher succeeded in opening up the possibility of an historical approach to subjectivity, wherein religion and historicity are intimately tied to one another.[53] The absolute, toward which spirit directs itself, appears only *as* historical. The importance of historicity, which became evident for Heidegger at the end of his study on Scotus, is taken up once again in relation to Schleiermacher's work. Yet as an actualization of the absolute, historicity demands its own approach. For Heidegger, religious experience must be engaged with its own means and according to its own criteria, rather than with scientific criteria imposed upon it from without. And Heidegger locates such criteria precisely in historical consciousness. "Religion, just as any world of experience, can gain its form only in historical consciousness."[54] It is not therefore possible to create a religion with philosophy as its ground (*erphilosophieren*), nor can philosophy here provide criteria for criticism. But if not philosophy, then what?

Here the phenomenological approach offers help: "Over and against this, only phenomenology can offer rescue in philosophical need."[55] A relation to god based on feeling can therefore direct the specific religious constitution of god as a 'phenomenological object.'[56] And this, once again, implies historicity: "The absolute — determinable only in the respective sphere of experience. Inside the respective sphere, it receives its full concretion only in the way that it shows itself in a *historicity*."[57] Therefore a phenomenological analysis must refer ever back to the historic as the primal meaning and determining element of living consciousness. Thus an interpretation of Schleiermacher, Heidegger sought to reformulate pious feeling in terms of phenomenology.

In this connection, Hegel's treatment of religion is also rejected. For Hegel, morality is the leading aim, which religion degraded to a means in its service.[58] Consciousness shows itself to be historical in the fulfillment of the moment, and not in the philosophy of the pure ego. In short, Heidegger took primal

experience as his focus, rather than derivative theoretical explication. It is at this point that Heidegger recognized the importance of the historical, which manifests itself throughout as the
determining moment of consciousness.

A Pious Atheist

Heidegger recognized that the religious object demands an
approach that is loyal to religious experience itself. In his commentary on Rudolph Otto's *The Holy,* Heidegger writes: "[T]he
holy may not be made into a problem as theoretical — also not
an irrational theoretical — *noema,* rather as correlate of the act-
character of 'faith,' which itself is to be interpreted only from
out of the fundamentally essential experiential context of historical consciousness."[59] Heidegger's phenomenology seeks to
justify the infinity of being, which Schleiermacher emphasizes
as a moment of meaning within religious life. The experience
and the observation of it are always, at each moment, historical. And as such, the historical is always a manifestation of
something other than what has come before. Thinking along
with Schleiermacher, Heidegger notes: "History in the most authentic sense is the highest object of religion, religion begins and
ends in it."[60] Religion here is, therefore, as an historical event,
a mystical moment of unarticulated unity between contemplation and feeling, which withdraws from all conceptual analyses
that metaphysical theology might attempt.

By following Schleiermacher's thinking on individuality,
Heidegger's phenomenology of religion translates the piety of
his youth into an analysis of religious feeling and experience,
without sacrificing his thinking before the altar of a philosophical concept of god. Here phenomenological analysis is pious
precisely because its subject, the prior, is pious. The moment
of the piety of faith is preserved but is transformed into a more
original sympathy with life that commits one to confronting

ultimate questions. Since observation does not necessarily accompany real questioning, what is essential to questioning is a personal stake, wherein a question can be actualized. As Heidegger writes in the winter of 1921, it is essential to know how to philosophize and to work in a phenomenological mode, "and in so doing, to be genuinely religious, i.e. . . . to take up factically one's worldly, historiological-historical task in philosophy, in action, and in a concrete world of action, though not in religious ideology and fantasy."[61] For Heidegger the question is not whether philosophy is religious, in the sense of pious, but whether philosophy is theistic or atheistic. To this he answers unequivocally: "Philosophy, in its radical, self-posing questionability, must be atheistic as a matter of principle. Precisely on account of its basic intention, philosophy must not presume to possess or determine God. The more radical philosophy is, the more determinately it is on a path away from god; yet precisely in the radical actualization of the 'away', it has its own difficult proximity to God. For the rest, philosophy must not become too speculative on this account, since it has its own task to fulfill."[62]

On the other side of this relation, Heidegger is careful not to reduce philosophy itself to a kind of art or religion. "The comparison of philosophy with science is an unjustified debasement of its essence. Comparing it with art and religion, on the other hand, is a justified and necessary determination of their essence as equal. Yet equality here does not mean identity . . . [W]e shall never grasp the essence of philosophy through these comparisons, either — however much art and religion are treated on a level equal to philosophy — unless we have already managed to look philosophy in the face to begin with. For only then can we differentiate art and religion from it."[63] Heidegger's determination of philosophy is prior to his determination of religion, precisely because he aims at a philosophical approach to phenomena.

As I have shown above, Heidegger clearly rejects a theoretical approach to understanding religion as a specific object for phenomenological philosophy; instead to identifying himself as a phenomenologist of religious experience. The most intimate experience of the self is understood here as a religious experience, and vice-versa; religious experience is the most intimate experience of the self.[64] Following from this idea, Heidegger maintains that the scholar who studies the history of religion understands Jesus as a pious person would regard him. That is, the comprehension of Jesus is preserved as a religious form of comprehension. The priority here lies in minimizing theory and maximizing the preservation of the original situation with the experience of the phenomenon itself in its originality.[65] Religion as a presentation of the absolute demands, then, a religious, i.e., a pious approach.

In order to resist theoretical theology and a theoretical approach in general, Heidegger grounds his thinking in a more personal stance. And in this stance, he finds the means for overcoming the timeless metaphysical framework that governed religious terminology as it had been passed over to him. Such a theoretical treatment was the result of the influence of Platonic-Aristotelian philosophy, which had been taken up into Christianity by Augustine, Aquinas, and their successors. As both believers and theorists, the early Christian thinkers saw a truth in philosophy that was not strictly separated from the truth of faith. It was precisely because of this nondifferentiation that Greek philosophy could be integrated into the truth of Christianity. This orientation of patristic philosophy to Greek thinking first took its direction from Paul's letter to the Romans, where he states: "Ever since the world began, His invisible attributes, that is to say, His everlasting power and divinity, have been visible to the eye of reason, in the things that He has made," (Rom. 1:20). Reason according to Paul has the capacity to trace God through His works, because God presents Himself in His works. This single idea fundamentally determined philosophical and theological thought for the next several centuries.

It is against this background that Heidegger's study of Luther must be considered. It is not by accident that Luther, as a forerunner of modernity, strongly resists the theological position that a harmony exists between faith and reason. In his *Heidelberger Disputationen* in 1518, Luther defends forty principles, of which twenty-eight are theological and twelve philosophical. In his resistance to a fusion of faith and reason he appears to refer to Paul's letter mentioned above. The nineteenth principle reads: "The man who looks upon the invisible things of God as they are perceived in created things does not deserve to be called a theologian." Access to the object of theology is not gained through metaphysical reflection. In other words, reason is not recognized here as a possible point of access to God. And in the twenty-second principle, this thesis reappears: "The wisdom, that looks upon the invisible things of God from his works, inflates us, blinds us, and hardens our heart."[66]

Heidegger's engagement with Luther in this regard deepened in Marburg, where he visited Rudolf Bultmann's seminar on Paul's ethics in the winter semester of 1923. In this course, Heidegger was invited to give a two-part lecture entitled, *"Das Problem der Sünde bei Luther."*[67] It was in this lecture that Heidegger aligned himself more closely with Luther in his critique of scholastic philosophy. He posed the question of how the calcified interpretations of scholastic philosophy can be overcome in order to revitalize the origin of that very philosophy. The key here, he concluded, is to return to the original messages of the text without falling back upon dogmatic doctrines. And Heidegger saw Luther himself as guilty of this failing where Luther remains averse to Aristotle's philosophy. Furthermore, this is a more general orientation within theology itself, as he states in *Being and Time:* "Theology is seeking a more primordial interpretation of man's Being toward God, prescribed by the meaning of faith itself and remaining within it. It is slowly beginning to understand once more Luther's insight that the 'foundation' on which its system of dogma rests has not arisen from an inquiry in which faith is primary, and that conceptually this 'foundation' is not only inadequate for the problematic of theology, but conceals and distorts it."[68] Therefore, it was not Luther's rejection of Aristotle that Heidegger supported, and it was moreover not Luther's religious faith that inspired him. He saw, rather, an attitude toward theoretical philosophy that was akin to his own. As philosophy does not offer knowledge of god, according to Luther, so Heidegger maintained in similar fashion that theoretical philosophy does not offer insight into factical life.[69] In the theoretical approach to religion and to god, the factical was displaced and concealed in the form of questioning after a metaphysical entity. Against this, Heidegger considered his own phenomenological approach to be pious and religious. A few years thereafter, a remnant of this pious prehistory was to emerge in *Being and Time,* where Heidegger notes that if one were to say anything about god's eternity, then, according to Heidegger, it could only be understood as a more primordial temporality that is 'infinite.'[70] The most primordial is the pre-historic, which precedes even prehistory itself.

For Heidegger, primary here is the explication of a basic attitude of the philosophical life that tries to understand life's real meaning. This attitude demands piety, lies at the basis of the inner call of phenomenology, and it must prove itself. In Heidegger's thinking, only by being true to these experiences of life can one free oneself from the concepts that have been alienated from life, yet at the same time serve as fetters for it.[71] This piety does not originate in the specific element of religion taken as the object of phenomenology. It is, however, connected with phenomenology, since the latter directs itself toward the matter at hand. And this matter is what Heidegger saw as the absolute, which is nothing other than one's own facticity. Heidegger describes this facticity in almost sacral words to Karl Löwith in 1921. It belongs to Heidegger's facticity that he is a Christian "theo*logian*" and that he is this in the circumstances of the "university."[72] Heidegger therefore seeks to take up a relation to himself from the standpoint of his facticity, which calls for a pious approach.

At this point, however, Heidegger's language with respect to religion is mired in structural ambiguity: where the object of phenomenology is concerned, he attempts to remain radically atheistic, yet when it comes to this same object, he seeks to be pious and devoted. The pious person here is the devoted ascetic who understands his object as it demands to be understood, i.e., from out of its factical character. Only when philosophy has become fundamentally atheistic can it decisively choose life in its very facticity, and thereby make this an object for itself.[73] Heidegger describes this philosophy as atheistic, "but not in the sense of a theory such as materialism or something similar. Every philosophy which understands itself in what it is must — as the factical how of the interpretation of life — know (and it must know this precisely when it still has some 'notion' of God) that life's retreat towards its own self (which philosophy achieves) is, in religious terms, a show of hands against God. But only then is philosophy honest, i.e., only then is philosophy in keeping with its possibility (which is available to it as such) before God; here atheistic means keeping oneself free from misleading concern which merely talks about religiosity." Because philosophy is concerned with the facticity of life, the philosophy of religion must be understood from that same perspective. Therefore Heidegger continues, "[T]he very idea of philosophy of religion (especially if it makes no reference to the facticity of the human being) is pure nonsense."[74] Such nonsense evolves out of a lack of piety, i.e., a merely theoretical approach that fails to attune itself to the facticity of life.

Heidegger maintains this precisely because for him, philosophy essentially directs itself toward the facticity of human being.

Through his explication of the notion of historicity, Heidegger was able to find a path leading out of the closed religious world in which he was raised. Through Schleiermacher's thinking, Heidegger was offered the possibility of isolating the religious as the absolute; and in so doing, he was led away from both theology and theoretical philosophy in his thinking. Out of this engagement, Heidegger was able to conclude that the religious is none other than the historical; the radicality of a personal position is only to be uncovered within history.

Heidegger was always resistant to the fusion of theoretical philosophy and theology, and he persisted in this conviction throughout his later thinking. As he states in 1935, "A 'Christian philosophy' is a round square and a misunderstanding."[75] Rather, he continues his understanding of thinking as piety. "For questioning is the piety of thought."[76]

Two

Heidegger and the
Philosophy of Religion

As we observed in the previous chapter, Heidegger directed his philosophy toward the facticity of human being. His approach to religion must be understood from the standpoint of this guiding interest. As the winter semester approached in 1920, Heidegger announced his upcoming lecture course, entitled "Introduction to the Phenomenology of Religion."[1] At the time, the theological literature of Rudolf Otto and Friedrich Heiler was widely circulated.[2] Husserl had found Otto's book, *The Idea of the Holy,* an impressive first beginning for a phenomenology of religion, albeit little more than a beginning. "It would seem to me that a great deal more progress must be made in the study of phenomena and their eidetic analysis before a theory of religious consciousness as a philosophical theory could arise."[3] As I will show later in this chapter, Husserl was committed far more to an eidetic orientation in the phenomenology of religion than Heidegger.

In this lecture course Heidegger presented an explication of the fundamental event of the Christian experience of life as it appears in the letters of Paul. In particular, Heidegger paid special attention to the fourth and fifth sections of Paul's first letter to the Thessalonians, with the aim of showing how this earliest contribution to the New Testament marks a decisive moment, wherein the Christian experience of life becomes manifest in and through the question of the coming of Christ. This coming is described as a sudden occurrence, like a thief in the night. The suddenness and unpredictability for which one must solemnly wait was a point of fascination for Heidegger. In particular, he focused upon Paul's notion of '*kairos*,' which signifies one's delivery to a moment of decision, a moment that cannot be reached through a calculation. The *kairos* does not represent a mastery of time, but rather the uncertainty inherent in the future. This defining characteristic of the *kairos* belongs to the history of life's actualization, which itself rejects any attempt at objectification.[4] In the moment of *kairos* one's life is at stake. Attempts at mastery or control of this moment express the wrong attitude with which this moment must be encountered.

The question here, however, is how Heidegger, as a philosopher, understood this conception within his philosophy of the facticity of life. First, he formalized the fundamental Christian experience of life. He does not choose a position with respect to the particular content of this experience, but rather limits himself to investigating the sustaining conditions of its possibility. Heidegger asks whether the kairological moment can be preserved within the history of the actualization of life and the unpredictability of the *eschaton*. It could potentially be understood as a possibility that we ourselves have or something that is under our control, so that the future that withdraws from us becomes part of our own planning. Yet, if it were to be understood thus, the specific character of the *kairos* would then be lost in a totalizing form of calculation. The future would then be conceived in the end as a horizon of consciousness out of which experiences evolve in a certain order. For Heidegger, the *kairos* has more to do with the conditions of the possibility of facticity, which it goes on to determine in a formal way.[5] For what takes place — the content in the moment of the *kairos* — can itself never be deduced. If it is possible to encounter properly the suddenness of the *kairos,* it must be accomplished without the aid of deduction.

Given his emphasis upon the kairological moment in facticity, how is one to understand Heidegger's position as a philosophy of religion? In a rough, Hegelian-inspired sketch, one could say that religion is the domain of representation, of the historical and situational context of human existence, and furthermore that philosophy is the domain of conceptual thinking, wherein one tends to withdraw from both representation and history. In this picture, religious representations are taken to refer to a content represented in the image, and the image itself is a representation of the concept. Yet is it possible to reproduce the representation of religion on the level of concepts? Is this conceptual approach the most suitable way to understand the representations of life as they are presented in Christianity? If so, then philosophy will certainly have a means for developing an understanding of religious images and representations. Of course, this demands that we know what philosophy is in the first place; only then can philosophy be a clear instrument for our aims. In Heidegger's thinking, philosophy as such has never been properly examined in terms of what it really is or should be. Precisely where Heidegger focuses his attention on religion, he also begins his thought on the difference between philosophy and science. He points out that philosophy carries with it a certain terminology that is, on the whole, less clear and stable than that of the sciences. Heidegger sees this ambiguity in philosophy not as a disadvantage, but rather as philosophy's own specific virtue.[6]

FROM THEORETICAL PHILOSOPHY TO FORMAL INDICATION

According to Heidegger, the primary which he seeks lies in the facticity of life, and is to be approached precisely as primary. Formerly, philosophy had not involved itself with studies of factical life and the experience thereof. "Insofar as philosophizing transcends factical experience, it is characterized by the fact that it deals with higher objects and the highest of them, with the 'first and ultimate things.'"[7] What distinguishes Heidegger's approach is that he is resolved not to take a theoretical path in order to reach the immediate experience of life, despite the fact that the theoretical road is acknowledged to be the highest expression of what philosophy is per se. Yet Heidegger understands philosophy including the philosophy of religion to begin and end in factical experience.[8]

After the decline of Hegel's objective idealism, historicism and psychologism rose to prominence in the academy. As I have discussed above, Heidegger had resisted these tendencies from the outset of his career. To develop an alternative understanding of religion, Heidegger referred to the work of Ernst Troeltsch. Against the proponents of psychologism and historicism, Troeltsch sought to demonstrate the independence, as well as the irreducibility, of religion by following Schleiermacher and the neo-Kantians. Troeltsch criticizes Hegel explicitly for failing to do justice to the element of experience in religion. Hegel's doctrine relies upon a pure metaphysical construction of reason and upon reason's immanent logical structure in order to deduce, through its inner necessity, the essence of history — and with this, the essence of religion. In Troeltsch's thinking, Hegel's reason could not adequately access historical reality, so a philosophy of religion had to take its point of departure from a psychological analysis of religion. Yet, in avoiding relativism and skepticism, this is, in Troeltsch's view, only one of four possible points of view — including the epistemological, historic-philosophical, and metaphysical — from which a philosophy of religion can inquire after the essence of religion. Psychology alone cannot address the question of whether truth is contained in religious phenomena, but requires an epistemology of religion as its supplement. This became the core of Troeltsch's philosophy of religion. Central to his philosophy is the concept of a religious a priori. He seeks to mark out religious life as a necessary element of human existence, so that religious phenomena could no longer be regarded as practicing a form of self-deceit, wherein one is imprisoned in one's own projected images. Therefore, any philosophy of religion must encompass two other aspects, namely the historic-philosophical and the metaphysical. The historic-philosophical aspect asks after the criteria of the history of religion. On the other side, the metaphysics of religion questions the way in which the idea of god, which for Troeltsch is only accessible by religious belief, is integrated with a larger body of knowledge. However, this means that the metaphysics entailed here must be other than classical metaphysics; it must be, in the end, a doctrine of faith.[9]

Heidegger finds fault with Troeltsch in the latter's consideration of religion from the beginning as an object — as in the practice of science — assigning it, in Heidegger's view, a false status upon this assumption. Here, the philosophy of religion is not determined from within the experience of religion, but from a certain concept of philosophy, and in particular, a scientific concept thereof and the concept of religion becomes secondary.[10] In Heidegger's view, any philosophical determination of religion cannot take place prior to a factical approach.

Heidegger's analysis of Troeltsch demonstrates that the relation between metaphysics and religion is no longer an obvious one. In fact, Heidegger takes them to be expressly separate spheres. As we saw in the first chapter, Heidegger found indications of this divide in Schleiermacher, yet he found at the same time a clear connection between religion and history. In his lecture course on the phenomenology of religion, Heidegger was unequivocally committed to a view of the historical as a core phenomenon of religion from the outset.[11] However, he failed to offer a legitimation for this view, seeming to accept it as if it were obvious.

For Heidegger, the motives of philosophical understanding are what we must identify, and these can be found only in the factical experience of life. Out of this self-understanding, constructing a phenomenology of religion is possible. This task is therefore bound up with the problem of historicity. And here there arises the danger of falling into the objective world of science, precisely because philosophy has tended to withdraw from historicity, almost as if the philosopher were concerned to defend himself against historicity. Historicity is particularly problematic for philosophy because philosophers of old neglected its influence in their search for eternal truths. Accordingly, the defense against history comes by way of neutralizing it, by turning it into an object with which one is theoretically involved. This can be called an understanding of history, yet, it is an attitudinal understanding and has nothing to do with phenomenological understanding.[12]

Nevertheless, it is this defense against history that leads to insight into the meaning of historicity. This possibility appears to resist the attitude of theory and to shed light upon the true dynamism of life itself in order to reveal the phenomenon of concern within factical life.[13]

In order to accomplish this, Heidegger develops a special terminology for the phenomenological approach as a means for resisting a purely theoretical relation to historicity. He introduces the concept of formal indication, which belongs to the theoretical aspect of phenomenology: "The problem of the "*formal indication*" belongs to the "theory" of the phenomenological method itself; in the broad sense, to the problem of the *theoretical*, of the theoretical act, the phenomenon of *differentiating*."[14] As a particular attitude, formal indication differentiates itself from the theoretical attitude, given the latter's insufficiency.

Therefore, according to Heidegger, the theoretical approach emblematic of philosophy becomes a problem to be overcome. We continue to question the specific way of thinking that needs to be adopted in philosophy because this questioning is itself part of philosophy. Heidegger writes, "Philosophy's constant effort to determine its own concept belongs to its authentic motive."[15] The question of what philosophy is, is a question that every philosopher must continue to pose anew.

The answer to this question cannot be given by describing various models of philosophy, whether past or present. Nor is it the actual state of affairs within philosophy. According to Heidegger, the way in which we philosophize — including the entire conceptual framework of philosophy as we know it — produces an approach that blocks the very entrance to authentic philosophy. For Heidegger, philosophy must start from the 'situation of understanding' in which the philosopher finds himself. Since the conceptual framework of philosophy hinders access to this fundamental situation of understanding from which philosophy itself is to begin, the question of method takes the highest priority of philosophy, and 'method' is to be understood in this connection in its original Greek sense, as a way of getting somewhere. From this aspect, one is in a better position to pose the questions, "Which way do we need to go?" "Must we take a detour to reach our goal?" and so on.

Once we really begin searching, we discover that philosophy is essentially an activity; it is something that we do, that we carry out. We learn what philosophy is by performing the act of philosophizing. It is, in short, a way of being. The way of being from which we start to philosophize — this is the 'situation' of our philosophy, the situation that Heidegger calls facticity. We philosophize from our factical situation. In a certain sense, this word serves as a precursor to what Heidegger will later interpret as 'historicality.' Philosophy, therefore, belongs to the lived immediacy of life; to the extent that it tries to locate its own situation of understanding, philosophy must clarify its own facticity. In asking about the specific nature and task of philosophy, the philosopher must also investigate the way of being of factical existence itself. Philosophy becomes, as it were, an introduction to the experience of life.[16] The philosophical entrance to life and its facticity are tightly interwoven within Heidegger's analysis.

Philosophy, then, is a way of being of factical life, but it also returns to factical life, precisely because our lived situation has become for Heidegger a subject of philosophical query. Factical life has to be understood from the experience of life, but the experience of factical life is oriented in different directions. Heidegger writes: "Philosophy's departure as well as its goal is factical life experience. If factical life experience is the point of departure for philosophy, and if we see factically a difference in principle between philosophical and scientific cognition, then factical life experience must be not only the point of departure for philosophizing but precisely that which essentially hinders philosophizing itself."[17] Philosophy, as a way of being of factical life, is hindered by a tendency that is characteristic of factical life.

To understand the obstructive tendency of factical life, one must take note of the particular way in which we are familiar with philosophy. It is familiar to us as a discipline at the university, as a part of our cultural heritage, as a complex of values and ideas, and as a critical method for discerning sense from nonsense. In the word 'philosophy,' a myriad of different activities come together. In general, however, we can say that philosophy is present to us in a rather obvious way. The obvious presence is an indication of the way in which we have philosophy at our disposal. But it reaches beyond this, since it is within the framework of this obvious quality of philosophy that we set about to understand life and ourselves. As a result, the way that we understand ourselves is itself never discussed or criticized. Factical life is understood within a conceptual framework that is not neutral; the way in which we understand ourselves has an effect on the way in which we live, as well as providing us with an orientation for leading our lives. The question that follows is what the orientation underlying philosophical discourse actually is.

The way in which we philosophize bears witness to the fact that while we are dealing with a theoretical relation to an object, such a theoretical relation is nonetheless embedded in the experience of factical life, which includes our actions, our dreaming, our feeling, and so on. These activities cannot be understood in isolation from the entities to which they are related. As relations, they can only be grasped from their orientation toward their respective entities. If we give up this orientation, we are left with only an abstraction that owes its very existence to this original orientation. When we speak of 'subject' and 'object,' for example, we are making such an abstraction. Though Heidegger does not reject this kind of abstraction out of hand, he goes beyond it by seeking a more primordial and fundamental relation to entities in human life, which he describes as 'care.'

Given that the relations we maintain in our factical life are not primarily theoretical, taking up a theoretical relation to entities obscures our understanding of facticity. Humans have various relations with other beings through seeing, feeling, smelling, and loving, just to name a few, and this is what the phenomenological approach repeatedly emphasizes. As an experience becomes a phenomenon one can ask about the content (*Gehalt*) of that experience, after the nature of the relation (*Bezug*) in which something is experienced, and, after the way in which this relation is enacted (*Vollzug*). A phenomenon is always given within these three orientations. In Heidegger's thinking, this means that a content-sense (*Gehaltsinn*) is always connected with a relational-sense (*Bezugsinn*).[18] A seamless connection of relational sense and content sense does not mean, however, that in the theoretical orientation entities are always characterized in the proper way. It means that the third orientation, the enactment-sense (*Vollzugssinn*), remains hidden.[19] The hiddenness of this enactment owes its cause to philosophy's primary preoccupation with its object. Yet factical life and authentic philosophy share the character of actualization; it is precisely this basic feature of philosophy that is blocked by a theoretical, purely conceptual approach.[20]

On the basis of the introductory sketch I have provided thus far, I will go on to give an account of the tendency in factical life that hinders philosophy's entrance to it and to history and religion as well. This hindrance is constituted by the way in which we keep philosophy at our disposal in our everyday lives, as we become absorbed in the world, in entities around us, and in all of life's 'pressing' matters. The unreflective adoption of the conceptual frameworks of traditional philosophy also belongs to these 'pressing' and 'important' matters and blocks the practice of authentic philosophy from access to the factical situation in which it is practiced.

FROM FORMAL INDICATION TO FACTICITY

Heidegger's quest to study human existence in its facticity and historicality breaks with the classical structure of philosophy in which concepts and theories are supposed to describe and lead to an understanding of life as we actually live it. However philosophy is situated in the facticity and fragility of human existence, which cannot be understood through obvious and familiar concepts. This is what we all too often tend to forget, especially when we use familiar concepts. Heidegger was perhaps the first to see how philosophy can be alienated from its own situation: that is, philosophy is in constant danger of becoming completely absorbed in its theoretical orientation. He states, "But exactly because the formal determination is entirely indifferent as to content, it is fatal for the relational- and enactment-aspect of the phenomenon — because it prescribes, or at least contributes to prescribing, a theoretical relational meaning. It hides the enactment-character (*das Vollzugsmäßige*) — which is possibly still more fatal — and turns one-sidedly to the content. A glance at the history of philosophy shows that formal determination of the objective entirely dominates philosophy. How can this prejudice, this prejudgment, be prevented? This is just what the formal indication achieves."[21] The facticity of human existence, in its quest for real life, through its repeated employment of familiar concepts and frameworks, calls for its own specific philosophical treatment. Formal indication is not a concept in the usual sense of the word. It is rather a reference or a guide that offers us a first glimpse of a particular phenomenon. For Heidegger, this situational actualization must be our original phenomenon of study, if we are to ask what philosophy actually is. We go wrong in attempting to apply objective concepts to a situational actualization, precisely because in doing so, we turn into a theoretical object that which cannot be an object. The formal indication directs us toward what we must actualize in our situational understanding of the world.

From this perspective, the formal indication has two overlapping functions.[22] First, it indicates a phenomenon in such a way that the phenomenon itself resists all premature or external characterizations.[23] Heidegger writes, "The formal indication prevents every drifting off into autonomous, blind, dogmatic attempts to fix the categorical sense, attempts which would be detached from the presupposition of the interpretation, from its preconception, its nexus, and its time, and which would then purport to determine an objectivity in itself, apart from a thorough discussion of its ontological sense."[24] That is, the formal indication expresses how a phenomenon is not to be understood. There is therefore always negativity in the formal indication, as we will see as well in Augustine (where real life is never this or that objective thing) and Paul (where the coming of Christ cannot be expected as an event at a certain moment in the future).

This negative function involves a second aspect: the provisional indication of the phenomenon. Here as well, the familiar habit of objectifying phenomena is resisted. What we seek after, real life, or that to which one is awake — the coming of Christ, to take Paul's example — cannot be objectified, but must be indicated in a specific and provisional manner. And because the very 'concept' of philosophy is transformed in this activity, so too is the philosopher himself transformed.

Heidegger uses the word 'indication' (*Anzeige*), because the indicated content is not something that we already have at our disposal, or something that we can grasp. Like a cue or a hint, it gives us a direction; it cannot be made concrete by way of examples. The indication, as a sign or a guide, precedes all examples. It belongs essentially to the question in giving it an orientation and a set of principles. Yet in preceding a question, it is never to be mistaken for the object of the question. Heidegger uses the term 'formal' here to emphasize that the philosophical concept, as formal indication, is not fixed in advance.[25] What is formally indicated is not presented as something brought to completion and understandable through comparison or classification; on the contrary, what is formally indicated is understandable only insofar as the philosopher himself realizes or actualizes a certain activity.[26] In this sense, the concepts serving as formal indications for what human existence is in its actualization remain empty.

Generally, we understand human existence without the need to pose questions. Yet it is precisely with respect to this general understanding that we need to win a distance, since, for Heidegger, existence itself is a question.[27] Therefore, philosophy means first and foremost asking, querying; it does not offer up any answers. The formally indicating character of philosophy serves to safeguard its own essence as questioning. These formally indicating concepts demand to be rethought from out of the philosopher's concrete historical situation, since one can understand something philosophically to the extent that one can understand it within the perspective of one's own situation. Therefore, formal indications are always put into play in reference to one's own historical facticity.

By reconstruing philosophy as formal indication, Heidegger's initial aim is not to remove the roadblocks within philosophy that hinder our understanding of factical life; rather, he wants to call attention to them as roadblocks. If we recognize their tendency to hinder questioning, philosophical concepts will provide access to what they conceal. The fragility and provisionality of factical and historical life is therefore taken up into the fragility and provisionality of formally indicating philosophy. For the character of factical life is such that it can only be indicated in this fragile, provisional manner. The question of philosophy, then, concerns actualizing this provisional life (*vorlaufend*), without getting mired in descriptive concepts.

To summarize what I have outlined above, formally indicating concepts are taken up ever again from out of the philosopher's concrete historical situation, precisely because I can only understand something philosophically when I understand it with respect to a concrete situation. And formal indications always refer back to the specific historical facticity out of which they arise.

For Heidegger, then, the philosopher must avoid the temptation to provide premature answers for questions about life, even if such answers are lucid insights. One takes it as his task, instead, to keep the primordial question of philosophy open. As

he states: "The formal indication renounces the last understanding that can only be given in genuine religious experience."[28]

In this respect, we must pose anew the question of Heidegger's relation to religion. As a philosopher concerned with factical life, he sees factical life in religion, the religion in which
he was raised, and which therefore belongs to the situation in
which he lives. The a priori is the prior situation in which he
exists, and not a general essential structure, as Troeltsch and
Otto believed.

If we turn for a moment to Otto's book, *The Idea of the
Holy,* we can see Otto's commitment to the direction set by
Schleiermacher, whose new edition of *On Religion* he supported in 1899. Otto found a point of departure for revealing
the holy by beginning in the experience of feeling, as an experience of unknown quality. We find this, accordingly, in his
determination of the holy: "Anyone who uses it [the notion of
the holy] today does undoubtedly feel the 'morally good' to be
implied in 'holy;' and accordingly in our inquiry into that element which is separate and peculiar to the idea of the holy, it
will be useful, at least for the temporary purpose of the investigation, to invent a special term to stand for the 'holy' minus
its moral factor, or 'moment', and, as we can now add, minus
its 'rational' aspect altogether."[29] Like Schleiermacher, for Otto,
morality and rationality are not points of entrance to the holy.
Rather, entrance to the holy is gained by way of a 'divination'
(*Ahnung*).

Otto's insights into the holy are not theological, as a kind of
science founded in supernatural revelation, but are instead scientific in the sense of a philosophy of religion. Otto refers to
a religious feeling as a religious a priori.[30] "Every religion
which, so far from being a mere faith in traditional authority,
springs from personal assurance and inward convincement (i.e.,
from an inward first-hand cognition of its truth) — as Christianity does in a unique degree — must presuppose principles

in the mind enabling it to be independently recognized as true. But these principles must be a priori ones, not to be derived from 'experience' or 'history'."[31] According to Otto, these a priori principles recognized as true are a *testimonium Spiritus Sancti internum.* On this assumption, he understands his philosophy of religion from the perspective of Christianity; the principles are first and foremost religious principles. Formal indication, on the other hand, is not religious; it is a concept used for gaining access to what is religious.[32]

Heidegger's rejection of the a priori as Troeltsch and Otto conceive it points to the fact that the philosopher qua philosopher is, in principle, unfamiliar with the concrete content of the experience that he investigates. Therefore, the explication of formal indication is necessary, because it refers to the motivating situation, and not to its given content. Husserl used the method of *epoche* to bracket our unreflective assumption of the reality of being (what Husserl calls the 'natural attitude') in order to carry out his phenomenological *Wesensschau.* In formal indication, Heidegger makes a similar move, by giving up the question of what is presupposed in the early Christian experience of life, in terms of the content of its faith. As he will later argue in *Phänomenologie und Theologie,* the problem of the truth of faith — and with this its value — that makes possible the kairological experience of life, is a problem that must be left to faith and to the theological studies involved in it. And this means in turn that the formal structure of temporality must be separated from the content of Christianity.[33] That is, formal indications have to be repeatable without actualizing the act of faith at the same moment.[34] In order for this formal indication to succeed, however, it demands an understanding of religion freed from its traditional theological-metaphysical framework.

Heidegger not only leaves this framework behind, but he also resists it as a philosophical framework for understanding facticity. Nonetheless, his commitment is completely philosophical. He imports new philosophical concepts in order to comprehend factical life.[35] These are not, however, new religious concepts, but rather concepts aimed at unfolding a new philosophy of facticity that resists all systems intent upon constructing a '*sub specie aeternitatis.*' To this end, he formulates a philosophical interpretation wherein he explicates early Christianity from the perspective of original temporality. This interpretation belongs to his overall commitment, which remains ontological. The explication of the experience of facticity is necessary in order to uncover the implicit ontology of early Christianity and furthermore to prepare a conceptual apparatus for a critical appropriation of the philosophical tradition.

Heidegger asks what a philosophy of religion's specific approach must be when it becomes a phenomenology of religion. It, too, must become a philosophy of facticity, which means that religion must be understood from out of factical life. This phenomenology is directed less toward its object, religion, than toward a philosophy that, in its actualization, makes use of particular concepts. Phenomenology must destroy philosophy and its framework if religion is to be understood from its own lived situation. Phenomenology's grasp of preoccupation is necessary to maintain its connection with history. It is particularly with respect to history that such preoccupation can block our attempts at gaining an original understanding.

In taking up this project, Heidegger lays out two basic determinations for the object of his philosophy of religion. First, early Christian religiosity is given in the early Christian experience of life and is itself an experience of life; second, the factical experience of life is historic, and Christian religiosity lives temporality as such ('live' being understood as transitive).[36] These determinations are not theses standing in need of proof, but rather phenomenological explications. As such, they must be taken formally, and moreover, they must be allowed their instability in the beginning, in order that they may be safe-guarded during phenomenological analysis. In the end, phe-nomenological explication unfolds the ontology that is implied in this experience of religion.

HEIDEGGER'S INTERPRETATION OF PAUL'S LETTERS TO THE THESSALONIANS

One may ask why Heidegger sees it necessary to analyze Paul and Augustine in his study of the facticity of human being. Looked at more closely, we can see how this direction stems from Heidegger's own position. There is a certain preju-dice in relation to Christianity, caused by the thrownness, which is part of the pre-structure of understanding as Heidegger will go on to work out in *Being and Time*. He writes in his lecture course on Paul: "Real philosophy of religion arises not from preconceived concepts of philosophy and reli-gion. Rather, the possibility of its philosophical understanding arises out of a certain religiosity — for us, the Christian reli-giosity. Why exactly the Christian religiosity lies in the focus of our study, that is a difficult question; it is answerable only through the solution of the problem of the historical connec-tions. The task is to gain a real and original relationship to his-tory, which is to be explicated from out of our own historical situation and facticity. At issue is what the sense of history can signify for us, so that the 'objectivity' of the historical 'in itself' disappears. History exists only from out of a present. Only thus can the possibility of a philosophy of religion be begun."[37] To catch a glimpse of this original facticity, Heideg-ger presents his explication of Paul's letters. Here the First Letter to the Thessalonians is central; by way of supplements he also looks at the Second Letter to the Thessalonians, as well as the Letter to the Galatians, and lastly, the Second Letter to the Corinthians.[38]

In his interpretation of these letters, Heidegger reveals the emergence of the actualization-sense, the third sense-orientation, in early Christian life. In an attempt to access itself, philosophy directs itself toward factical life. Heidegger emphasizes the relation-sense in its directedness toward a meaningful content, yet it is of utmost importance to understand life within the coherence of all three sense-orientations.[39] The first two, as I noted above, tend to conceal the third, actualization. Based on the concept of '*parousia,*' the second coming of Christ, Heidegger demonstrates how the actualization-sense is to be understood. An essential moment of the orientation of factical life shows itself in the articulation of the actualization-sense, and it does so as historicality. That is, the meaning of the orientation of human existence appears in existence as historicality. Thus, the way in which factical life lives time is historicality's actualization.

In early Christian life, the actualization of factical life coheres with the two corresponding sense-orientations; without the coherence of these three, the essential facticity of factical life cannot become visible. Heidegger locates a presentation of factical life in Paul's appeal to the community of faith of the Thessalonians, an appeal to Christian life. Paul's letter is essentially a proclamation, in the form of an announcement to the Christians of Thessalonia. This proclamation can itself be understood as a kind of relation; it concerns a public announcement of a specific content, and it takes place within a relation between an individual and a specific audience. Important here is that this proclamation is not simply a relation with a content, but an actualization. This actualization is what Heidegger prioritizes in his interpretation. This approach carries with it a number of significant consequences, especially with respect to how the preacher and his message are to be understood. From the perspective of the relational sense, the preacher is the announcer, and what is preached is the announced content. This perspective takes up the structure of two entities between which a relation exists. But when this preaching is understood as actualization, then both the preacher and what is preached are understood as particular moments in the event of preaching. Heidegger writes: "Object-historical understanding is determination according to the aspect of the relation, from out of the relation, so that the observer does not come into question. By contrast, phenomenological understanding is determined by the enactment of the observer."[40] Phenomenological understanding, determined by the actualization of the observer, refers to the situation from which the observer listens.

By 'situation,' Heidegger does not mean the biography of the person who speaks, but rather the circumstances in which that person speaks. The aim here is to explicate this situation, since it is only understandable from the perspective of the actualization sense. Paul experiences himself as a fellow sufferer and as a member of the community of faith in Thessalonia. This is the situation from which he speaks. The community of faith of the Thessalonians is coming into being, and the community is aware of this coming into being. This emergence of the Thessalonians' community is connected with Paul's appearance in Thessalonia. This coming into being is the acceptance of his appeal, and with it, the devotion to God. That is, in this event, the Thessalonians became Christians. For being a Christian is not merely having an opinion about life, according to Heidegger; it is a way of behaving, a type of factical life. It concerns the "how" of behavior. The genesis of the Thessalonians, with their devotion to God and their aversion to idols, is connected with Paul's own genesis — as the one who is a disciple — in and by preaching. Paul's speaking is not a theoretical speculation, of which he himself would not be a part. His destiny is united with the destiny of the community. From this 'situation' of solidarity, he speaks to the community. His own place is part of his speaking. Paul speaks in a situation of need, and this need is the concern about the coming of Christ.

This need is strengthened all the more by his knowledge of Satan as the one who fights against God's will.

The need from which Paul speaks, the situation of the preacher, cannot be isolated from that about which he speaks. The need in which Paul finds himself and out of which he speaks, as well as the coming of Christ as the content of which he speaks, are moments of his preaching as actualization. The crucial question in this connection, however, is: how are we to understand the coming of Christ as a moment of actualization? From the perspective of the content sense, the coming of Christ is the content of an image that refers to a future event. The sense orientation is that both the coming and that in which the coming is to take place — time — are represented as entities that are present at hand. In this case, relational sense and content sense link up perfectly. Thinking means, then, having or creating representations. A representation is filled with a content that refers to something that will take place in the future.

However, Paul does not give heed to this particular aspect. This is not because he is unaware of it, but because his concern is not with a coming that will take place at a certain time. He writes, "For you know perfectly well that the day of the Lord comes like a thief in the night."[41] This knowing refers to the actualization-sense of the coming. Against this background, Paul stands opposed to two groups and two ways of living. The first group is made up of those people who see the coming of Christ as something that is to happen at a certain time. This way of living is one that looks for certainty and peace; it is the life of those living in darkness because they lack the illumination of authentic knowing. They are unaware that Christ comes like a thief in the night. Members of the second group are those who know about the coming of Christ as something indeterminate, and they live in insecurity and uncertainty. According to Heidegger, this latter is a moment of actualization-sense.

Actualization is connected to historicality as the whole in which this process of understanding takes place. It is necessary to understand the actualization sense from the perspective of the historicality of human existence. This is the point where the two opposite ways of living become explicit. The apostates do not accept this truth; they see the coming as something that will happen in the foreseeable future. According to Heidegger, they make the mistake of concealing the actualization-sense by bringing only the relational-sense and the content-sense together. And in this turning to the content of the world, the turning away from the actualization sense is presupposed. Where the apostates think that they can hold out for Christ's coming, the true Christians attune themselves to the uncertainty of the coming; they understand it as an indication of the way in which they have to live. This opens them up to the unexpected; they do without an understanding of the coming as a particular content contained within a future moment. In this way, they avoid neutralizing historicality. Those who do not accept this truth are therefore unable to recognize the Antichrist, who clothes himself in the mere appearance of the divine. Heidegger interprets the coming as an indication of factical and historical existence.

One significant aspect of historicality in this sense is that Christian life extends itself between a beginning and an end. The beginning of Christian life is preaching and the devotion to God; the end is the coming of Christ. This beginning and end, however, are not events, but rather moments of the actualization itself. And in this actualization of devotion to God, which must be actualized again and again, human existence becomes historical.

Humanity can give up the meaningful world in which it lives, for factical life also means being absorbed in the world. 'Being absorbed in' means being oriented to entities which only appear meaningful. This does not change in Christian life, where relational sense and content sense do not change, but remain as they are. The difference here is that they no longer determine Christian facticity. Together, the relational sense and the content sense form the supporting orientation toward meaningful entities. Due to this meaningfulness, the actualization sense remains hidden. But if the perspective of content is given up, the 'empty content' can indicate the way in which Christians are to live their lives. Again, what is coming is not some anticipated future moment. Christian life means standing before God, in a devotion that must be ever renewed. In and through this actualization, Christian life becomes historical. Christians are those who relate to the world "as if they do not."[42] As an explanation for this, Heidegger borrows from Paul's letter to the Corinthians: "What I mean, my friends, is this: the time we live in will not last long. While it lasts, married men should be as if they had no wives; mourners should be as if they had nothing that grieves them, the joyful as if they did not rejoice; those who buy should be as if they possessed nothing and those who use the world's wealth as if they did not have full use of it."[43]

This 'as if they do not' does not mean that the Christian has to give up his relations to the world. It belongs to the facticity of life that one becomes absorbed in the world and it is impossible for the Christian to have relations other than the worldly. This 'as if not' refers specifically to the actualization-sense. Christian facticity cannot be experienced from the content-sense. That is, Christian understanding lies not in the representation of God, not in the coming of Christ, nor does the essence of Christian life lie in preaching as doctrine, dogma, or theoretical standpoint. It refers instead to breaking through the all-embracing tendency toward entities that is typical of theoretical representation. As a result of such breaking-through, the actualization-sense can be made to appear. But this turning does not mean that the theoretical approach as a mode of caring can be eliminated, either. It is simply not possible for Christian life to be lived purely in actualization. But out of the conversion to God, the fragility of life becomes visible. This fragility is typical of authentic Christianity, which, according to Heidegger, points to the facticity of human existence. Heidegger writes: "Christian life is not straightforward, but is rather broken up: all surrounding-world relations must pass through the complex of enactment of having-become, so that this complex is then co-present, but the relations themselves, and that to which they refer, are in no way touched."[44] Living a Christian life means understanding life's fragility, which means being aware of the discrepancies within the sense orientations of factical life. In the final analysis, factical life is this discrepancy of sense orientations, which for the most part goes unnoticed. The meaning of this turn to the actualization-sense of factical life lies in the fact that the relational-sense, in its orientation to the content as such, comes to light. This happens as a result of the distance opened up between actualization-sense and content-sense. Through this distance, the relational-sense can be uncovered in its tendency toward the world of meaningful entities. But this also entails that the actualization sense is directed to 'something meaningless.'[45] It is not by chance that Heidegger will go on to speak of 'no-thing.'

As I have shown above, the normal orientation in which humanity lives is indicated as the connection between the relational and the content-senses. In his situation, factical life does not bear witness to its own actualization. The implication here is that it lives indifferently both in relation to the actualization of factical life itself, and in relation to the all-embracing absorption in the world. Humanity has to stay in the meaningfulness that is and has been the adage of normal life up through the present. The same goes for philosophy and science. The statements made in those fields have to be both meaningful and correct. In everyday life and in everyday philosophy, humanity is concerned with this correctness. "In a specific situation, I can factically listen to scientific lectures and, in the course of this, than talk about quotidian matters. The situation is essentially the same, except that the content has changed; and yet I do not become conscious of a specific change of attitude. Scientific objects, too, are always first of all cognized with the character of factical life experience."[46] The connection between the relational sense and the content sense refers to all modes of speech.

In philosophy, however, it is important to demonstrate the all-embracing character of these sense-orientations. For this, philosophy must withdraw from this content orientation, which draws us into absorption. To this end, it seeks a context in which this all-embracing character of speaking, as well as the appearing of beings, can be experienced. If the all-embracing character of the relational-sense and the content-sense resisted all attempts to access it, philosophy itself would be rendered impossible. The question of the possibility of philosophy depends upon the possibility of finding a standpoint from which the orientation of factical life can be understood.

In his interpretation of Paul's letters to the Thessalonians, Heidegger tries to understand the coherence between the relational-sense and the content-sense on the one hand, and the actual-ization sense on the other. This coherence of the moments of the orientation of human existence is found in its fragility. Whenever this fragility of factical life is misunderstood due to the tendency toward objectivity, the essence of the facticity of human life is misunderstood. If one wants to remain true to this fragility, the concepts that indicate factical life stand in need of revision.

For Heidegger, the faith of the Thessalonians is not a concern here, nor is the content of their faith. He is involved first and foremost in the experience of historicity, which is implied in such faith, as well as in the ontology implied in this experience. However, it remains in question whether this experience of historicity is accessible at all if we consider it in isolation from its content: that is the unpredictability of history with respect to the Christians' hope for the coming of Christ. It recoils utterly from calculative manipulation. This period of waiting is oriented instead to a sudden, startling event, which nullifies everything that we take to be predictable, certain, and secure. Human beings live and die in the face of a future that rejects objectification. Values, meaning, and totalities cannot be deduced on the basis of this Christian experience of time.[47]

HEIDEGGER'S INTERPRETATION OF AUGUSTINE

Heidegger masterfully brings out the obstructive tendency of philosophy in his analysis of Augustine's *Confessions*. This analysis was part of a lecture course he taught in the summer of 1921, entitled "Augustine and Neo-Platonism."[48] According to Heidegger, Augustine, like Paul, approaches life from the perspective of facticity.[49] Augustine does not consider the *beata vita* (the beatific life) from the perspective of its content, as something in the external world, but from the actualization of looking for it. Augustine transforms the question of how to find God into the question of how to find the beatific life. This was possible for him because he regarded the beatific life as real life, and real life is the true life that he calls God. Heidegger sought to illuminate the way in which people are related to the content of beatific life, most commonly by looking forward to it and hoping for it. Here we see that Heidegger 'historil-izes,' to use a neologism, the relation that a believer maintains to God.

While Augustine approaches the quest for God from life's facticity, he also displays a tendency to move away from fac-ticity. This, however, as we shall see, is part of Augustine's conception of facticity. According to Heidegger, Augustine does not radically question his quest for God because his situation is such that he operates with an objective conception of know-ing.[50] Nevertheless, Augustine knows that the beatific life is not present in the way that, for example, the town of Carthago is present for someone who has visited it and subsequently retains a mental image of it. The beatific life is present to us in such a way that our understanding of it compels us to want to make it our own. But it is difficult to find oneself in the right posi-tion with respect to this authentic truth after which we search. Augustine explains in his *Confessions* why it is so difficult to put oneself into the right position, even though the quest for truth seems to us to be so natural and straightforward. In fac-tical life, people by and large operate according to their own prima facie opinions. These may be determined by tradition, fashion, convenience, or fear. The truth is hidden from human-ity, in part because humanity itself flees from it. Yet on the other side of this flight, Heidegger sees a concern for truth, despite the fact that it is primarily hidden. This care, which is typical of factical life, is actualized within a horizon of expec-tations. For Heidegger, most important is the observation that this care is actualized historically.[51] The human self is seen from the perspective of historical experience because care itself is historical. In the tendency characteristic of care, there is also a constant danger of falling into inauthenticity. This means that the individual is no longer directed toward God as the true beatific life.

Heidegger especially sees a Neo-Platonic influence in Augustine in the longing for pleasure because beauty, in Augustine, belongs to the essence of being. Something is pleasurable and provides enjoyment if it does not refer to anything beyond itself, and if it is chosen purely for itself. Such pleasure is directed toward eternal and unchangeable goods. This results in a stance toward the world wherein peace and tranquility are the true aims of life; real life is seen as the realization of peace and tranquility. This aim is actualized historically because life actualizes itself in the direction in which its expectations move. Nevertheless, it is difficult for the individual to actualize his life in an authentic manner, because of the difficulty involved in distinguishing one's own tendency toward the true beatific life from the tendency toward other kinds of pleasure and enjoyment. To overcome this difficulty, Augustine proposes an order of values, which Heidegger regarded as theoretically motivated, and Greek in its origin.

The basic orientation of Augustine's values is connected not only with Neo-Platonism, but also the doctrine of the *summum bonum*. He ties this Greek theoretical approach to the Christian message. Heidegger points out, as we saw in the previous chapter, that Paul's text, in the Letter to the Romans at 1:20, sets the foundation for patristic philosophy as a whole. The fathers of the early Christian church laid down the Christian doctrine within a Greek philosophical framework that has endured up to the present. And because of the undeniable Platonic influence on Augustine, it would be a mistake to think that we could arrive at an authentic Christianity by simply going back to Augustine.[52]

Through this Greek influence, we can detect an ahistorical conception operative in Augustine's quest for the beatific life. But Augustine is aware that the *beata vita* cannot be found in what humans find easy to believe, in humanity's 'convenient' tendencies. In the quest for the true *beata vita* and the danger in following convenient tendencies, the individual must eventually confront the question of who he or she is. This question becomes exigent when one sees oneself undertaking things that one does not want to carry through, and conversely, wanting to do things that one finds oneself unable to do. That is, there are processes at play within oneself that are beyond one's own control. This places a certain burden (*molestia*) on humanity, a burden that belongs to the very facticity of human existence. According to Heidegger, philosophical activity must start from this aspect of facticity and not from theoretic notions like 'body,' 'soul,' 'sense,' 'reason,' and so on.

Understanding that there is a dark side, as it were, within us means realizing that the individual is not completely accessible to him or her self. It is not possible for me to see myself in such a way that I am completely transparent; part of me remains hidden from such attempts. I can never say what I actually am in a moment where I have completely penetrated into my own heart because I may always fall back again into concealment in the next moment. Therefore, this moment of having total self-awareness, if possible at all, is always only a movement in the direction of life; it is both a moving forward and backward. Yet it would be wrong to represent this total self-awareness as a kind of hyper-reflexive solipsism. The self is completely historical; it is not a tranquil, theoretical moment, but rather historical actualization. In the theoretical approach to philosophy, Heidegger sees humanity's tendency to fall back into its enjoyment of obvious things.

Augustine describes three such tendencies that we, as humans, are subject to. The first he calls *concupiscentia carnis,* the second, *concupiscentia oculorum,* and the third, *ambitio saeculi.* In our quest for the beatific life, we are moved to put ourselves into question. However, the danger in questioning myself is that I may not really carry out authentic questioning, but rather become carried away by the pleasure I find within my quest. Such is the case, for example, when one sings in praise of the Lord, where one forgets the praise itself and begins simply to enjoy the pleasure (*concupiscentia carnis*) of the singing itself — the beauty of the tones and the songs. This intertwinement of carnal life and truth in factical life comprises the danger of being directed toward something other than true life. Against this background, there is a long tradition in which god is seen as the highest light, and the highest form of self-possession, wherein god is joyfully witnessed as the highest beauty. The being of god is understood in this tradition from the perspective presentation, of standing before someone's eyes. Thinking that is oriented toward seeing is directed toward what can be presented, consequently missing the irreducible historical actualization. What is visible is only what lasts and subsists. This image is clearly expressed in the *visio beatifica* of the scholastic tradition.

These Greek elements in philosophy hinder the understanding of factical life: the theoretical approach is not able by itself to undo its Greek framework in order to grasp factical life.[53] But as god is experienced in the actualization of the quest for him, in the quest for the true life, the distance from the 'highest' god as beauty and light, grows. The quest for the *vita beata,* rather than seeing beauty in a thing (*in re*), is directed toward what we hope for, what we do not yet have in our grasp. The question for Augustine is how to win access to God. God is 'present' in the concern and care for the self's quest for life.[54] Any metaphysical representation of god as a 'thing' is to be avoided. But in Heidegger's view, Augustine's explication of the experience of god is Greek, in the sense that all of our philosophy remains essentially Greek.[55]

The second tendency, the *concupescentia oculorum,* has to do with the pleasure of the eyes. As we saw above, singing to praise god can be reduced to the pure enjoyment of notes and sounds. A similar occurrence can take place with respect to our eyes. Pure seeing as such, seeing out of sheer curiosity, can overtake the quest for truth. This seeing is a mere looking, a witnessing, informing, or objectifying. In this case, the relational sense is overtaken by seeing.[56]

The third tendency, the *ambitio saeculi,* is worldly ambition. In this tendency, the self, which is sought, takes itself to be its prime object. Even though the quest for truth is directed to the self, this self must not be considered from the perspective of self-interest. The self in relation to the other sees itself as superior or looks for respect and esteem from others, demanding the other's praise. This enjoyment of praise is a form of self-interest, and as such, a falling away from searching for the true self. This happens most frequently when one is no longer sure of oneself, where one stands in need of the praise of others as a means of compensation. In asking after one's real self, one must discard one's self-interest. It is precisely at the moment where one approaches oneself with empty hands that the true self can appear.

Against the background of these tendencies, humanity always tends to fall into the objects of life; this is the *molestia* of factical life. *Molestia* is a burden and an obstacle to self-possession. This burden is not something objective, a thing that one could simply cut away. The individual is in danger of losing himself in objective things. In concrete, authentic actualization there lies the possibility of a fall and yet at the same time the possibility to receive true life. This means that the self should be seen as important, yet the danger of self-interest is always lurking around the corner. This burden is part and parcel of life, and it belongs to human facticity, as it belongs to Augustine's notion of facticity. The tendency to understand the beatific life within a Neo-Platonic framework therefore also belongs to Augustine's facticity. The radical possibility of falling is built into the care for the truth of the self, yet it also provides an opportunity for finding one's true self. Although we can be sure of ourselves, we are nevertheless fundamentally unsure beings; we do not know how long we will live, whether life will let us down, and so on.

In his analysis of Augustine's description of the three tendencies, Heidegger demonstrates how it is that we are always absorbed in the world. The fact that factical life is absorbed in the world does not mean that we are dealing with two separate elements, namely factical life and the world. These two elements are actually moments of one and the same movement, which cannot be broken down into separate components. The tendency toward absorption nullifies any distance between the self and factical life. Being engrossed in the world destroys all distance to the self as well as to factical life in the world. The interdependence of relational sense and content sense is the orientation in which everything happens, an orientation that is so obvious and all-embracing that it is not seen as such. Distance is necessary in order for this orientation to become visible. The tendency of life toward the world, with its objects of pleasure, of beauty and of praise, understands itself from the world as an entity of the world; there is no motivation to search for another means of understanding oneself. Every possibility for life to understand itself out of another way of being disappears in and through the tendency toward being absorbed in the world.

This absorption in the world stems, once again, from the connection between the relational sense and the content sense in factical life. It is also out of this orientation of life that philosophy usually originates, because it starts with concepts that are already at hand in the world. However, philosophy not only originates from factical life, but is also hindered by the way in which factical life is carried out. The relational sense as an orientation to the world — insofar as it understands life as an entity within the world — blocks access to the true way of being, and from this perspective, it hinders the task of philosophy. The relational sense, due to its one-sided orientation toward its content, conceals the actualization sense of factical life. Heidegger writes that "factical life experience manifests an indifference with regard to the manner of experiencing. It does not even occur to factical life experience that something might not become accessible to it. This factical experience engages, as it were, all concerns of life."[57]

As I have shown, Heidegger's interpretation of Augustine points out that the quest for true life tends to ossify as a result of humanity's devotion to obvious sensual preoccupations.

Heidegger's quest for truth is no longer devoted to the highest being, as was the case during his early studies in Freiburg. In Heidegger's thinking, the orientation toward the highest is instead reformulated as a historical orientation. The historicity of religion has to be understood out of its own situation and out of the presuppositions contained within it. It should not be taken up from a philosophical framework, as if from the standpoint of some highest being, precisely because as we have noted, the philosophical idea of a highest being hinders our understanding of facticity, and with this, religion as an expression of facticity. We see this change actualized in Heidegger's earliest writings, and it involves as well the philosophical paradigm with which he approaches religion. What we are left with, then, is a religion that is an expression of historicity.

The idea that Greek philosophy corrupts the original Christian faith is an idea found especially in Luther's Protestantism. However, this is not Heidegger's position. Heidegger looks for a better philosophy, but not for a new faith that would be a faith without philosophy. Instead, the metaphysical paradigm is put into perspective, where one can see how it opposes the understanding of facticity. There is a collision between two philosophical approaches, but not a collision between faith and philosophy. Heidegger seeks an atheistic philosophy, or at the very least, a philosophy without an a priori conception of god.

THREE

Philosophy and Theology as Mortal Enemies

*I*n this chapter I will focus upon a text by Heidegger that has received relatively little attention.[1] *Phenomenology and Theology* is a short volume consisting of two texts: a lecture and a letter.[2] The lecture "Phänomenologie und Theologie" was presented on March 8, 1927, in Tübingen, and then repeated in Marburg the following February. The appended letter, written in regard to an upcoming debate at Drew University from April 9 to 11, 1964, dates from March 11, 1964, and it offers a set of reflections upon what Heidegger calls "The Problem of a Nonobjectifying Thinking and Speaking in Today's Theology."[3]

Heidegger presented the lecture during the period that *Being and Time* was first appearing in publication, and the concept of phenomenology in the lecture is grounded solidly in the account given in that work.[4] He resists seeking the difference between philosophy and theology in the separation between faith and knowledge, between revelation and reason. If this were the case, then philosophy would simply be the interpretation of the world free from revelation and belief; taken in this light, the problem of the relation between philosophy and theology would be reduced to the relation between two different, competing worldviews. Heidegger shifts the entire problematic to a question of the relationship between two sciences. He proposes an ideal construction of both sciences wherein the specific subject of each can be sought and isolated. This idealization contrasts with the particular mode of understanding within modern science, which takes the form of logically valid statements. Instead, science in Heidegger is seen as the unconcealment of a certain isolated domain of being or of entities, akin to Aristotle's search for the specific domain of first philosophy in the doctrine of being qua being in his Metaphysics. Here, every domain demands an approach and a set of concepts corresponding to its own particular nature. To Heidegger, the primary distinction to be made is whether one is dealing with a science of entities or a science of being. The latter he terms philosophy. Sciences of entities, on the other hand, have the presupposition of a positive[5] entity, both present and available, always already revealed to us in our understanding in one way or another. Philosophy, however, does not have a specific entity but rather being in general as its field of research. In making this distinction, philosophy radically differentiates itself from all other positive sciences. Theology, too, falls under the category of the positive sciences, and as such is essentially other than philosophy. "Our thesis, then, is that theology is a positive science, and as such, therefore, is absolutely different from philosophy."[6]

Since this perspective classifies theology as a science of entities, it is as such closer to natural science than it is to philosophy. This is, of course, a rather extreme proposal on Heidegger's part. Yet it was necessary for Heidegger to break from the popular conception of philosophy's relation to theology, as if both shared the same theme, but one took it up from the standpoint of faith and the other from reason. Nevertheless, Heidegger has certain reservations in describing theology as a science: for him, the essential question is: is theology a science, and does it have to be? This question, raised almost in passing, is not as innocent as it appears, because he maintains that a philosopher has a different object of research and cannot answer such a question.[7] In his lecture, Heidegger points out the fact that faith does not necessarily ask for scientific explanation. Thus, Heidegger's proposal is best read as a kind of draft, should faith ever require a scientific approach. By sketching an image of theology as a science, it is easier to evaluate the question of whether or not it should become a science at all. Because each science of entities deals with present entities, i.e., the *positum,* theology can only be seen as a positive science. And Heidegger does not refer in any way to the possibility of a natural or philosophical theology as the domain of the question of being, as an element of metaphysics or ontology.

What is this positive character of science in Heidegger's conception? Here we can lay out three fundamental determinants:

1. There is an entity present to us, revealed in a particular way. This entity is a possible focus of theoretical objectification and research, as Heidegger has shown in the concept of science given in *Being and Time.*[8]
2. This present entity is already grasped on a prescientific level. This understanding is already implied in the specific scientific field itself, as well as in the nature of the being of this entity. Preceding all theoretical understanding, it is more or less unconsciously taken up into an understanding of being.
3. This prescientific understanding implies a prior understanding of being which determines the entity to be uncovered. According to the way in which the uncovered entity, the understanding of entities, and the understanding of the being of entities vary, the theme of the science will change as well.

The problem where theology is concerned, is how to get from the second determination listed above to the third. Because the prereflexive understanding of being mentioned in the third determination is explicated in the analysis of being (fundamental ontology), it can thereby function as the basis for the prescientific approach mentioned in the second. But this given is especially problematic when the *positum* of a science is not given from a domain that was earlier (a priori) uncovered as human being (Dasein).[9] The *positum* characteristic to theology is not something that Dasein can understand a priori. This is all the more problematic because Heidegger himself rejects religious a priori phenomena in general, as we observed in regard to Otto and Troeltsch in the previous chapter. Thus, Heidegger is forced to reduce the ontological elements of theology to something that can be only formally indicated without the content of its theological message.

Despite these difficulties, Heidegger seeks to determine a relation between philosophy and theology. And in order to carry this project out, he must determine the scientific, positive character of theology. But what is the given *positum,* of theology? Answering this question will not take us all the way to a characterization of the whole of theology as a science. Yet only on the basis of this answer can we go on to ask about theology's scientific character.

The Positive Character of Theology

When we ask about the positive character of theology, we do not have in mind those aspects of it that are determined by a particular set of values. Positive science is the uncovering of a present entity, already uncovered for us in one manner or another. If we were to describe what theology's *positum* is by saying that it is Christianity as a historical phenomenon — as the history of religion and culture would confirm it — we would have to direct ourselves, then, to Christian customs, rites, and so on. But this approach is insufficient, precisely because theology itself belongs to Christianity. Therefore, Heidegger distinguishes theology from a science of religion. Theology is something that develops historically within Christianity; it belongs to the history of Christianity, it is supported by Christianity, and it determines Christianity in turn. But theology does not belong to Christianity insofar as it appears on the scene within the general structure of a given culture; neither is its *positum*, as one may suppose, God.

Theology is the knowledge of that which first makes something like Christianity possible as an original, world-historical event; it is a knowledge of what is termed 'Christianness'.[10] Following Kierkegaard, Heidegger will make use of this distinction between Christianity and Christianness in his subsequent work.[11] But what, then, is Christianness? "We call faith Christian. The essence of faith can formally be sketched as a way of existence of human Dasein that, according to its own testimony — itself belonging to this way of existence — arises not from Dasein or spontaneously through Dasein, but rather from that which is revealed in and with this way of existence, from what is believed. For the 'Christian' faith, that being which is primarily revealed to faith, and only it, and which, as revelation, first gives rise to faith, is Christ, the crucified God."[12] Faith is Christian. It is a mode of existence of human Dasein, which by virtue of its own testimony does not stem from Dasein itself. This way of existence, according to its testimony, arises out of what in and through this way of existence reveals itself: faith. This entity is revealed for Christian faith and only for it. What is revealed only for faith is Christ, the crucified God; Christ determines the relation of faith in the cross as Christian. This crucifixion is a historical event, one that is documented in its specific historicity for the believer in Scripture. Only a believer "knows" this event. What is revealed in this way has a certain message for those who factically and historically exist, a message independent of whether its recipients exist contemporaneously with it or not.[13] As an announcement, the message (Mitteilung) does not convey knowledge of real events, past or future, but allows one to partake in the event, which is the revelation itself; such is the message revealed in it. Here content and form come together and are inseparable. This taking-part, actualized only in existence, is as such always only expressed as faith, as given by faith. In this taking-part of the event of crucifixion the complete human Dasein is placed as Christian. This means that human Dasein is drawn to the cross, placed before God. With this, touched by revelation, human existence becomes aware of itself in its forgetfulness of God. Being thus placed before God means a turn of human Dasein in, and through the mercy of God that is grasped in faith.[14]

I am sticking closely to Heidegger here in his ideal construction of theology. Faith understands itself thus only faithfully. The believer never understands his specific way of existence based on theoretical constructions of his inner feelings. The believer cannot become a believer out of a theoretical or philosophical reflection. As we will see as we move on further, there is no rational, philosophical, or ontological reason for faith. Faith is the only entrance to faith. In and by faith human existence is touched by the possibility of an existence that human existence does not possess solely on its own. However, whether this is a Paulian-Lutherian view will not be taken up here.[15] First and foremost, the relation between philosophical reflection and faith has to do with insight into the relation between philosophy and religion. As we have seen, Heidegger notes tendencies in Luther which emphasize the deconceptualization of theology, that Heidegger himself defends.

It is difficult to determine the relation between philosophy and faith out of Heidegger's analysis of Dasein. In what way can something be drafted in faith which can neither be preunderstood by the analysis of Dasein, nor preunderstood in Dasein itself? What relation does a philosopher have to this problem? How does the philosopher relate to something that happens to Dasein, like faith? He understands it as a possibility that is given to Dasein. But with regard to its content, the philosopher remains aloof. He is only interested in the formal indications to the extent that they can indicate the ontological presuppositions of a phenomenon like faith. Once the message of faith is accepted, the believer understands himself over and against his prior situation, understands himself as rebaptized. Since the philosopher does not follow the content of faith, he cannot therefore follow such rebaptism. How are we to understand this moment of rebaptism?

Against the background of our previous chapter it becomes clear that Heidegger continues his understanding of history in his understanding of faith. In his interpretation of Paul's letters, the kairological moment was a precondition for understanding early Christianity. The temporal experience of original faith is characterized by the expectation of the *parousia*. Unpredictability and suddenness belong to the *parousia*. In the expectation of its arrival, the actualization of life through the original believers is no longer characterized by a chronological order of events, in which the present holds a dominant role. In the expectation of the *parousia,* the believer is placed in a field determined and limited by the expectation of the decisive arrival. This arrival of an undetermined future is explicated and ontologically formally indicated in *Being and Time* as the authentic future. The relation of time and history is changed by it: in the chronological understanding of time, history with all its events is classified in the indifferent stream of time. In the kairological understanding, it is just the opposite: the stream of time is structured from the historical, or from events that are to be expected in history.

It is obvious that the analysis of time in the early lecture courses is developed in the direction of what appears later in *Being and Time*. The destruction of the history of ontology in section six of *Being and Time* is dedicated to the unconcealment of the temporal meaning of being. Nowhere does Heidegger expressly contrast the meaning of the early Christian experience to the Greek experience of time; he finds the kairological moment of consciousness in Aristotle as well. It is important to see that this experience of time implies, in addition, an experience of history.

Heidegger ascribes a specific historicality (*Geschichtlichkeit*) to the Christian faith in its original deconceptualized form. The specificity lies in the kairological understanding of history, an understanding that has both an existential and an existentiell character.[16] It is existentiell insofar as it has to do with a concrete content which cannot be isolated from the life-world. It is existential because it is, as the Christian understanding of time, a figure of understanding of being that remains unthematized. Christian messianism, which is based in constitutive historic events for Christian faith, is only understandable for a philosopher from the perspective of a kairological understanding of history. This kairological understanding, however, is only made possible by events that are to be expected, i.e., the coming of Christ. In this way there is a mutual implication of concrete content and historic understanding. Yet Heidegger has no existentiell relation to the Christian faith. He has an existentiell relation to existentiality as it is explicated in *Being and Time*.

In accepting the message of revelation no knowledge is conveyed about the reality of past or future events. Rather, there is an existentiell commitment to what is revealed. In this commitment the *kairos*-moment is actualized. This actualization is faithfully carried out as a rebirth. "Rebirth does not mean a momentary outfitting with some quality or other, but a way in which a factical, believing Dasein historically exists in *that* history which begins with the occurrence of revelation; in *that* history which, in accord with the very meaning of the revelation, has a definite uttermost end."[17]

The authentic actualization of the existence of faith is consequently rebirth as a mode of historical existence of the factical, faithful Dasein. This history begins with the event of revelation. The event of revelation, which is handed down to faith and consequently actualizes itself in faith, unveils itself only to faith. Faith, as appropriation of revelation, is itself the Christian event. Faith is that way of existence that determines factical existence in its Christianness. *"Faith is the believing-understanding mode of existing in the history revealed, i.e., occurring, with the Crucified."*[18] Factical existence offers the pregiven possibility of the kairological moment, which receives, in turn, completion from faith's content.

So rebirth stands at the beginning of a new history, strangely for someone who is not born twice — namely, the philosopher. But it is possible to understand it ontologically as a new history from the pre-given possibilities of Dasein. The content determined by Christianness remains alienated from the question of the ontological presuppositions that make it possible in the first place. The image of rebirth announces a separation between an old and a new existence. Nevertheless, it is also necessary to see the continuity between them. It is not a matter of an old and a new Dasein, but of the continuity of an already given Dasein, which is regarded with a new kind of view. The idea of the *kairos,* which is connected to authentic temporality, takes shape by an acceptance of the revelation of faith. The existential structure of factical Dasein is actualized by a content of faith, and also by an existentiell commitment to it. But the philosopher is not bound to actualize this existential structure through faith.

No authentic understanding of temporality can guarantee the truth of the content of faith. Heidegger clearly separates philosophical analysis and faith because there is no philosophical reason for faith. Accordingly, Heidegger's understanding of historicality assigns no place to faith which originates from the claims of thinking. Therefore, the understanding of historicality leaves the question of the truth of faith completely to the credibility of faith itself.[19]

The whole of entities uncovered by faith is the *positum* of theology. In this *positum* faith itself belongs to the connection of events of the faithfully uncovered entity. If we presuppose that theology is imposed on faith, out of faith to serve faith, and if we presuppose as well that science is a conceptual uncovering objectification, then theology consists in thematizing faith together with what is uncovered in it, i.e., what is revealed.[20] In other words, theology as a science is created only from faith. As far as theology is imposed on faith as a science it can only find its motivation in faith. If faith is not capable of understanding and explicating conceptually, as science does, then theology is completely inappropriate to its object, faith. Without conceptual explication science is impossible. This also means that theology cannot be deduced from a rationally drafted system of sciences.[21]

In "Phenomenology and Theology," Heidegger writes about theology in very concrete terms. What he writes, for instance, on the theology of the cross implies a certain theology. Such perspectives on faith are only possible if one is familiar with faith. One could say that Heidegger writes here as a theologian, although I have already shown this not to be the case, in view of the fact that he separates the character of the message from its content. Furthermore, the difference between theology and philosophy is not neutralized here. At the end of his lecture, Heidegger speaks quite consistently about a mortal enmity (*Todfeindschaft*) of both.[22] So the problem bears upon the one who wants to maintain both positions, not the one who is to take the position of the philosopher, as Heidegger does. Only a

ratio that abandons the revelation of faith is capable of actualizing the philosophical way of thinking. The existentiell commitment to faith alone will never find the formal indications for
understanding the ontological structure of factical Dasein. Only
through the ontological analysis does it become understandable
that theology presupposes something that is not pre-given in
Dasein, or in being. Heidegger will go on to repeat this: "The
unconditional character of faith, and the problematic character
of thinking, are two spheres separated by an abyss."[23] Heidegger will claim that the question of being does not exist for the
believer because this question is already answered out of faith:
"For example, anyone for whom the Bible is divine revelation
and truth already has the answer to the question 'Why are there
beings at all instead of nothing?' before it is even asked:
beings, with the exception of God Himself, are created by
Him."[24] This makes clear that the question of being should not
be confused with what is indicated as god in faith. The word
'faith' is for Heidegger only oriented to an existentiell commitment
to belief in revelation. A philosophical belief in Jaspers' sense[25]
does not exist for him.[26] Thinking and belief cannot be reconciled in a unified concept, nor in a third given that encompasses both. "'Being' — that is not God," is for Heidegger the
only thing that counts as valid.[27]

As a philosopher, Heidegger unfolds an existential, ontological analysis of Dasein. He continues this when he speaks
about theology. Religion, the ontological presuppositions of which
he seeks, takes place at the existentiell, ontic level.

THE SCIENTIFIC CHARACTER OF THEOLOGY

What does it mean that theology is a science of faith?

1. It is a science of what is revealed in faith, namely that which
   is believed.

2. With this, theology is a science of faithful comportment itself, faithfulness; faithfulness that exists as a revealed relation.
3. Theology is a science of faith because it originates from faith; it legitimates and motivates faith out of faith.
4. Theology is a science of faith because the objectification of faith aims at building faithfulness.

Faith is, in its relation to the crucified, a mode of historical human existence. Faith is historical in a history that discloses itself in faith and only for faith. From there, theology exists as the science of faith, as a way of being that is historical in itself. It is a historical science of a specific kind, according to the historicity that is implied in faith, namely the occurrence of revelation.[28] Theology aims at what is revealed in faithfulness and at the transparency of the Christian event, which is set within its limits by faith itself. The object of this historical science is Christian existence in its concreteness, and not a system of valid theological statements on general relations within some particular region of being. Rather, the transparency of faithful existence is an understanding of existence and refers only to human existence. This means that the process of making transparent is founded in a capacity of Dasein, as understanding is a possibility of Dasein. As far as the understanding of faith is a hermeneutics, it is given from a possibility of Dasein. "In hermeneutics what is developed for Dasein is a possibility of its becoming and being for itself in the manner of an understanding of itself."[29] In the same moment, theological statements are faithful to their content. The particular state of affairs of the object of theology demands that the theological knowledge adjusted to it can never take effect as a separate knowledge of another matter.

Heidegger understands theology as a self-clarification of faith, and not a harmonizing of faith and reason. With this attitude he continues to resist the kind of harmonization of philosophy and faith that is characteristic of neo-scholastic theology and Christian philosophy. Therefore theology cannot found faith in its legitimacy and strengthen it. It cannot lighten in one way or another both the affirmation of faith and faithfulness itself. Theology can only render faith more difficult; this means that faith can only be attained by faith itself, and not by theology as a science.[30] All other sciences are incompetent in the field of theology because they do not grasp the *positum* of theology. This applies also to philosophy, Heidegger's thinking included. An apologetic science or philosophy is seen as an impossibility, in view of the specific nature of theological science: "Likewise, the shortcomings of the non-theological sciences with respect to what faith reveals is no proof of the legitimacy of faith. One can allow 'faithless' science to run up against and be shattered by faith only if one already faithfully holds fast to the truth of faith."[31] If faith can be found in no way by thinking, nor even made plausible, then there is for the non-believer and for the believer alike no external reason for belief. If there were a necessary philosophical reason for belief, this would be what Heidegger refers to as the strike of lightning that would oblige him to close his philosophical workshop.[32] In this case, we would expect that there is a question of a kind of leap from philosophy to faith to contend with.[33] Yet Heidegger never made this leap. If thinking were to lead to faith, faith would then be determined by thinking and thereby lose its specificity. An existentiell commitment in thinking would not be possible anymore, precisely because the answers would already be determined by faith, which aspires to bring the ultimate contents of the whole of reality to words. Even if the content of this ultimate word of faith were to be determined by thinking, the initiative would no longer lie in faith; for faith would no longer stand in its own roots, as Heidegger formulates it.

Theology is, according to its *positum* and from the specific historicity of faith, a historical science. This does not mean that a practical and systematic theology is out of the question but that theology is historical theology in all of its disciplines. Theology is a conceptual explication of Christian existence. "To grasp the substantive content and the specific mode of being of the Christian occurrence, and to grasp it solely as it is testified to in faith and for faith, is the task of systematic theology."[34] Theology is not systematic because it divides the whole of the content of faith into small pieces in order to summarize it systematically and show its validity. Where it attempts to uncover the inner coherence of the occurrence of Christ, theology is systematic in avoiding a system. "The more historical theology is and the more immediately it brings to word and concept the historicity of faith, the more it is 'systematic' and the less likely is it to become the slave of a system."[35] Systematic theology succeeds to the extent that it explicates the concepts and their coherence out of the nature and the specific state of affairs of the entities it objectifies. Systematic theology must understand faith in its original historicity. Heidegger clearly distances himself from an external system that could be imposed upon faith or from a system of meaningful statements that aim at eternal claims. The deconceptualizing that Heidegger applies to philosophy in order to do justice to human historicity is also to be applied to theology, as an explication of the historicity of faith. Eternal truths should not slip into the explication of temporal existence. The systematic design of theology has to correspond to the inner historicity of its *positum*. "The more unequivocally theology disburdens itself of the application of some philosophy and its system, the more philosophical is its own radical (*eigenbürtigen*) scientific character."[36] It's scientific character originates in and is born out of its *positum*.

In the first instance, theology as a systematic and historic discipline has as its object the Christian occurrence in its Christianness and its historicity. This occurrence distinguishes itself as a mode of existence of the believer. Existence is always action and praxis. Therefore, "theology in its essence has the character of a practical science."[37] As the science of the acts of god in relation to the faithfully acting human being, theology is always homiletical and preaching. Therefore, theology can constitute itself as a practical theology, both in homiletics and catechetics. It is not practical because of the need to apply its theoretical propositions to a practical sphere. Theology is historical, systematic, and practical because of the nature of its *positum*.

With the foregoing claims in mind, it is obvious that in this draft of theology, certain ideas about what theology is are excluded. God is not the object of theology in the way that animals are the objects of zoology. Theology is not speculative knowledge of god, or at least not within the project of theology as a positive science. Theology could be a speculative knowledge of god as a project of metaphysics, as ontotheology. There it answers the question of the highest and first being. Nor is the object of theology the relation of god to human and vice-versa. In that case, theology would simply be a science of religion. Moreover, theology is not a science of human beings and their religious situations or experience, as a psychology of religion would have it. According to such an analysis, god would be found in human being. None of these interpretations of theology is drawn from the proper *positum* of theology. They are derived instead from nontheological sciences such as philosophy, history and psychology. However, it remains difficult to determine the limits of theology from out of its object, in the way in which the limits of every science are determined from out of its fundamental concepts. The specific difficulty is that the basis of theology cannot be found in the field of philosophy. "Rather, theology itself is founded primarily by faith."[38]

Theology is specifically characterized by its *positum*, not only with regard to the access it has to its object, but also with regard to the evidence of its claims. Its specific conceptuality can only arise from the *positum* itself. It cannot lean on other sciences in order to radicalize or strengthen its evidence, nor can the evidence of faith by increased or justified by another science.

If one reads *Being and Time* as a transcendental fundamental ontology, then this universal science of being is constitutive for all other sciences of entities. It would found these sciences. But the *positum* of theology is not given from Dasein as a possibility that is already pre-given in Dasein from the start.[39] However, the formal structure of temporality, in which the content of the revealed message is received, is given in Dasein a priori. The formal structures of temporality also determine the structures of hermeneutics as the interpretation of an announcement that addresses Dasein. If there is a possible understanding and hermeneutics of faith from out of faith, then it has to follow the dictates of hermeneutics. Yet it is not possible from the perspective of fundamental ontology to decide whether the scientific character of theology is in accordance with its *positum*. Whether and how the *positum* of theology has to be developed scientifically has to be answered by theologians, and not by philosophers. Thus Heidegger rejects all religious a priori in Dasein. What is given in Dasein, however, is a means for dealing with the *positum* of theology.

THE RELATION OF THEOLOGY, AS A POSITIVE SCIENCE, TO PHILOSOPHY

Faith has no need for philosophy. This state of affairs changes when the explication of theology sets itself the task of becoming scientific. Science of faith needs philosophy in a very particular way. As a science, theology's concepts must appropriately reflect the entity that it has undertaken to interpret. But is that which has to be understood conceptually here not inconceivable from the very beginning? Even so, this inconceivability can be unconcealed in the proper way; otherwise, it remains utterly meaningless. Such inconceivability should not arise from a lack of reason, but from the nature of the *positum* itself; it is not something to be understood. It is not a matter of the 'thinkability' of faith, but rather of its 'credibility.'

But wouldn't it be better to leave faith to itself? Why is there a need for philosophy here? Heidegger writes: "Every ontic interpretation operates on the basis, at first and for the most part concealed, of an ontology."[40] Theology is an ontic operation. It is led by a more or less hidden understanding of being. But the question of being is not raised in theology. Is it possible to understand the meaning of the cross, of sin and grace in another way than in faith? Faith cannot become the criterion of knowledge for the philosophical-ontological question. However, the basic concepts of theology are not completely isolated from philosophical questioning. The explication of basic concepts is never an isolated matter, which, once isolated, can be passed around like coins. How are to we to regard this relation between the basic concepts of theology and philosophical questioning?

As we have noted above, Heidegger indicates faith as a rebirth. Does this mean that the pre-faithful existence of Dasein has disappeared? Heidegger answers: "Though faith does not bring itself about, and though what is revealed in faith can never be founded by way of a rational knowing as exercised by autonomously functioning reason, nevertheless the sense of the Christian occurrence as rebirth is that Dasein's pre-faithful, i.e., unbelieving, existence is sublated (*aufgehoben*) therein."[41] This sublating does not mean that prefaithful existence is removed, but that it is lifted up into a new form, in which it is kept and preserved. The ontological conditions of the prefaithful human being persist in the faithful human being. In faith pre-Christian existence is mastered at an existentiell level as rebirth. This means that in faithful existence the conquered pre-Christian Dasein is implied, not discarded, but is at one's disposal in a new way.

Heidegger's use of the term '*aufheben*' here immediately calls Hegel to mind. Does this mean that the relation between religion and philosophy must be understood from a Hegelian perspective? Obviously not, since in Hegel religion is regarded as something preserved in the rationality of spirit. Religion is not different from spirit; only the form differs. There isn't a considerable difference between religion and philosophy in Hegel because the content of religion and that of philosophy remain one and the same.[42] In Heidegger, on the other hand, continuity exists between the two at an implicit ontological level, yet at the ontic level, the difference between them is decisive, as we shall see in what follows. In Heidegger's analysis, what is existential-ontological remains implied within what is religious. This is also the reason why formally indicated temporality as an ontological presupposition can be found in the historicality of the occurrence of faith.

We can see the relation as follows: "Hence we can say that precisely because all basic theological concepts, considered in their fully regional context, include a content that is indeed existentially powerless, i.e., ontically sublated, they are ontologically determined by a content that is pre-Christian and that can thus be grasped purely rationally."[43] The believer remains anchored in the ontological presuppositions of Dasein. Theological concepts necessarily include an understanding of being that human Dasein possesses to the extent that Dasein exists. Heidegger adds a key remark on the kinship between theology and philosophy in a footnote: "All theological concepts of existence that are centered on faith intend a specific transition of existence, in which pre-Christian and Christian existence are united in their own way. This transitional character is what motivates the multidimensionality of theological concepts."[44] The transition characteristic to Dasein is obviously distinguished by Christian existence in a particular way. Because of this, theological concepts possess an ambiguity in which one can see pre-Christian concepts in and through Christian ones. As a result, the meta-phor of rebirth gestures toward the characteristics of the first birth, existentiality.

The concept of sin, for instance, is only meaningful within faith; only the believer can exist as a sinner, since sin in Christianity also presupposes a belief in the revelation of God. However, if one wants to explicate sin in a conceptual way, then it demands a step backward to the concept of guilt. In other words, if one wants to explicate sin, one has to turn to the original ontolog-ical existential characteristics of Dasein. In these existential characteristics of existence, Dasein is determined as guilty. The more originally and appropriately the basic condition of Dasein is explicated and brought to light, that is, the more originally and ontologically the concept of guilt is understood, the more this concept of guilt can serve as a guide for the theoretical explication of sin. Sin arises as a concept within the world of faith when the act of the believer is seen in the light of a revealing and forgiving god. It is an interpretation added to what is ontologically experienced as guilt. Guilt arises in a new light, namely in the light of a transcendental god. Guilt be-comes sin, and the ambiguity of sin allows one to see guilt within it. Sin is the faithful and existentiell interpretation of what is existential-ontologically founded in the concept of guilt.

Heidegger presupposes that the theological explication of sin must remain oriented towards the ontological concept of guilt. This does not mean that theology is patronized by philosophy: "For sin, in its essence, is not to be deduced rationally from the concept of guilt."[45] Theology needs the ontological concept of guilt from the pre-faithful Dasein, which is in turn sublated in faithful Dasein. In Hegel the sublation proceeds from relig-ion to spirit; in Heidegger it goes from philosophy to religion and is not philosophically necessary. If the concepts of faith are to be philosophically explicable, and are not to remain in a specific, yet meaningless, conceptuality, then what is said must be understood from an existential-ontological perspective. In *Being and Time* Heidegger expresses this as follows: "Ontically, we have not decided whether man is 'drunk with sin' and in the *status corruptionis,* whether he walks in the *status integritatis,* or whether he finds himself in an intermediate stage, the *status gratiae.* But in so far as any faith or 'world view' makes any such assertions, and if it asserts anything about Dasein as Being-in-the-World, it must come back to the existential structures we have set forth, provided that its assertions are to make a claim to conceptual understanding."[46] Elsewhere Heidegger formulates this separation even more sharply: "The existential analysis of Being-guilty proves nothing either *for* or *against* the possibility of sin. Taken strictly, it cannot even be said that the ontology of Dasein *of itself* leaves this possibility open; for this ontology, as a philosophical inquiry, 'knows' in principle nothing about sin."[47] The concept of guilt remains silent about sin; not even the possibility of sin receives a better understanding from it. "The theological concept of sin as a concept of existence acquires that correction (i.e., codirection) that is necessary for it insofar as the concept of existence has pre-Christian content. But the primary direction (derivation), the source of its Christian content, is given only by faith. Therefore ontology functions only as a corrective to the ontic, and in particular pre-Christian, content of basic theological concepts."[48] The philosopher who wants to understand the concepts of faith has to understand them out of and by means of philosophical concepts. These philosophical concepts are formally indicating concepts, which are always empty not only with respect to religion, but also with respect to all human concerns. Therefore, the question whether theological concepts are right is not for the philosopher to judge.

Theological concepts, then, are examined only with regard to their ontological presuppositions, not their specific content.

We have already observed this in Heidegger's analysis of the *parousia*, where Heidegger analyzes the specific understanding of temporality that plays a role in the expectation of the coming of Christ. For Heidegger, it has to do with the underlying ontology of temporality. However, the possibility of this specific understanding of being is connected with a certain faith: the expectation of the coming or arrival is connected to the concrete possibility of the coming of Christ. Yet, according to Matthias Jung, a sharp distinction between historic genesis and ontological validity cannot be made here,[49] due to the very facticity of the religion in which Heidegger himself was raised. That is Heidegger's hermeneutical departure. Heidegger, as a philosopher, singles out the *kairos*-moment in a religious context, and uses his analysis of the understanding of being in order to do it. On the basis of this, he can also find in Aristotle's philosophy the *kairos*-moment.[50] This results in the concept of the moment in *Being and Time*.[51] At that point it has to do with pure formal structures, emptied of all content.

Heidegger, as we have seen, uncovers essential structures of Dasein from certain religious phenomena and contexts. The world of the believer offers an expression of more fundamental existential structures. In themselves, such structures have nothing to do with religion. This point legitimates Heidegger's entire intention. He does not, however, answer the question of whether the ontological implications of these religious phenomena are meaningful for the validity of faith. It is true that Heidegger's philosophy of guilt and the future is essentially developed from out of his interpretation of Christianity, but it is his explicit intention to analyze its philosophical meaning. His project is not about theology, nor Christian faith, nor religion in general; his references to the religious are always oriented toward, and for the sake of, the ontological analysis.

For Heidegger, philosophical concepts can function as a corrective for the understanding of theological concepts. And faith, in its turn, can give direction to empty philosophical concepts. This indicates the specificity of theology with regard to other positive sciences. "Here one must note, however, that this correction does not found anything, in that way, for example, that the basic concepts of physics acquire from an ontology of nature their original foundation, the demonstration of all their possibilities, and hence their higher truth. Rather, this correction is only formally indicative; that is to say, the ontological concept of guilt as such is never a theme of theology."[52] The ontological concept of guilt indicates the formal character of the region of being in which the concept of existence moves, and it is here that the concept of sin has its proper meaning. The ontological concept of sin determines the space in which sin can move in order to be ontologically understandable. For its part, ontological understanding is neutral and atheistic. The relation of philosophy to the other positive sciences, however, is far more directive: "On the other hand, it can be shown that philosophy, as the free questioning of purely self-reliant Dasein, does of its essence have the task of directing all other non-theological, positive sciences with respect to their ontological foundation."[53] The ontologically precedent (a priori) openness, which is given with regard to the other sciences out of Dasein, does not apply to theology. It has a *positum* in the revelation of faith that is *sui generis,* a *positum* about which philosophy cannot speak. Therefore, it is not possible to find the content of faith, the Christianness, in the analysis of Dasein.

In Heidegger's analysis of Paul's letters, the ontology of temporality was derived from Christianity as formal indication. Here, in "Phenomenology and Theology," ontology as formal indication of Dasein offers the limits within which the religious concepts must be preserved as concepts of existence. Ontology provides a formal indication, i.e., an indication free of ontic representation, of the pre-Christian form of basic concepts of theology. In theology, concepts like guilt, which according to

Heidegger are philosophically seen as formal indicating concepts, are interpreted anew as a whole by the sublating character of faith. The concepts are, as it were, born again. But the theological conceptual contents are thus not an addendum to what is philosophically understandable. In the concept of sin the concept guilt is preserved, but it receives a new content. In faith the pre-faithful Dasein is sublated. A comprehensive understanding of this sublation is necessary in order to understand the relation of philosophy and theology as Heidegger sees it.

Because theological concepts always have out of their region of being an ontologically determined and therefore philosophical, content, all religious concepts imply an understanding of being that human Dasein has out of itself. From this understanding of being, philosophy can eventually function as a corrective for the ontic content of the basic concepts of theology, but it cannot speak about its theological content.

Furthermore, it is not necessary for philosophy to serve a corrective function with regard to theology: "But it is not of the essence of philosophy, and it can never be established by philosophy itself or for its own purpose, that it must have such a corrective function for theology."[54] In the ontological concepts as formal indications there is no reference to, and also no direction for, a possible meaning in theological terms. As ontology, philosophy offers the possibility to function as this corrective for theology, "if indeed theology is to be factical with respect to the facticity of faith."[55] If theology wants to belong to the facticity of Dasein, then it must stay within the ontology of facticity; without this, it can never be understood from the perspective of an ontology of facticity. This is the reason that Heidegger states early on that philosophy of religion is only understandable from the perspective of an ontology of facticity. He persists in this conviction: "the very idea of a philosophy of religion (especially if it makes no reference to the facticity of the human being) is pure nonsense."[56] That theology seeks to answer to this demand to limit itself within the borders of facticity does not originate from philosophy itself, but rather originates from theology, which strives to understand itself scientifically. Out of itself, philosophy is not aware of a possible meaning for theology because the theological *positum,* the revealed faith, does not belong to its domain.[57] It is important to bear in mind here Heidegger's hesitation with regard to the question of whether theology has to be a science. The need for philosophy to serve as a corrective for theology arises only when theology insists on being scientific.

Heidegger thus distances himself from religious philosophical approaches, in which a religious a priori is supposed, following Otto and Troeltsch. He distances himself as well from a conciliation of faith and reason that would reduce faith to reason, as is the case in the philosophies of Kant and Hegel. Nor does he assume the harmony of faith and reason at which Thomistic philosophy aims.[58]

Heidegger understands faith as the natural enemy, as it were, of philosophy: "This peculiar relationship does not exclude but rather includes the fact that *faith*, as a specific possibility of existence, is in its innermost core the mortal enemy of the *form of existence* that is an essential part of *philosophy* and that is factically ever-changing."[59] What we see here is the fundamental opposition of two possibilities of existence, which cannot be realized by one person in one and the same moment. Faith as a possibility of existence, implies death to philosophy as the possibility of existence. This does not mean that the scientists in each field must behave like enemies: neither excludes a factical and existentiell taking seriously of the other. The existentiell opposition between faith, on the one hand, and philosophical self-understanding, on the other, must be effective in its scientific design and in its explications. And this must be done in such a way that each meets the other with mutual respect. This can be undertaken more easily where one sees the different points of departure more sharply. Christian philosophy, therefore, is in Heidegger's view a "square circle."[60]

In an early lecture from July of 1924, where he addressed the Marburger theologians, Heidegger put it thus: "The philosopher does not believe. If the philosopher asks about time, then he has resolved to understand time in terms of time or in terms of the '*aei,*' which looks like an eternity but proves to be a mere derivative of being temporal."[61] Therefore he mentions expressly that his considerations are not theological. In a theological sense — and theologians are at liberty to understand it in this way — a consideration of time can only mean making the question concerning eternity more difficult, preparing it in the correct manner and posing it properly.

Quite aside from whether the theological answers are true or untrue from the perspective of faith, it can represent no answer at all to this question, precisely because it bears no relation to it. For faith, asking such a question is simply a form of foolishness. Yet according to Heidegger, philosophy consists in such foolishness. A "Christian philosophy" may well be a round square and a misunderstanding. However, one can use theology to thoughtfully question and work through the world of Christian experience, the world of faith. Heidegger sees in theology's dependence on philosophy a lack of greatness in theology itself. "Only ages that really no longer believe in the true greatness of the task of theology arrive at the pernicious opinion that, through a supposed refurbishment with the help of philosophy, a theology can be gained or even replaced, and can be made more palatable to the need of the age. Philosophy, for originally Christian faith, is foolishness."[62]

There remains, however, a problem: if one wants to remove all reflection from theology, claiming it is not allowed objectively, then theology falls into a number of difficulties. What about a language of swearing, or when one expresses oneself as a poet? Does the sense of speaking not become a question of taste? The danger of arbitrariness and anarchy that threatens in such cases is a considerable objection. For they do not admit the power of evidence; it is impossible to refute or reject what is expressed in them. The criterion here would then be the authenticity of speaking itself. One ends up here in a kind of subjectivist swamp. Would Heidegger even place theology in this category? Reason as a kind of general authority of control seems to disappear here. Obviously we know that theological speaking does not speak out of itself, but the longing for insight into the origin of this speaking brings with it a natural tension. Is there more than a purely charismatic speaking?

FOUR

Aristotle's Ontology as Theology

H eidegger's main motive is to raise the question of being. Questions about being seem to have been discredited, not only in the past century, but in the whole of Western philosophy. Therefore, Heidegger very appropriately starts *Being and Time* with a reference to Plato's Sophist: "For manifestly you have long been aware of what you mean when you use the expression 'being.' We, however, who used to think we understood it, have now become perplexed."[1] After this quotation, Heidegger continues: "Do we in our time have an answer to the question of what we really mean by the word 'being'? Not at all. So it is fitting that we should raise anew the question of the meaning of Being."[2] The question about being characterizes philosophy.

As Plato in relation to Parmenides turns the previous understanding of being, Heidegger announces at the beginning of *Being and Time* the end of the tradition initiated by Plato. Heidegger wants to be loyal to the tradition of the question of being. The question, "What is the meaning of being?" is possible, on the one hand, by raising the question again, and on the other hand, by going back to knowing about being. In such a repetition, the metaphysical tradition is neither simply assimilated, nor forgotten, not left behind, but recalled.

To understand Heidegger's intention, first it must become clear in what sense the present-at-hand ontology is no longer tenable. Second, we must attend to how the question of being is raised again by Heidegger's analysis. Once one sees that the calcified tradition is a possible answer to the question of being, then it is visible as a construction. Seeing the tradition of metaphysics as an answer to the question of being is not possible when only one "real" perspective is permitted. The metaphysical tradition must be understood as one response to the question of being. If we see metaphysics as a possible, rather than necessary, answer to the question of being, then every biased perspective is at stake.

Against this background, Heidegger differentiates between the motive of philosophy (the original question of being) and its tendency (the factical filling-in of the question). This difference contrasts what is originally intended, and the concrete direction in which the ontology is worked out and filled in. The tendency of the ontology is no longer tenable, not because of an external or anti-metaphysical criticism, but because of the motive of the question of being itself. Heidegger takes this motive, the question of being, as a not-yet-actualized possibility of ontology. The tendency of the tradition hitherto can no longer be maintained, because the way in which the motive of the question of being has yet to be followed is foreign to this tradition.

The metaphysical-ontological question is, according to Heidegger, the core of Western philosophy. Terms like 'philosophy' and 'metaphysics' are used interchangeably in Heidegger's thinking. In the following, I work out the way Heidegger analyzes Western philosophy as an ontology that is understood more and more as a theology. This view of Western metaphysics was not, however, grasped all at once. It took several steps before it landed in Heidegger's essay "Onto-theo-logical Constitution of Metaphysics."[3] In this work, Heidegger sees philosophy and metaphysics as chained in an ontotheological structure. The possibility of an atheological philosophy, which the early Heidegger saw in Aristotle, has completely disappeared. This possibility is saved for what the later Heidegger calls 'the thinking of being,' as opposed to philosophy and metaphysics.

THE THEOLOGICAL AS THE HIGHEST

For Heidegger, Greek philosophy reaches its climax in Aristotle, and will never be surpassed in the tradition that follows from it. Therefore, Aristotle's thinking is a normative point from which the philosophical tradition can be determined more precisely. The well-thought-out way in which Aristotle follows the motive of philosophy marks the limit of the whole tradition, which becomes visible now as a finite possibility for thinking and as a temporary answer to the question of being.

In his earliest writings, Heidegger emphasizes the relation between ontology and theology in Aristotle's first philosophy.[4] In this earliest presentation from 1922, Heidegger sees the metaphysical tradition as an ontotheological tradition that follows from the tendency for philosophy to forget its original motive. Because understanding has its concrete possibility for being actualized in being free from daily concerns, the possibility of theorizing is placed against the background of the facticity of life. "*Theorein* is the purest movement which life has available to it. Because of this, it is something 'god-like.' But for Aristotle the idea of the divine did not arise in the explication of something objective which was made accessible in a basic religious experience; the *theion* is rather the expression for the highest being-character which arises in the ontological radicalization of the idea of being that is moved."[5] The highest way of being has to be the highest way of moving: it is *noēsis noēseōs*. This being must be pure beholding, free from every emotional relation. Therefore the divine cannot be envious, not because it is absolute goodness and love, but rather because in its being as pure movement it can neither hate nor love at all.

Being is understood from a normative perspective, from the perspective of the highest way of being. Connected with this is the highest way of moving, which is pure thinking. This also determines the way Christianity speaks about the highest being of God. The divine being is understood as *actus purus,* which also relates to the inner-godly life, the Trinity. The *actus purus* also determines the way human being understands its relation to god and the way human being understands being as proper to itself. According to Heidegger (in 1922) this means: "Christian Theology and the philosophical theology and the anthropology which always also develops within such contexts all speak in borrowed categories, categories which are alien to their own field of Being."[6]

In the winter semester of 1924/25, Heidegger wrote a long interpretation of Aristotle before he started an extensive commentary on Plato's Sophist. He mentions the duality in Aristotle's first philosophy; the first philosophy is both *theologikè* and the science that considers *on hē on.*[7] Theology as well as ontology claim to be first philosophy. This duality can be found through the Middle Ages until the ontology of the modern period. The question is why ontology and theology become the two basic Greek sciences. According to Heidegger, "Theology has the task of clarifying beings as a whole, the *holon,* the beings of the world, nature, the heavens, and everything under them, to speak quite roughly, in their origins, in that by which they properly are."[8] Clarifying beings as a whole, by means of an unmoved mover, has nothing to do with proving god through a causal argument. Theology has the whole, the *holon,* as its theme, as does ontology, which considers its *archai*. As the Greek understood it, both take their departure from beings as a whole, as the *holon*.[9] Theology considers beings according to what they are already in advance, i.e., according to what constitutes, in the most proper and highest sense, the presence of the world. "The most proper and highest presence of beings is the theme of theology."[10] The theme of ontology is beings, insofar as they are present in all their determinations, including everything there is — mathematical beings as well as physical — that which constitutes presence in general. According to Heidegger and his interpretation of the Greeks, the problem here is not that first philosophy is theology, but that it is ontology as well. The question is: "what is the sense of the characters of Being which pertain universally to all beings insofar as they are, in relation to the individual concrete being?"[11] From Aristotle and the Greeks up to the present, this question has not come one step forward. In fact, the opposite is the case: "the position the Greeks attained has for us been lost and we therefore do not even understand these questions any longer."[12]

For a more complete sketch of Heidegger's earlier interpretation of Aristotle, I turn to a lecture course from the summer semester of 1926, entitled "Die Grundbegriffe der antiken Philosophie," in which Heidegger offers an overview of Greek philosophy and explicates more precisely the central ideas in Aristotle.[13]

At the beginning of this lecture course, Heidegger announces his intention, to penetrate the understanding of basic scientific concepts. These not only made possible but have determined decisively Western philosophy until today.[14] From this perspective, philosophy starts with a repetition of the tradition. In this analysis, he shows that the tradition formed by the Greeks neglects the question of the being of factical life. In order to raise the question of being more radically it is thus necessary to counter the tradition.[15]

Heidegger often explicates the question of being by a comparison with the sciences, by which he means the positive sciences. In science, the object is always already given, already there before it is approached scientifically. Without this already-given object, science is not possible. The object of philosophy, however, is not and is never given. It is only there by differentiating between entities and being. Because of this, Heidegger speaks of philosophy as a critical science (*krinein* = discern). In philosophy, being is discerned from entities, without, however, understanding being as a positive given. Being concerns something that is not there.[16] Being always remains the being of an entity; nevertheless, it can be distinguished from it and understood as such. In the same way the characteristics of being, which can be sought, must not be understood as entities themselves.

In Aristotle, philosophy is determined as the question of being. He is the first who asks about being qua being, for being as such, insofar as it is. On the one hand, he gathers together and completes the whole tradition that precedes him. On the other hand, with this question and the way he works it out, Aristotle determines the orientation of the whole tradition that comes after him. This outcome is unsurpassed. According to Heidegger, Aristotle unites the basic motives of the previous philosophy, but after him there is only decline.[17]

In Aristotle's *Metaphysics,* the question of being is formulated and worked out normatively. This first philosophy is characterized in two ways as both a science of being (ontology) and as a science of the highest and most authentic being (theology). Theology is the inquiry into the being that is most proper, that corresponds in the highest way to the idea of being.[18] For its part, ontology endeavors to determine the being of entities.[19] Thus, theology is also the search for an entity. They both concern a double concept of fundamental science: the science of being and the science of the highest and authentic entity.[20] But whereas in ontology an explication (understanding) of being is intended in which the found characteristics are not to be understood as entities, in theology there is an ontic explanation of being. In this case being is reduced to an entity, and the difference between being and entity is not maintained. And precisely this difference — between being and entity — characterizes and motivates philosophy.

Heidegger notices a strange moment of ambiguity between the two different approaches of the question of being in Aristotle.[21] He understands this hesitation or wavering as a consequence of the way in which Aristotle begins from the tradition that precedes him. According to Aristotle, his predecessors already ask about being as the first causes of entities. This is the question from which being as such is to be determined.[22] This question can lead to an ontical explanation, to find a perfect entity as an instance of being, but it can also lead to the maintained difference of being and entity. Heidegger interprets this wavering or hesitation as a tension between the motive of philosophy and its factical tendency. Aristotle works out the question of being as a search for the entity that really and completely has being. The result of this dominant tendency in the motive of first philosophy, Heidegger points out, is that the highest entity is determined as complete and perfect effectiveness.

Aristotle develops this idea of the highest entity against the background of his search for causes and principles. The themes of first philosophy are the *arche* and *aitia,* translated by Heidegger as the first grounds and causes, as well as their quantity and essence.[23] Aristotle says that there are four causes, but according to Heidegger the necessity of this is not shown. The investigation of these four causes follows from the question of being: what is really intended here is an investigation of the causes of entities beyond entities. However, Aristotle interprets his predecessors' questioning of being as a question into the ground of entities. He tends toward the ready-to-hand answers, a tendency from which he could not free himself. Heidegger sees this hesitation and wavering between ontology and theology as the highest possibility for Aristotle's thought.

Heidegger then raises the question of why the inquiry into being has taken the perspective of ground. Why is there a why, a ground?[24] The Greeks did not raise this question: it is strange to Greek thinking. Heidegger sees in this tendency an answer to the question of being that motivates philosophy. This demands an inquiry into the connectedness of ontology and theology in Aristotle.

According to Heidegger, Aristotle's ontology becomes more explicitly a theology with his explication of being as possibility and actuality. With the terms *dynamis* and *energeia*, Aristotle thinks movement (*kinesis*), which is proper to being as a whole and which is, as such, eternal. Every movement has a *telos*: a goal and a completion. An eternal movement cannot be ended; nor can it near its goal. The eternal movement of being as a whole has to have a *telos*, if this eternal movement is to be possible. But it is a goal from which it is always and continuously removed.[25] Aristotle characterizes this *telos* as the first mover, which cannot be moved by something else because then it would be incomplete and imperfect.

Such a first mover, which is in no way characterized by possibility or incompleteness, is pure energeia: pure, real presence.[26] It is an independent and continuous presence.[27] The ontology ends in the idea of an entity that possesses being in the most perfect way. With this, the ambiguity of ontology and theology is decided in favor of the latter. The explication of being becomes an explanation from the perspective of an entity that has being in the highest degree. Heidegger explains that Aristotle looks for a more specific characteristic of this entity, which he finds in pure contemplation (*theorein*). This pure contemplation is subsequently explicated as thinking thinking itself (*noēsis noēseōs*). It refers to the knowledge that is proper to the highest entity, which is understood by Aristotle as a pure and lasting contemplation of nothing other than this contemplation itself. First philosophy in this respect is the kind of knowledge that belongs to a perfect entity. Sophia is the highest understanding and the authentic science; it is the most divine because it has the divine in the most authentic way and refers to something divine. God is, before all, something like origin and ground. This science is absolutely free contemplation; because of this, it belongs in the first instance to god, which itself is everlasting contemplation, and contemplation of this contemplation. Sophia is, in the end, theology.[28] Heidegger emphasizes that Aristotle calls the unmoved mover the divine and real being, but that it is not a religious consideration about the relationship of a personal creator-god to human beings and the world. Only since Augustine, and after him in Scholasticism and finally in Hegel, has the idea of the first mover been united with the idea of the Christian God.[29] And yet this misses the point, because the Aristotelian philosophical and conceptual framework offers a preconceptuality that is inappropriate as an approach to the Christian faith. Theology, according to Aristotle, is knowledge of the authentic and most real entity, and accordingly a neutral science of being.[30]

Next, Heidegger raises the decisive questions: Why is the problem of being necessarily pushed to the question of the most authentic entity? Is there an ontology that is developed without an orientation to a most excellent entity?[31] How is it possible that the question of being (the motive of philosophy) is worked out as the question of the authentic entity?

In Aristotle, the question of being becomes the inquiry into the entity that represents being in the most perfect way. That means: being has the meaning of perfect being. Being is interpreted as complete efficacy (*energeia*); it has pure actuality. Therefore, Aristotle writes that reality (*energeia*) is earlier than possibility (*dynamis*), and earlier than all of this is presence.[32]

In *Metaphysics* VI.1.1026a29 he says: ". . . but if there is a sub-stance which is immutable, the science which studies this will be prior to physics, and will be primary philosophy, and uni-versal in this sense, that it is primary." This science intends to investigate being as being (as ontology), but in fact it does so as theology, because from the beginning it understands being from the perspective of an entity that has being in the highest way.

The science of being qua being poses an entity in which the authentic being is shown in the purest way. Only out of this entity can the idea of being be understood. Therefore, a disci-pline is needed that studies the entity that is considered to have authentic being. It is a science of what being really means, and as such it has an ontological orientation. So first philosophy is the science of being, and at the same time, a science of the highest entity.

This ambiguity is characteristic; it is not confusion or the side-by-side existence of two perspectives that are not con-nected. It comes from the inner necessity of the problem, which was not formulated or addressed by Aristotle and fell into oblivion after him.[33] The pure ontological problem has still not been mastered completely — namely, whether every under-standing of being presupposes an ideal entity in order to under-stand the specific character of being.

Why is Aristotle then normative for the tradition of meta-physics? From the beginning, being means for Aristotle pure and permanent presence. Therefore, what Aristotle presents as first philosophy is ambiguous; it is ontology and theology at the same time. The question of being is also the question of the perfectly qualified being. Aristotle started this project: the inter-twining of the question of being that has to be distinguished from entities and the question of the perfect quality of being as something specific to the highest entity is the matter of meta-physics. Heidegger will unravel both questions and think, in this way, against the tradition of metaphysics; but he will keep them together as well, and continue metaphysics with it.

Aristotle is normative both because of his project of first philosophy and because his determinations of being have never been equaled. But he is especially so because he does not work out the hesitation and the ambiguity between ontology and theology, which cannot be articulated. It appears that he was aware of the limits of his first philosophy, when he saw that ontology and theology could not be distinguished. He could not unravel both because the question of being, according to the tradition in which he was situated, is also the question of perfect being, namely *energeia*. With this position, Aristotle came to the limits implied in the problems of Greek philosophy.[34] Aristotle's hesitation was the deepest insight possible within the horizon of the Greek understanding of being: he doubled that the question of being *ipso facto* meant the question of the being in the highest degree. After him, however, this hesitation is forgotten and being is explicated as ground and efficacy until Heidegger. At the other side of Aristotle's hesitation, Heidegger starts again. To Heidegger, the question of being and the question of god — ontology and theology — belong together but are not the same.

So Heidegger sees in the theological question the inquiry into a being. This is the knot of the problem: the double concept of a science of being as both ontic explanation and ontological explication. When the causes of entities are asked for, the subject of the question is being. However, when the causes of being are asked for, the subject is an entity.[35] The question of the highest and most authentic entity is an ontic question. The question of being itself is an ontological question. The ontic question means explanation; the ontological question means explication.

In this lecture course of summer semester 1926, Heidegger mentions explicitly the possibility of the question of being without a theology. This possibility is presupposed in order to raise the question of their connectedness. The possibility of an atheological ontology leans on the hesitation with regard to this question that Heidegger sees in Aristotle.

PHILOSOPHY AS THEOLOGY

Later on, in his last lecture course in Marburg in summer semester 1928, Heidegger chooses to start with Aristotle in understanding the origin of metaphysics[36] because Aristotle framed the elements of basic philosophical problems. As such, Aristotle's philosophy contains a wealth of truly undeveloped and, in places, completely hidden possibilities.[37] But Aristotle is far from providing fulfillment or final clarity. According to Heidegger this is seen in his very characterization of philosophy: "There is a definite science which inquires into being as being and into that which belongs to it as such."[38] This is the first philosophy; it is philosophy of the first order and genuine philosophy. But the meaning of 'being' seems to remain obscure. Almost everything is an entity, but it is difficult to identify the being of an entity. "Being as the theme of philosophy is indeed obscure. It can only be said negatively: the object of philosophy is nothing belonging among beings as a particular being."[39] So the original motive of philosophy as the question of being would be kept alive if the answer were not prematurely found in an entity or in a highest entity.

Aristotle, however, not only sees in philosophy an ontology and a theology; he also calls the whole project of first philosophy a theology.[40] *To theion* refers to the heavens: the encompassing and overpowering, that under and upon which we are thrown, that which dazzles us and takes us by surprise, the overwhelming. It is clear that if the divine is present anywhere, it is present in this kind of entity. Furthermore, the noblest science must deal with the noblest type of being; the highest science must be science of the highest, the first. Heidegger now understands Aristotelian first philosophy within a twofold perspective: knowledge of being and knowledge of the 'overwhelming' — Heidegger's translation of the Greek *theion* (the all-prevailing).[41] He links this with the twofold character in *Being and Time* of existence and thrownness.[42] Heidegger thinks from the perspective of the overwhelming character of existence and throwness in order to avoid understanding it as an entity in the world. It is the kind of knowledge that never can become a fixed possession but has to be sought anew each time. First philosophy is ontological in its investigation of being as being; it is theological insofar as it investigates the overwhelming. However, Heidegger does not work this out further.

What does it mean that philosophy is also theology? Is it an appendage, a finishing touch, a worldview? Is philosophy only a theology so as to have a conclusion? Or is it both at once? Does that which is sought under the term 'theology' in fact reside in the essence of philosophy understood totally and radically? Or is what arises in Aristotle as theology simply a remnant of his early period? These questions, raised by Heidegger, mirror the discussion of Aristotle in the 1920s.[43] With the Aristotelian twofold description of philosophy as 'ontology' and 'theology,' either nothing is said or everything, according to our original possibilities of understanding. To what extent theology belongs to philosophy can only be understood if we radicalize the notion of ontology.[44] But as shown in the last chapter in Heidegger's ontology, which he simultaneously develops and unfolds in *Being and Time,* there is no place for theology as an ontic science in philosophy.

From the time of his interpretation of Kant and of German Idealism, Heidegger seems to correct his earlier radical interpretation concerning two disciplines in Aristotle's Metaphysics.[45] From then on, the two disciplines seem more united and connected with each other. A doubling (*Doppelung*) appears precisely in the determination of the essence of "first philoso-phy." It is both knowledge of 'being as being' and also knowl-edge of the most unique region of beings out of which being as a whole determines itself. Both belong together as the lead-ing problem of a first philosophy of being. Understanding being means understanding it from the perspective of the high-est entity that determines the whole of being. Therefore, Heidegger can determine metaphysics in the wake of Aristotle as "the fun-damental knowledge of beings as such and as a whole."[46]

In the same year, in his inaugural lecture "What is Metaphysics?" Heidegger understands metaphysics as "the inquiry beyond or over beings that aims to recover them as such and as a whole for our grasp."[47] With this definition Heidegger summarizes the tradition that started with Aristotle. Heidegger writes: "This is how the matter stands in Aristotelian philosophy. Philosophizing proper is for Aristotle this dual questioning: concerning the *on katholou* and concerning the *timiōtaton genos,* concerning beings in general, concerning being, and concerning that being which properly is. Yet the way in which these are intrinsically connected was not further elaborated by Aristotle, and we find nothing in what has been handed down from him that would provide us with information as to how this unitary problematic looks which takes as its object *physis* in this dual sense, nor are we given any information as to how that problematic is explicitly grounded from out of the essence of philosophy itself."[48]

So the question of the divine as a philosophical question is not a religious question according to Heidegger's analysis. This philosophical theology, used as a paradigm in the structure and further construction of the theological dogmas of the Middle Ages, was made easier because Aristotle himself, in the sixth book of the *Metaphysics,* divides first philosophy into two fundamental orientations of questioning, without making their unity itself into a problem.[49] The question is to what extent the dual ori-entation of this questioning constitutes philosophising proper in a unitary way. "This question is open and is open to this day, or rather is not even posed any more today."[50] Heidegger opposes the philosophical concept of god for which he develops a counter-paradigm. For Heidegger the intrinsic connectedness seems to be obvious and becomes more and more the paradigm for Western philosophy as such. Thus, Heidegger no longer asks why philosophy landed as ontology and as theology, but he asks about the original unity of both disciplines.[51]

THEOLOGY AS THE SEARCH FOR GROUND

In summer semester 1930, Heidegger starts to speak more explicitly about the highest being as the ground of being.[52] The words 'world' and 'god' are only used as orienting titles for the totality of being and the ground of the totality. Heidegger indicates the highest being as that being that is the most in being, the beingest (*seiendst*).[53] He also mentions, once again, that in Aristotle the real is higher than the possible.[54] Here Heidegger's philosophical opposition is fully directed against Aristotle since Heidegger explicates in *Being and Time* that the possible is higher than the real. From this perspective, Heidegger develops a less open interpretation of and counterparadigm against Western metaphysics. The more Heidegger interprets philosophers of modern times, the more he sees the unity and connectedness of ontology and theology. He also emphasizes, more than before, the notion of the ground as the theological element of ontology.

Heidegger understands philosophy more and more as theology. He finds an expression of this in Hegel:[55] "For philosophy, too, has no other object than God — and thus is essentially rational theology — and service to God in its continual service to truth."[56] In Hegel, according to Heidegger, ontology becomes the speculatively grounded interpretation of being, in such a way that the actual entity (*Seiendes*) is the absolute *theos*. It is from the being (*Sein*) of the absolute that all entities are determined. Heidegger refers here to Aristotle, who already brings philosophy (in the genuine sense) in very close connection with *theologikè episteme*. But where Heidegger sees unity, he claims that Aristotle is unable to explain the relationship between the question concerning being qua being and the question of god.

Especially in his 1936 lecture course on Schelling, Heidegger emphasizes the connectedness and unity of ontology and theology: "Theo-logy means here questioning beings as a whole. This question of beings as a whole, the theological question, cannot be asked without the question about beings as such, about the essence of being in general. That is the question about the *on hēon*, 'ontology.' Philosophy's questioning is always and in itself both onto-logical and theo-logical in the very broad sense. Philosophy is Ontotheology."[57] Here Heidegger skips the reference to the highest being. The question of being as such immediately implies the question of being as a whole, because it presupposes an understanding of an entity that represents the highest being, the beingest, which determines the whole of being.

In the question of being, the truth of being is asked for: that which makes being in its essence open at all and thus comprehensible. This question of the truth of being is the fundamental question of philosophy in general, as long as philosophy is determined as the question of what being is. This is the original motive of philosophy; this question is therefore prior to every concrete answer to it. The question of the truth of being is thus essentially more primordial than the way this question is answered by Aristotle and later thinkers. Aristotle, however, first makes explicit the question that had always been asked by philosophy, and he forces it into the formulation of what being qua being is.[58]

Heidegger places the tension between the question of being and its possible answers in such a way that he can use the words 'ontology' and 'theology' for the basic movement of Western philosophy. For him ontology means "only the question into the truth and the question into being, and theology means for us the question into the being of ground. The essential is the inner connectedness of both questions."[59] Heidegger's concept of ontotheology as a unity of being and ground implies pantheism where being and ground are united. This concept belongs to the heart of Western metaphysics: because the question of being cannot remain by itself, it turns into the question of the being of the ground, and this is again the theological question.[60]

Heidegger's interpretations of Aristotle, explicated above, are ambiguous concerning the question of whether ontology has to be theology. In his later period, he says that it is because metaphysics has an ontotheological structure that the question of being has not been raised. "Ontology means the question of the truth and the ground of being, and "theology" means for us the question of the being of the ground. What is essential is the inner connectedness of both questions."[61] The inner movement of the questioning is a continuous playing back and forth between the theological question of the ground of beings as a whole and the ontological question of the essence of beings as such, an onto-theo-logy revolving within itself.[62]

This interpretation of Western philosophy as ontotheology becomes more and more clear for Heidegger; in the later Heidegger, for instance, to say that philosophy should not be ontotheological is tantamount to saying that philosophy should not be philosophy. In his 1944–46 treatise, "Nihilism as Determined by the History of Being," Heidegger begins to understand the ontotheological structure of metaphysics from the perspective of the history of being. Ontology and theology are then forged together: "Because metaphysics, thinking the being as such, is approached by Being but thinks it on the basis of and with reference to beings, metaphysics must therefore say (*legein*) the *theion* in the sense of the highest existent ground. Metaphysics is inherently theology. It is theology to the extent that it says the being as being, the *on hē on*. Ontology is simultaneously and necessarily theology."[63]

In the "Introduction to 'What is Metaphysics?'" (1949), metaphysics is characterized as "twofold and yet unitary" on the basis of its ontotheological structure. "Because it represents beings as beings, metaphysics is, in a twofold and yet unitary manner, the truth of beings in their universality and in the highest being. According to its essence, metaphysics is at the same time both ontology in the narrower sense, and theology."[64] Metaphysics is the insight that being immediately refers to beings in their totality, since with the beingness of being, one refers to all entities. Understanding being as a whole presupposes a normative concept of being, in which an understanding of a highest entity is implied. "In this manner, metaphysics always represents beings as such in their totality; it represents the beingness of beings (the *ousia* of the *on*). But metaphysics represents the beingness of beings in a twofold manner: in the first place, the totality of beings as such with an eye to their most universal traits (*on katholou, koinon*); but at the same time also the totality of beings as such in the sense of the highest and therefore divine being (*on katholou, akrotaton, theion*)."[65]

When he writes "The Onto-theological Constitution of Metaphysics" (1959), the insight into this structure is completely settled. In this essay, Heidegger definitely decides that the ambivalent relationship and ambiguity of ontology and theology are characteristic of first philosophy. Heidegger refers back to his inaugural lecture, "What Is Metaphysics?" defining metaphysics as the question about beings as such and as a whole. The wholeness of this whole is the unity of all beings that unifies as the generative ground. "To those who can read, this means: metaphysics is onto-theo-logy."[66] Heidegger, without explicitly saying it, but with his references to Spinoza and Hegel, continues here his pantheistic interpretation of Western metaphysics. Being and ground are two sides of the same coin. In the sixties this insight does not change for Heidegger; in fact becomes more and more obvious in his analysis.[67] In the early Heidegger, ontology without a theology was thought to be a possibility of philosophy. But because he raises the question of whether ontology should be theological, in his later writings ontology as theology belongs to the very constitution of philosophy. It becomes obvious to him: ontology is theology.

How does the question of god belong to philosophical thinking? To what extent does theology belong to philosophy? How and why does the philosophical question of god enter the tradition? These questions are prepared in Aristotle, to whom Heidegger was most oriented, in order to sharpen his ideas with respect to the ontotheological question. But during the years of his interpretation of Aristotle, Heidegger loses openness with regard to that question, insofar as it is a metaphysical question. He does not see this possibility of the question of being any longer in metaphysics. "Metaphysics has this twofold character because it is what it is: the representation of beings as beings. Metaphysics has no choice. As metaphysics, it is by its very essence excluded from the experience of being."[68] It seems to me that Heidegger contradicts himself here. Because the ontotheological structure of metaphysics is an answer to the question of being as the motive of philosophy, without an experience of being, the ontotheological structure could never be an epoch of the history of being. It may hinder the question of being, but it could never make it impossible — otherwise, Heidegger could not read Aristotle and the whole of Western philosophy from the perspective of the question of being.

The question, "How does the deity enter into philosophy?" is not to be answered with the idea of a god that comes from outside. The god always is already in metaphysics. It belongs to the question of being which is characteristic of philosophy as such. With the question of how the godhead enters into philosophy, Heidegger discusses questions, which, once they are well thought-out, make it possible to isolate the philosophical question of god from religious speaking and thinking. Generally the question into the gods and the godhead is both intentionally and unintentionally understood within an ontotheological paradigm. This paradigm determines from the beginning the place of religious speaking as the highest speaking. By defining philosophical speaking in its ontotheological structure, it is possible to isolate this classic metaphysical anchoring from religious speaking.

The question whether there is ontology without a theology for Heidegger is, however, no longer a question within the domain of philosophy and metaphysics. Rather, it is within what he calls the domain of 'thinking.' The motive of philosophy, strictly speaking, has disappeared from philosophy, but it has been preserved in the thinking of being. This domain of thinking is, in a sense, a counterparadigm to philosophy in which the question of being is not answered with an entity that represents the highest way of being, the whole of being and the cause of being. In the 1955–56 lecture course, "The Principle of Reason," Heidegger refers to the mystical words of Angelus Silesius: "The rose is without why: it blooms because it blooms, it pays no attention to itself, asks not whether it is seen."[69] The "without why" is the counterparadigm of metaphysics with which Heidegger presents an atheological ontology.

FIVE

The Ideal of a Causa Sui

H eidegger's criticism of the metaphysical concept of god is especially directed toward the concept of god as cause.[1] In the wake of Aristotle, being is understood as *actualitas*. The highest representation of *actualitas* is an entity, which has this *actualitas* in the purest way as a determining characteristic. This means that it is *actus purus*.[2] Being in the first and the purest way is proper to god.[3] Such a metaphysics does not transcend the level of entities, because it does not understand the ontological difference. On one hand, it speaks about being as a characteristic of entities and is only understood as this characteristic (*actualitas* as determination of the dominant understanding of an entity). On the other hand, it sets as the ground of entities another entity, which possesses the criterion for being an entity in the most perfect way. In a certain sense, god is an exemplary instance of being as *actualitas,* of something that actualizes completely. This idea of actualization is also present in the modern ideal of the self-actualization of the human being.

Classical metaphysics is ontotheological. In Aristotle it is still both ontological and theological insofar as it understands the whole of being from the perspective of a ground. The unthought unity of metaphysics lies in this idea, because the question into the ground of entities gives rise both to the question into being as such and into the highest entity. In this way, Thomas Aquinas presents the unifying moment of god and the separate entities in being, understood as actuality. The relationship between god and the separate entities lies at the level of the formal similarity of characteristics between two entities.[4] Being itself is identical to god's goodness.[5] Aquinas explicates the metaphysical concept of creation in accordance with Aristotle's concept of the *causa efficiens*.[6] The transcendence presented here is between entities, and does not touch the problem of the ontological difference. He understands it as an emanation of the whole being from a universal cause, which is god, and it is this emanation which we indicate with the word 'creation.'[7] This concept of creation remains within the domain of causality. "The real appears now in the light of the causality of the *causa efficiens*. Even God is represented in theology — not in faith — as *causa prima,* as the first cause."[8] Heidegger wants to transcend this with his understanding of being. Aquinas distinguishes several forms of causality, but does not question causality as such. He interprets god within this paradigm as *causa universalis*. "The causal character of Being as reality shows itself in all purity in that being which fulfills the essence of Being in the highest sense, since it is that being which can never not be."[9] It always refers back to "the question of God's existence in the sense of the *summum ens qua ens realissimum*."[10] Because Christian theology works with this metaphysics, it has to reinterpret all entities. The being of entities means in this case being created.[11] Therefore, Heidegger's specific understanding of the divine, about which he later speaks, cannot be explicated with this kind of characterization of being.

The ontotheological structure of Western philosophy takes on a specific form in modernity: it no longer refers to god as

the highest entity, but to human being. Especially in his interpretation of Nietzsche, Heidegger shows how ontotheology
leads to radical subjectivism in modern thinking. Anthropology is the starting point for understanding reality in modernity.
The paragon of this is Giovanni Pico della Mirandola (1463–1494).
In 1486, at the beginning of modernity, he writes a text that is
typical of the modern Western ideal of humanity. In his *Oratio
de dignitate hominis,* God speaks as follows: "We have given
to thee, Adam, no fixed seat, no form of thy very own, no gift
pecularly thine, that thou mayest feel as thine own, have as
thine own, possess as thine own the seat, the form, the gifts
which thou thyself shalt desire. A limited nature in other crea-
tures is confined within the laws written down by us. In con-
formity with thy free judgment, in whose hands I have placed
thee, thou are confined by no bounds; and thou wilt fix limits
of nature for thyself. I have placed thee at the center of the
world, that from there thou mayest more conveniently look
around and see whatsoever is in the world. Neither heavenly
nor earthly, neither mortal nor immortal have We made thee.
Thou, like a judge appointed for being honorable, art the
molder and maker of thyself; thou mayest sculpt thyself into
whatever shape thou dost prefer. Thou canst grow downward
into the lower natures which are brutes. Thou canst again grow
upward from thy soul's reason into the higher natures which
are divine."[12]

Mirandola represents God as permitting humanity to have
what it wishes and to be what it wants. Man's will determines
what he is: he is able to make and to mold himself. In making
himself, the human being does not have a fixed abode, a face,
or a special task. He is completely in his own hands. The
human being is understood as an entity that is a *causa sui:* a
being that causes itself. The only fixed ground, as something
from which the human being can live out his life, is what he
makes of himself. The only certainty for human beings is

human beings. Modernity is driven by the idea that human beings produce their own reality.

The moment of subjectivity dominates the philosophy of modernity with regard to religion as well. This can be seen explicitly in Feuerbach's work. He understands religious reality as an image of humanity, placed by a human being outside of himself, and which the human worships as god.[13] Humanity makes an object out of its essence, which it considers to be another entity. Feuerbach writes in *The Essence of Christianity;* "The object of any subject is nothing else than the subject's own nature taken objectively. Such as are a man's thoughts and dispositions, such is his God; so much worth as a man has, so much and no more has his God. Consciousness of God is self-consciousness, knowledge of God is self-knowledge." Feuerbach adds to this: "By his God thou knowest the man, and by the man his God; the two are identical."[14] Thus, for Feuerbach theology is anthropology.

Feuerbach was not solely responsible for subjectifying the philosophy of religion. Freud's work and the existentialist interpretation of phenomenology influenced the field as well. This anthropological approach to religion and theology became widely accepted. It was seen as progress — as an answer to god-is-dead theology. That it would be seen as a definitive form of nihilism, as Heidegger interprets Nietzsche, was almost impossible to imagine at that time. Nowadays the anthropological interpretation of faith and religion is present in the field of health, where faith seems to be important for mental health. Heidegger refers to this in his letter to Erhart Kästner from January 1, 1954, when he writes that nowadays the theologians work together with psychoanalysis and sociology.[15]

Heidegger sees ontotheology as a movement that little-by-little has been applied to the human being. Therefore, he writes in winter semester 1930/31: "The inquiry into the *on* was ontological ever since its beginning with the ancients, but at the

same time it was already with Plato and Aristotle onto-theo-
logical, even if it was correspondingly not conceptually developed. Since Descartes the line of inquiry becomes above all
ego-logical, whereby the ego is not only crucial for the logos
but is also co-determinant for the development of the concept of '*Theos*' as it was prepared anew in Christian theology.
The question of being as a whole is onto-theo-ego-logical."[16]
Human being becomes, as an ego, the ground of reality par
excellence.

GROUND

The ultimate concern of human beings is to determine a
fixed ground and first and highest cause. In modernity, man
himself becomes these. Against this background, I will discuss
the concept of causality, especially the phenomenon in modern
thinking in which only what can be given an explanation and
a cause is considered valuable and to have the right to exist.
This requires making visible the hypertrophy of causality in
fields where causal thinking is not appropriate. In what follows,
I will consider the ideas of perfection and progress in the
human experience of sense and meaning.

Modernity searches for complete certainty in its knowledge
of reality. It is not surprising that in this period of Western
thinking, more than ever before, the principle of sufficient reason was used to validate a judgment, an observation or a phenomenon. All kinds of causality can be reduced to one cause,
in accordance with the principle of sufficient reason: everything
that exists has to have a cause, why it is and why it does not
not exist.[17] For Western man it is not difficult to understand the
claim, "nothing is without reason" because our understanding is organized in such a way that our reason, when it understands something, always and everywhere asks for its cause.
Only founded claims are accepted and are understandable. In

this constellation humans automatically look for causes: often only the most obvious, sometimes also the more removed causes, and in the end also the last and first cause. In this context, it is not important to distinguish different types of causality in order to get a better insight into it. Indeed it is hard to gain insight into causality with a collection of the meanings of the word cause,[18] since a preunderstanding of causality is prior to the possibility of collecting different 'causes.'

Still, to get a definition of the concept, it is useful to enter into it with an everyday meaning, since that is the logical or epistemic ground. It indicates the place where the truth of a judgment can be founded. In this, the principle of sufficient reason is operative: the principle that nothing is without reason and that no claim can be made without ground.[19]

Everything that is suitable to legitimize the truth of a judgment can be called ground in one way or another. This foundation can lean on other judgments already accepted as true, in which logical deduction is a possible but certainly not exclusive way: epistemic grounds are not necessarily logical grounds. Judgments are also acknowledged as founded and grounded when they are in accordance with experts, or with traditional or historical connections. In a stricter sense, only the objective, logical legitimations of a judgment are to be called 'grounded'. For example, sentences or judgments are accepted as grounded when it is possible to deduce them logically from other sentences or judgments accepted as true.

In all cases, the foundation is given by gathering the judgments into a connection with other judgments that are accepted as true. The principle of sufficient reason means that, with regard to claims, one has to look for a foundation as far as possible. It has to be the most satisfying in accordance with the circumstances.

This postulate of founding is connected with the modern Western understanding, that what is not founded is simply incomprehensible.

Therefore, when something has to be made understandable, it must be connected to and founded in an already existing connection of thoughts.

Foundations do not normally appear isolated on the scene but belong to a more encompassing connection of a theory of foundations, in which general premises are deducible from even broader presuppositions. From this perspective, one seeks final insight. This is present most explicitly in the Cartesian effort to achieve an unshakeable ground for all knowledge. The absolute foundation — the unshakeable and fixed ground — is found in the thinking ego, which becomes the fixed ground for all judgments.

Leibniz formulated the ideal of absolute foundation through the principle of sufficient reason. Every being has a reason to be. The first, which causes all the others and gives them reason to be, also has a reason to be. The highest being only can be understood by Western man as being there when it is understood as caused, since without being caused or founded, all that exists does not really exist. Therefore, in Western thinking, the highest being that bears all reality and all sense is, in the end, thought and represented as caused by itself. In this formula, the idea of the *causa sui* gets its definitive form from Spinoza: "By that which is self-caused I mean that whose essence involves existence; or that whose nature can be conceived only as existing."[20]

Initially, the principle of sufficient reason applied both to judgments and to the reality that corresponded to the judgments; in modern epistemology causal relations are no longer aspects of reality itself. It has become unusual to understand the relations that are formulated as causal explanations, as relations of real grounds and their results. The rejection of this realistic interpretation of causality leads to a reinterpretation of the principle of reason. One begins to speak of a postulate of explanation. According to its realistic interpretation, the principle of causation says that "everything necessarily has a cause" (meaning a cause in reality). But according to the principle of explanation, the formula is: An adequate scientific explanation has to be found for everything.[21]

This can be criticized from the realistic point of view. Causal explanations assume a reality that is independent from thinking. A thinking that wants to apply a subjective logic in the understanding of real objects in the end does not have a criterion to which it can measure its knowledge. It remains captured within the projects and the limits of human thinking.

Thus, once the ground of knowledge is found in the modern thinking subject, a gap appears with regard to reality. Reality itself is no longer the criterion for knowledge; rather, a subjective logic becomes the ground from which reality is understood. Modern philosophy finds the answer to the inquiry into being and the meaning of objects in the constitution and construction of things for a human subject. The conditions for the possibility of knowledge are found in human subjectivity.

With the shift from the objective, realistic foundation to the subjective approach, the principle of reason changes. In the subjective approach, human subjectivity as the ground of reality makes objectivity possible. Human subjectivity appears as the ground *par excellence*. When Kant asks for the conditions of possibility of knowledge of reality, Heidegger sees this as a further explication of the question of sufficient reason.[22]

Against this background is also the question of meaning and sense from the perspective of subjectivity. The moment of the unity of the manifold within a whole of meaning lies in the constitution of the objects. This unity of a whole of meaning cannot be observed empirically, but results from a spontaneous act of subjectivity which accompanies all representations.[23] The synthetic effect of the "I think" is the ground on which objective experience is possible. It is a question of whether there is experience of an object since all objectivity is already a project of the subject. The human subject realizes the ground of meaning on which experience is possible. This is continued in Neo-Kantianism and in Husserl's phenomenology. All that is, is only there for a human subject with the help of the acts of a consciousness, which means by a constituting intentionality.[24] Human subjectivity is the supporting ground of all reality. This also means that the whole from which reality is understood and illuminated is constituted by human — and individual — subjectivity.[25] In the end, the meaning of reality is the meaning that the individual self gives to it. The principle of reason gets its point of departure in the human being: a being is grounded insofar as it is grounded in human subjectivity.

The principle of reason, as formulated by Leibniz, reads: "nothing is without reason." This principle has become so obvious that everyone is used to it and fails to notice its peculiarity. Heidegger speaks, therefore, in the wake of Leibniz about the great and mighty principle of sufficient reason.[26] He means that, within Western thinking, asking for the causes of things leads to the idea that a thing or a reality whose reason or ground cannot be shown does not have the right to exist. Entities only have the right to exist when they are founded.

This means that everything that can be said to exist has to have a ground or a cause. This principle is also the '*principium reddendae rationis,*' which means the principle of justification and rendering account. All entities that exist can and must be accounted for in principle. *Ratio* does not mean the same as "cause," but it does indicate that every entity is embedded in account and justification, motivation and connection, need and intention, aim and destiny, meaningfulness and ground.

This principle has mastered the whole of modernity. Modern science and technology are only possible because of the dominance of this principle. Technology is understood by Heidegger as an utterly rationalized practice and as a way of thinking which is capable of understanding everything by calculating and taking into account.

The modern university is based on this principle as well.[27] The university sees it as its task and purpose to do research and to educate. In these endeavors, everything has a cause or a reason. The raison d'être of the university is the principle of sufficient reason. Thus, without knowing it, scientific research and education may be embedded in a framework that limits their freedom and creativity.

THE PROCESS OF SUBJECTIFYING

Heidegger understands the subjectivistic and anthropological approach as a symptom of nihilism. The phenomenon of people wanting to live in a meaningful world could only appear on the scene because meaning has disappeared as a given. This, in turn, is connected to the phenomenon of subjectifying. Heidegger has precisely articulated the phenomenon of a meaningless world as a situation in which human beings do not feel at home anywhere and find a ground for their existence nowhere. Human beings are in danger of becoming homeless, and disinherited, without dwelling, possession, or tradition. "The loss of rooted-ness is caused not merely by circumstances and fortune; nor does it stem only from the negligence and the superficiality of man's way of life. The loss of autochthony springs from the spirit of the age into which all of us were born."[28] The phenomenon of homelessness is typical of the time we live in and is essentially connected with the subjectification of reality.

Heidegger expresses this precisely in his interpretation of Nietzsche. He sees the uprooting and the loss of meaning in connection with the subjectification of meaning, which is, according to him, the peak of meaninglessness. When everything has to do justice to human beings, then the era of complete meaninglessness begins.[29] In several places in his work, Heidegger points out that the anthropological character of meaning is characteristic of modernity: "Today, then, anthropology is no longer just the name for a discipline, nor has it been such for some time. Instead, the word describes a fundamental tendency of man's contemporary position with respect to himself and to the totality of beings. According to this fundamental position, something is only known and understood if it is given an anthropological explanation. Anthropology seeks not only the truth about human beings, but instead it now demands a decision as to what truth in general can mean."[30] In this modern age, we only know what something means when we know what it means for human beings. In such a constellation or framework, all search for truth becomes anthropology, as does the theological search for truth, and the truth of religion.

Why is the phenomenon of subjectification a reason for Heidegger to speak about meaninglessness? Meaninglessness is first characterized by the fact that being does not come to truth. One can see this phenomenon in the important thinkers of the modern age, such as Descartes and Kant. Modern humanity does not know entities in their being, but only itself as the one who determines its being. We see this also in Dilthey's early concept of hermeneutics: everything the human being talks about and expresses is an expression of himself.[31] Meaninglessness is the phenomenon of being not brought to light. Being does not come into the open, because the truth of entities is already decided in anthropology. Wherever the essence of the truth of entities is decided, there the reflection on the truth of being does not take place. Truth becomes certainty and is formulated as that which is relevant and makeable for a human subject. Human subjectivity decides what entities are and which entities are; furthermore, it decides about truth and about what is true. Understanding entities as produceable, as makeable material, and understanding the human being as such an entity is characteristic of modernity. Entities are modeled on their surrender to unconditional planning, calculation, and organization. Modern humanity sees its reality as produceable. Applied to humanity,

this means that it makes itself. The idea of humanty as produceable by and for itself figures in the idea of the *causa sui,*
which generally refers to complete self-determination and self-
actualization.

The idea of *causa sui* is connected with the ontotheological
structure of Western thinking. Thinking means thinking of
being, but within the ontotheological framework it means that
if something exists, it is thought as something that has to have
a cause. Even the highest entity that exists has to have a cause.
From there it is decided that the highest only exists insofar as
it has its cause in itself: the first cause causes itself. The idea
that something could exist gratuitously and without reason disappears from the scene. Grace becomes an exclusive theme of
theology.

Freedom is also understood from the perspective of *causa
sui.* Someone is free who exists because of him or herself.
Causa sui expresses the image of man who strives for his independence. All kinds of dependency are, from the perspective of
this image of man, held in less esteem; even the dependency
of a needy body should be avoided. This is the ideal of a completely
undetermined human subject isolated from history, shaped in
modernity, who is able to place reality opposite to him as an
object.

Initially, the idea of the *causa sui* was not applied to man,
but to god as the highest and first entity. In modernity this idea
is applied to the human being as the first and highest entity.
Human beings produce themselves by their own labor; humans
are the starting point of their own being; humans considered as
their own cause, have as their ideal total self-actualization.
Thus, modernity teaches that humans are both, the root and the
highest being.[32] Karl Marx writes: "To be radical is to grasp
the root of the matter. But for man the root is man himself . . .
The criticism of religion ends with the teaching that *man is the
highest being for man.*"[33] But Heidegger asks: How does one

come from the first to the second thought, i.e. that man is his own root, and that man is the highest entity for man — isn't an intermediate thought missing, namely that man is all there is? A lot of people have already decided that this is the case. Not without rhetoric Heidegger asks: "From where is this decided? In what way? By which right? By which authority?"[34] Man as an entity that produces himself is confronted with the question of motivation. Why and for the sake of what does man produce himself?

Modern man seeks the answer to these questions in the general structure of entities. In Western metaphysics generally, the relation between meaning and entities is deduced from entities themselves. Entities are characterized by self-persistence. Spinoza puts this clearly: "Each thing, in so far as it is in itself, endeavors to persist in its own being." Furthermore, "The conatus with which each thing endeavors to persist in its own being is nothing but the actual essence of the thing itself."[35] Every orientation to a purpose, goal, or motive is understood as an offshoot of an entity's own self-persistence.[36] The idea of finality, which is criticized in modernity, is placed within the immanent efficacy of the entities. The outcome is always the result of a pregiven program.[37] This means that man is not able to transcend his own domain.

The modern age is of the opinion that, as a consequence of the idea of self-persistence, the criterion for and the answer to the question of meaning is to be found in the human being as a needy entity, who finds his destiny in the satisfaction of all his needs.[38] In all dimensions of human existence, something becomes meaningful on the basis of human need. Meaningfulness becomes an economic question that has as its answer, the total satisfaction of needs.

Heidegger understands the relation between meaninglessness and anthropologism against this background. Where the machination (*Machenschaft*), or makeability of everything, and meaninglessness rule, the disappearance of meaning has to be replaced by posing aims and values.[39] Everything of value will be under the control of the human subject because something has a value only insofar as man assigns one to it. One of the most important consequences of the experience of meaninglessness, according to Heidegger, is that being becomes a value: this means that it comes under the control of human subjectivity. Nihilism, the era of meaninglessness, is the unauthorized claim that being, instead of existing as a ground, is under the control of human subjectivity. The idea that everything gets its value and meaning from human subjectivity presupposes that entities are originally placed in a state of indifferent worthlessness, that on their own, things would not have meaning and value. They are saved from this state by the meaning-giving and valuing subject.[40]

Since the nineteenth century, history has been understood in the same way. One acts as if human beings on their own could give meaning to history, which presupposes that history on its own is meaningless and has to wait for human beings in order to become meaningful. What man can do with regard to history, according to Heidegger, is to be aware that history withholds and hides its meaning from man.[41]

In our era, entities as a whole are determined by meaninglessness, because the being of entities is already determined by the 'machination' of the human will to power. Because the question of being is forgotten, entities are handed over to an unleashed machination that decides what they are. Humans not only have to live without truth, but the essence of truth — that something is revealed to them — has fallen into oblivion. The era of complete meaninglessness has, according to Heidegger, more talent for invention, more activism, more success, and more plans to publicize all of this, than any previous era before. Therefore, it has to fall back on the claim that it can give a meaning to everything, a meaning to which it is worth dedicating oneself. The era of complete meaninglessness will fight its own essence the hardest, with the claim that it is able to give a meaning to everything.[42] Modernity has as its dominant characteristics, "first, that man installs and secures himself as *subiectum,* as the nodal point for beings as a whole; and secondly, that the beingness of beings as a whole is grasped as the representedness of whatever can be produced and explained."[43] When man becomes the giver of meaning, then being is meaningless.

The turning of the question of meaning into its giving and causation is an effort to banish the crisis of meaning. Humanity seeks the solid ground of meaning in itself. However the subjectification of meaning increases the crisis of meaning rather than answering it. When metaphysics, religion, and theology are understood and explicated as anthropology then they are in line with modernity, which is characterized by subjectivization, anthropologism, and psychologism.

HUMAN BEING THAT CAUSES ITSELF

Let me turn back to the idea of '*causa sui.*' *Causa sui* generally indicates self-determination and self actualization.[44] It refers to the idea of a radical freedom with which an entity posits and makes itself. Someone is free, who is because of himself.[45] Freedom, then, means self-causation with regard to acting. How current is Pico della Mirandola's ideal?

In modern philosophy, the idea of *causa sui* is applied completely to human beings. Man is produced by man's own activity. This implies the total self-realization of man. Subjectifying the principle of sufficient reason in modernity leads to the human being as the source and the site of the production of meaning. As a result, humans become the center of reality in two ways. First, they are the ground from which reality is actualized. Second, as this ground, they are the most important material and therefore the primary object of investigation. Humans become raw material for humans, with all its consequences: "Since man is the most important raw material, one can reckon with the fact that some day factories will be built for the artificial breeding of human material, based on present-day chemical research."[46]

The principle of sufficient reason has its biggest application in technology. Therefore it is important to describe the consequences that technology has in the domain of the experience of ultimate meaning. To what extent are perfection and progress active in the domain of ultimate meaning? History, which appeared in Christian culture as the history of a process of salvation, was rebuilt in a quest for a state of inner worldly perfection. History became a narrative of progress. The ideal of progress, however, has no content; it is empty. The ultimate goal is to create conditions in which an ever-new progress and perfection can be achieved. But with this, the question to what purpose remains unanswered.[47] The world of the perfecting of technology is without a purpose. It develops into a world in which the same happens all the time and in which there is no experience of meaningfulness.

Heidegger understands this situation from the perspective of expanding nihilism. It is a process in which, in the end, the being of entities no longer appears. This is not to be understood as the consequence of an error, of a deceit or self-deceit of knowledge, but as a result of the oblivion of being. Heidegger understands the most dominant characteristic of the general experience of meaninglessness comes from the development in which being becomes a value. Everything of value comes under the control of the human subject. This is also the case in the principle of sufficient reason: the cause is only acknowledged insofar as human beings acknowledge the cause. It is this presupposition that in fact is at work in nihilism: things are nothing in themselves. The place entities take is determined by technology. Everything that exists is prepared for production and is material for the needs of human subject.

In technology what counts is the success of technical acting. Everything that is important for man must be important for technical success. The question of whether this leads to a simplifying of the concept of being no longer arises. The *homo faber* itself is also an object of technology. This means that the inventor and perfector of everything ingeniously perfects himself, thus completing human power. The application of technology to man implies the perfection of the inventor and cause of technology. Technology becomes the perspective on being as such. The consequences of the progress of the total technologization of man, however, run up against the finitude of human existence.

The idea of progress in technology and science inherently looks forward to an endless progress of its movement into the future. Progress, as a movement produced by itself, presupposes that what comes after outperforms that which preceeds it. In that sense, technology is always progress. It is a pursuit of permanent self-surpassing toward an endless goal. Because of this ceaseless repetition, the question arises whether a basic mood of boredom prevails in the technological society.

Man cannot be moved forward into a shade-less clarity because of the given of human finitude. Here lies the error of the technological ideal: it is unable to give meaning to the 'now' because it is always anticipating what is to come. This is because every present is seen as a pre-history, in which everything ever again is a means to an end in an endless future. Every present is, in principle, inferior from the perspective of future technical perfection. In this way, technological perfection carries along unspoken, destructive power with regard to every actual present.[48]

MEANING AND FINITUDE

It is characteristic of Heidegger's philosophy that human being is understood as a finite entity that cannot found and cause itself. "The Self which as such has to lay the basis for itself, can *never* get that basis into its power . . . Thus Being a basis means *never* to have power over one's ownmost Being from the ground up."[49] Human being cannot overtake its own conditions of possibility which are more original and earlier. The conditions of possibility are understood as that which makes possible: they are a whole that always precedes human being, and they offer the space within which human being can be. "According to *Being and Time,* "meaning" designates the realm of projection, designates it in accord with its own proper intent (that is, in accord with its unique question concerning the "meaning of Being"), as the clearing of Being, the clearing that is opened and grounded in projection. Such projection is that in the thrown project which propriates as the essential unfolding of truth."[50] Thrown projection is that which makes possible our understanding of being, but we cannot appropriate it, and we are not it in the end; it is earlier than us. This condition of possibility is always earlier and prior and precedes all wanting and planning of man. Asking for the meaning of being means, according to Heidegger, asking for that which already precedes as the way or the space that makes man possible as a historical being. This space is the ground on which everything rests, that which is already present and supports all entities.[51]

Heidegger calls the question into the meaning of being a trek. This trek is not an adventure but a turn homeward into that which always already has preceded. In reflection, that is, asking for meaning, we arrive where, without knowing it, we already are. We enter a site from which the space that determines our doings opens for us.[52] Reflection as a question about meaning asks about the place where we are, in light of which we appear as present. This place itself, however, cannot be observed; it precedes us as that which reflection makes possible.

Especially in the reflection on the being of humanity, the ground and the place on which it stands and which makes possible its existence is asked for. Out of this space humanity is able to approach itself as a self, and it is able to come to itself. Sometimes humanity loses itself in its worries and the things of the world; in that case humanity has no time for it self. Someone who has time for his self understands the space in which he already is. Out of the time and the space that humanity has at its disposal, humanity is able to appear as a self, and it can throw a light on its self, experience itself as an entity, and is able to reflect upon itself. It can do this only out of the time handed down to it.

The quest for meaning is a quest for the whole space in which man can exist. This whole cannot become a fixed property. In the end, we are not that which makes us possible, for it is earlier than and prior to us. Humans are understood by Heidegger as entities that cannot appropriate the whole of their conditions of possibility, because they cannot appropriate a time which is always earlier.

The project out of which someone experiences his life really anticipates a *temporary* destination or a *provisional* end. This provisional end provides the actual present with meaning and place. The whole from the perspective of which someone understands his life is not something that he himself can wind up and cause. The future can hold a lot of possibilities, and things can develop in a completely other way than what one ever expected. The provisional and temporary whole that we constantly anticipate mostly happens to us — it is handed down to us, which means it is not the result of planning and calculation. This temporary meaning generally appears for living human beings unexpectedly and suddenly. It is given to them, approaches them, or is handed down to them. This is the reason why Heidegger speaks in *Being and Time* about 'destiny' and 'inheritance.'[53] Therefore, meaning as embedded in tradition does not belong to the kind of "things" that one can make, control, found, or bend to one's will. Meaning and sense are beyond the range of a planning and making will, but presuppose a receptive openness toward that which is handed down to someone.

The question into meaning is not approachable by a calculation. Meaning, in which human beings live, cannot be made a fixed possession; it belongs to them, as finite entities to whom the meaning is handed down. The ideal of Giovanni Pico della Mirandolla was an important development in the modern age, but it misses the fact than human beings cannot make themselves. Rather, it is important for human beings that they learn to be the mortals that they are. For Heidegger this means "those to whom being appeals. Only such beings are capable of dying, that means, to take on death as death."[54]

Six

Heidegger's Interpretation of the Word of Nietzsche: "God is Dead"

*T*his chapter will work out the implications of the onto-theological structure of metaphysics, which leads to the subjectification of reality in modern times, on the basis of Heidegger's interpretation of Nietzsche. Nietzsche also remains under tribute to metaphysics. I will pay special attention to the notion of the death of god.

In the text "Phenomenology and Theology," discussed in the third chapter, Heidegger begins with a reference to Nietzsche's *Thoughts Out of Season* wherein "the glorious Hölderlin" is mentioned. He also refers to Franz Overbeck's *On the Christianness of Today's Theology,* which establishes the world-denying expectation of the end as the basic characteristic of what is primordially Christian. Heidegger continues with a discussion of Nietzsche's phrase "God is Dead," "European Nihilism," and "The Determination of Nihilism in the History of Being,"[1] demonstrating that his understanding of theology and its relation to philosophy are in line with his later works.

The theme of the death of god plays an important role in Nietzsche, often interpreted and commented upon. Heidegger also mentions the death of god, in reference to Nietzsche, in his inaugural Rectorial address.[2] But I focus here on Heidegger's treatment of this theme in his essay "Nietzsche's Word: 'God is Dead.'"[3] This text, in which Heidegger interprets the story of the madman from *The Gay Science,* was written in 1943. Its content is based on the Nietzsche lecture courses that Heidegger taught between 1936 and 1940.[4] In a sense, Heidegger offers in the essay a summation of these lecture courses. That is the reason why this text is very significant for Heidegger's interpretation of Nietzsche. In these lecture courses, Heidegger understands Nietzsche's thoughts as the completion of Western metaphysics. This completion does not mean that Nietzsche no longer belongs to metaphysics; on the contrary, the completion belongs to it as the end belongs to a route that has to be covered.

In the preceding chapters, I presented the ontotheological constitution of metaphysics. The *logos* as a logic is seen as the exclusive entrance to being in metaphysics and marks the execution of an unspoken decision. For Heidegger, the *logos* in its original meaning is "the gathering of beings and letting them be."[5] The *logos* structures that which is into a possible unity or connection (*ordo entium*).[6] In its turn the connection motivates the search for foundations and dependencies. Something is not accepted as a being until it is presented as founded in something else; in this way the whole refers to a last, all-founding ground. The anticipation of this founding of the whole lies in the *logos*. In this way the tendency toward something like unity, ground, and foundation is laid in the *logos*.

According to Heidegger, the connection of ontology and theology that is characteristic of metaphysics is a given because at the very beginning of metaphysics, the openness of being is actualized as *logos*. Metaphysics is logic because its ontology and its theology have to be in accordance beforehand with the *logos:* "They account to the *logos,* and are in an essential sense in accord with the *logos*."[7]

As ontology, metaphysics thinks being in an undetermined and general way, as that which is merely and purely present (*ousia*). As theology, it understands this being of pure presence as caused by the highest being. Therefore metaphysics thinks "of the Being of beings both in the ground-giving unity of what is most general, what is indifferently valid everywhere, and also in the unity of the all that accounts for the ground, that is, of the All-Highest."[8]

The *logos* guarantees for metaphysics the openness of everything, and by virtue of its nature tends towards unity and ground. Therefore, in the light and the openness of the *logos,* being appears at its most general; and this generality is explained from an entity as if it were an entity itself. As the last ground of being, only that entity is appropriate that is to be thought in the presented order of entities as the highest entity, as *summum ens:* "This highest and first cause is named by Plato and correspondingly by Aristotle *to theion,* the divine. Ever since being got interpreted as *idea,* thinking about the being of beings has been metaphysical, and metaphysics has been theological. In this case theology means the interpretation of the 'cause' of beings as god and the transferring of being onto this cause, which contains being in itself and dispensing being from out of itself, because it is the being-est of beings."[9] From the beginning, metaphysical theology has thus determined the essential characteristics of the divinity of god.

The metaphysical god is characterized as the highest entity. It is the being-est amid all entities; it is the *ens realissimum* and *plenitudo essendi*.[10] This means god is the entity that most corresponds to the meaning of being and embodies this, because metaphysics, within the horizon of its *logos,* thinks being as presence.[11] Therefore metaphysics thinks god as an entity that, as pure presence, excludes every absence, as that to which metaphysical thinking always can return. As pure presence and as everywhere present it is always available as ground. The first in itself is at the same time the most fixed and as such the most knowable.[12]

Against this background, god is determined as *causa prima.* This implies that god as *causa causarum* is also the ground of all causality. So the metaphysical god appears as the guarantee for the principle of sufficient reason. God as first cause is at the same moment determined as that cause that cannot be caused from outside, but, as absolute cause, is the cause of itself.[13] All that exists appears in the light of the *causa efficiens.* In this chain of causalities, god has the place of the first cause, as *causa prima.*[14]

The understanding of god as *causa prima,* together with the fact that causality is understood as *facere* and *efficere,* has made it easier for philosophical theology to enter into Christian dogma.[15] Therefore Heidegger considers the *ens creatum* as a philosophical concept from the beginning. The *ens creatum* is a determination of the caused entity for a certain period, but the idea of entities as created disappears in modernity when the idea of being as subjectivity or as objectivity for a subject arises.[16]

The ontotheological structure thinks being within the whole of entities and from there within the perspective of a highest entity. Under the influence of Christianity, this highest entity is understood as the cause and producer of entities; all that exists is caused by God the creator. All entities are reduced to the cause that is the highest entity, called the divine. This, how-ever, does not mean that the highest entity always appears on the scene with that same name in metaphysics. It also appears as '*idea,*' '*energeia,*' 'substantiality,' 'objectivity,' 'subjectivity,'

'the will' and 'the will to power.' In every epoch it is understood and presented as the highest or ultimate entity.[17]

In metaphysics all that exists is present for a divine or
human subject (the Middle Ages and modernity, respectively)
or is present for a transcendental subject. By positing a highest
entity, an order of ranking appears in entities: higher and lower
entities, real and unreal entities, entities that are observed with
senses and entities as such (as they are for god). Connected
with this doubling, forced by the order of ranking, is a notion
of truth. Something is true if the represented corresponds to the
real, or conversely, if the real corresponds to the represented.
Things correspond to the idea of them that exists in god. This
was the case especially in the Middle Ages. Human representation has to correspond to the thing in order to be correct. The
thing is correct insofar as it is in accordance with the intention
of god's creation.

It is true that these moments are not immediately the most
important characteristics of the ontotheological structure of
metaphysics; nevertheless they are essentially connected with
it. Therefore, Nietzsche, who wanted to live on this earth very
intensively and remain loyal to it, announces the end of this
highest and doubled world. In his loyalty to this earth he
rejects the supersensible world and preaches the death of god
as the highest entity. It is in the wake of this thinker that
Heidegger shows the dominant characteristics of metaphysics.

CHRISTIANITY AS PLATONISM

Nietzsche thoroughly discusses Plato and Platonism, and he
shows Platonic philosophy in all its consequences. Plato separates
the true world — the intelligible world of the ideas — from the
sensible, visible world. This true world is placed beyond the
visible world and is not attainable by everyone. When this true
world gets lost, it becomes a postulate of practical reason, as

is the case in Kant. What exists outside scientific knowledge is not denied, but operates as *idea,* as thinkable thought. When, after Kant, observation becomes the authority in thinking, ideas and the supersensible world remain effective due to the influence of theology, which is formulated according to a Platonic paradigm. Platonism is then conquered to the extent that the true world as the supersensible world is abolished. The principle of the true world is abolished; in its place positivism shows up. Positivism, however, remains in the double world, insofar as it resists every supersensible world. Nietzsche solves this problem; he abolishes the true world together with the apparent world, in order to turn radically away from Plato.[18]

The difference between the true and the apparent world is the basic condition for metaphysics. In being as a whole, there is a gap that separates one from the other. Plato's philosophy creates these two worlds that are so determinative for Western thinking. The division that Christianity makes between a perishable earth and an eternal heaven refers back to this division between the true and the apparent worlds. Nietzsche's criticism of Christianity presupposes a Christianity that follows the Platonic line. In this context, Heidegger agrees with Nietzsche's statement that Christianity is Platonism for the people.[19] Nietzsche considers the *ideai* and the supersensible to be values. In his interpretation, all philosophy since Plato is a metaphysics of values. Only the supersensible is acknowledged as a real entity. This supersensible can be defined in multifarious ways: as the Creator God of Christianity, as moral duty, as authority of reason, as progress, or as happiness. Ever again the observable is judged from the perspective of the ideal. This is why Nietzsche considers all metaphysics to be Platonism: Christianity is just a popularized form of it.[20]

Christianity especially follows in the track of Platonic-metaphysical thinking with the doctrine of creation a doctrine still effective today. The real entity is reason itself as the creating and ordering spirit. Entities are the creation of this creator.[21] The gap between supersensible and sensible worlds and the concept of truth that is connected with it are two of the moments in metaphysics that are determined by Plato for the whole of Western thinking. That representation is correct that is directed towards the object, and this correctness of representation is in turn equated with truth. According to Heidegger, Plato creates the possibility for this concept of truth in the "allegory of the cave" at the beginning of the seventh book of the *Republic*.[22] The 'looks' that show what things themselves are, the *eidō* (ideas), constitute the essence in whose light each individual entity shows itself as this or that.[23] The being of entities is understood as the idea.

The interpretation of being as *idea* has dominated all Western thinking throughout the history of its transformations up to the present day. Truth becomes a correctness of vision, of apprehension as representation.[24] As correctness of vision, truth becomes a characteristic of the human relation to entities. The locus of truth becomes the assertion, and the essence of truth lies in the agreement of the assertion with its object.[25] An assertion is correct if it corresponds; the truth is this correspondence. On the one hand, the thing accords with the representation or assertion. On the other hand, what is meant in the assertion accords with the thing.[26] Entities are true insofar as they correspond to the prethought order of creation of god. Because god also creates human understanding in correspondence with the ideas, human beings are able to have true knowledge. The correspondence means an agreement with the order of creation.[27] This concept of truth as correspondence was present in the Middle Ages. Even when the Christian worldview disappears, these characteristics of truth remain in force.

The god-creator is replaced by universal reason, which provides entities with their essence. Truth is a correspondence between reason and the nature of entities. An unreasonable truth is no truth at all. Propositional truth is always, and always exclusively, this correctness.[28] Judgment becomes representing in the right way. Heidegger asks what the nature of this representing is, which means positing for oneself. Herein Heidegger sees an all-controlling will to be operative. Representation extends over all that is, and determines it.[29] Only what becomes an object in this way, *is,* and is seen as existing. Since the beginning of the modern age, the being of an entity has been understood from the perspective of will, which is understood by Nietzsche as will to power. The will to power is the last ground of entities. It is because of this that Heidegger interprets Nietzsche as a metaphysician. In the end, Nietzsche's criticism of metaphysics remains within metaphysics. "As an *ontology,* even Nietzsche's metaphysics is *at the same time* theology, although it seems far removed from scholastic metaphysics . . . Such metaphysical theology is of course a negative theology of a peculiar kind. Its negativity is revealed in the expression 'God is dead.' That is an expression not of a-theism but of ontotheology, in that metaphysics in which nihilism proper is fulfilled."[30]

Heidegger approaches Nietzsche and his declaration that "God is dead" from the perspective of nihilism. He places Nietzsche within Western metaphysics — significantly, at its end. In a certain sense, Nietzsche executes the end of metaphysics. What happens when the history of metaphysics ends? One of its dominant characteristics is that the supersensible becomes a product of the natural; in other words, the supersensible is reduced to the sensible. Therefore the discrepancy disappears between sensible and supersensible, idea and observation. This devaluation, this pulling-down or reduction of the supersensible, ends for man in a world without meaning. This means that the framework and the space from which human beings can live disappears. This meaninglessness, however, remains the unthought and unconquerable presupposition of the blind effort to withdraw from meaninglessness by the mere giving of meaning. The project of giving meaning and valuing, in which everyone nowadays has to be and wants to be engaged, is itself a symptom of a history of metaphysics that has become meaningless.[31]

The truth of being has changed and altered in the course of history. Nietzsche observes a change in the history of metaphysics; that is to say, he sees a change in the history of ontology, the interpretation of all that exists. The fact that he sees the rise and unfolding of nihilism means that Nietzsche himself has a theory of the being of entities. A reflection on Nietzsche's metaphysics enables us to better understand the situation and the place of present human beings. This is especially so because the actual situation of present human beings is hardly expressed or experienced, as is the case with all things that are most near: they are first overlooked.

It is important to explore the land and the ground on which metaphysics could reach its full growth. Metaphysics, through its dominance, forgets to think the truth of being; it thinks while forgetting the ground on which it stands. It forgets the space in which and through which it grows, its specific presuppositions. Therefore, a reflection on Nietzsche's metaphysics asks for what remains unthought as presuppositions of his metaphysics.

Nietzsche's metaphysics is characterized as nihilism, a doctrine of the being of entities that Nietzsche recognizes as dominating for centuries and up to the present. Nietzsche summarizes the interpretation of it with the word: "God is dead."[32]

This is not only a personal position of the so-called atheist Nietzsche, whom one can contradict by pointing out church attendance or Christian political parties, and add the fact that Nietzsche became insane in 1888. Rather, Nietzsche expresses something that has been implicit and unspoken for a long time in Western metaphysics. It is a judgment about the destiny of Western thinking, something that is not easy to change.

Nietzsche expresses the word "God is dead" most clearly in the story of the Madman in the third book of *The Gay Science.* It is the story of a man who in broad daylight walks into a market square with a lantern in his hands, and constantly calls that he is looking for god, while the bystanders ridicule him. The text is from 1882. During the same time, Nietzsche starts to compose his main work, which he provisionally indicates as "will to power" with the subtitle "Attempt at a Re-valuation of all Values" (*Versuch einer Umwertung aller Werte*). This subtitle is important for Heidegger's subsequent interpretation.

However, the idea of the death of god was not completely new in 1882. One can find this idea already in the young Nietzsche. In some notes from the time of the origin of his writing *The Birth of Tragedy,* Nietzsche writes in 1870: "I believe in the ancient German saying: 'All Gods must die.'" If one goes further back in time, preceding Nietzsche, one reads in the young Hegel, in his essay *Faith and Knowledge* (1802), the following sentence: "the feeling on which rests the religion of the modern period — the feeling God himself is dead."[33] Also Blaise Pascal (1623-1662) writes in a reference to Plutarch: "*Le grand Pan est mort*" (Great Pan is dead).[34] Gods can die and disappear; they are as perishable as human beings and eras are. Against this background Heidegger develops the notion of "the last god," which makes space for the coming god.[35] This theme will be discussed in the next chapter. So far nothing new is said in Nietzsche's phrase, that gods are mortal and can disappear was more or less already present in the consciousness of Western philosophy.

Four years after the publication of the four books of *The Gay Science,* Nietzsche completed them with a fifth, which starts by saying: "The greatest recent event — that "God is dead," that the belief in the Christian God has become unbelievable — is already beginning to cast its first shadows over Europe."[36] With these words it becomes clear that by the death of god Nietzsche means the death of the Christian God and the supersensible world.[37] God is the name for the domain of the ideas and the ideals, since Plato and Christian Platonism, considered to be the true and real world. This world is opposed to the world of change, appearance, rhetoric, and power. That god is dead means that this supersensible world no longer has sense and strength. Metaphysics, seen from the perspective of Plato, comes to an end. Thus Nietzsche understands his philosophy as an anti-Platonism. When god, as the supersensible ground and purpose of all reality, is dead — when the supersensible world has lost its compelling and constraining powers, its inciting and constructive capacities — then there is nothing to which human beings can direct and orient themselves. Therefore it is written in the story of the Madman: "Are we not straying as through an infinite nothing?"[38] This nothingness means the absence of an ideal and obligating world.

NIHILISM

The death of god and nihilism are connected in Heidegger's interpretation of Nietzsche. To understand that the word "nihilist" is not only a term of abuse, it is important to know what it means in Nietzsche. The word "nihilism" is brought to the philosophical scene by Jacobi (1743–1819). Nihilism according to Nietzsche is thus a historical movement, something that happens in the history of Europe. But it is not just one movement among others; it is the movement of European thinking as such. It is the destiny of the modern age and of modern man, but it does not simply belong to the nineteenth and twentieth century or to certain countries or groups. It belongs to the ominousness of this cheerless guest that it cannot recognize: its own origin.

Nihilism is not defined by the denial of the Christian God, the suppression of Christianity, or the preaching of atheism. As long as one sees in the death of god only the phenomenon of unbelief, which turns away from Christianity and all that is connected to it, one looks at it from the outside; this theological-apologetic perspective misunderstands what Nietzsche wants to say from the beginning. The story of the Madman demonstrates that the death of god has nothing to do with the chatter of the unbelievers who are unaware of it. According to Nietzsche, the death of god is a pronouncement upon the end of the ideal world and its meaning for human beings.

The event of the death of god is, according to Nietzsche, something that happens in metaphysics. Metaphysics has determined the being of entities as the supernatural world, the ideal, god, moral law, the authority of reason, progress, and the happiness of the majority, respectively. This framework now loses its constructive power and falls down.

In one of his notes from the planned but never completed major work, *The Will to Power,* Nietzsche asks, "What does nihilism mean?" He answers: "That the highest values are devaluing themselves."[39] He explains that there is no longer an aim in reality and that there is no answer to the question of the 'why.' God, the supernatural as the true real world that determines everything, the ideal, the aims, the reasons, etc.: all of these become worthless. This process of devaluating is not a sign of decline but is, rather, the basic process of Western thinking. Thus Nietzsche is not worried about the result, which he considers to be the inner logic of Western history.

Nietzsche thinks that human beings will inevitably assign new values. Now that the highest values have fallen down, a revaluation of all values will occur. The 'no' against the old values arises from the 'yes' with respect to the new ones. This new valuation is also seen by Nietzsche within the perspective of nihilism. Indeed, he designates the new valuation, next to other characteristics of nihilism, as the complete (*vollendete*) nihilism.[40]

When the position of god is emptied it does not mean that the position itself disappears. The empty position invites reoccupation and the filling in of new ideals. Examples of this, according to Nietzsche, are theories concerning universal happiness, socialism, and other utopian ideals. This is incomplete nihilism, which changes the old values, but leaves the metaphysical framework as it was. Attempting to avoid nihilism without revaluating radically the old values does not change anything in the end. Thus complete nihilism must change the positions of the values and revaluate them. In this figure of nihilism another valuation of life is hidden.

Nietzsche's nihilism centers around values: their founding, devaluation, revaluation and creation. The highest purpose, the causes and principles of entities, the ideals and the supernatural, god and the gods, all of this is understood in terms of value. Therefore, according to Heidegger, knowing what Nietzsche means by value is the key to understanding his ontology.

At the beginning of the last century a philosophy of values arose under Nietzsche's influence. It spoke of an order or priority of values (Hartmann, Scheler). While in Christian theology God is considered as the highest entity, the highest good, and the highest value, Nietzsche's metaphysics considers a value to be a precondition from which one is able to maintain and increase life.[41] Therefore, a value always represents a certain perspective, namely the perspective from which one can maintain and increase life. As such it is part of the whole of growing life.[42]

Values are not first something in themselves, they are only valid to the extent that they are assigned, given, or founded as a precondition of that towards which one is directed. In Western philosophy since Leibniz this perspective is understood as striving, from which every perspective or representation is determined. According to Heidegger's interpretation of Nietzsche, values are always preconditions for maintaining and increasing, because they are constitutive of life. If an entity's striving were limited to just maintaining itself, then it would already be decreasing. This maintaining and increasing are parts of the whole of life's constitution. Becoming is the permanent change that Leibniz already identifies in the entities.

Nietzsche considers this becoming to be the basic characteristic of all entities, which he understands as "the will to power." The will to power is the basic feature of life. Will to power, becoming, life, and being all mean the same for Nietzsche.[43] This will shows itself in forms of power such as art, politics, religion, science and society. Therefore Nietzsche says that a value is always connected to the perspective of the increase or the decrease of these centers of power. The values and the changes of values are connected to the growth of power of the one who lends or gives the value.[44]

Now we know that the source of values is the will to power. This will to power means for Nietzsche a new foundation of value. It is new because it manifests itself with its own name; what had always already been working in the background now appears on the scene. At the same time from the perspective of the older values it s a revaluation of all values, because the old values were realized from the supernatural, which was determinative for metaphysics. With this new insight, metaphysics is turned round and Nietzsche claims this turn to be the overcoming of metaphysics. Heidegger argues, however, as we shall see, that this turn remains within metaphysics.

We have already discussed nihilism as a process of devaluating the highest values. This devaluation is seen from the perspective of a revaluation of all values; this means that Nietzsche sees nihilism within the possibility of lending or founding values. This leads to the conclusion that the death of god is only understandable from the perspective of the will to power. Therefore the question arises: What is the meaning of the will to power?

WILL TO POWER AND THE OVERMAN

Nietzsche talks about the will to power in the second part of *Thus Spoke Zarathustra,* which was published a year after *The Gay Science* (1883). He writes, "Where I found the living, there I found Will to power; and even in the will of those who serve I found Will to power; and even in the will of those who serve I found the will to be master."[45] Being a servant means wanting to be a master. This will is not a wish, but a command. As a command it is about disposal and the ability to dispose. The possibility of total self-disposal lies in obedience to someone else or to oneself. The will to power, in the end, is the desire for total self-disposal. In this way the commander is always superior. In the end, the will wants itself. Therefore Nietzsche writes that wanting means wanting to become stronger, wanting to grow. This means more power but is only possible through ever-increasing power, because only then does it remain power. Standing still means falling down.

The will to power is the inner essence of the being of entities, by which we mean entities as a whole. Wanting means wanting the means to become stronger. The means are the preconditions founded by the will to power, and these preconditions are the values. Therefore Nietzsche can say that in all wanting lies a valuing. So the will to power is understood as a value-founding will. Nietzsche determines the will to power as the ultimate truth about the being of entities. Therefore Heidegger can say that Nietzsche, despite all turns, remains on the path of metaphysics with his theory about the truth of the will to power as the being of entities. In Nietzsche, truth is used by the will to power. It is a necessary value because everything is always related to maintaining and increasing of the will to power.[46] But, according to Heidegger, because Nietzsche sees metaphysics as the history of the foundation of values, he cannot think the essence of nihilism.[47] This means that he does not see the ground on which he stands.

Nietzsche understands nihilism negatively as the devaluation of all values, but also positively, as the revaluation of values. This revaluation overcomes nihilism in its completion. The will to power becomes the origin and measure of all founding, giving, and lending of value.

In the story from *The Gay Science,* the Madman says, concerning the act of human beings by which god is killed: "There has never been a greater deed; and whoever will be born after us — for the sake of this deed he will be part of a higher history than all history hitherto."[48] Man moves over to another history, because in the new and other history, the principle of the foundation of value, the will to power as the principle of the being of entities, is accepted. With this, modern man takes a final step: he wants himself, as the executor of the unconditional will to power. Incomplete nihilism, in which the higher values are devaluated, is conquered. The name of this higher history is Overman (*Übermensch*).

Without knowing it, man is poised to take control over the earth. Formerly, human beings did not experience the will to power as a characteristic of being, nor did they adopt it. The new human being takes over the will to power in his will. This means that everything that exists, every entity, exists as founded by and in this will. The old ideals and aims lose their efficiency. They do not give rise to life any longer: the world of ideas and ideals itself became lifeless, dead, inefficient. That is the meaning of the metaphysically intended claim that god is dead. The first part of Nietzsche's *Thus Spoke Zarathustra* from 1893 ends with the words: *"Dead are all Gods: now we will that overman live."*[49]

This does not mean that man takes the place of god. The position that the Overman takes is another domain: it is the domain of subjectivity.[50] From this position every entity becomes a represented object, an object for the I, the *ego cogito*. Everything that exists, becomes something that exists for a human subject, even the human subject itself. Human beings, who take the position of subjectivity, make an object of the world. The earth is only visible and understandable, then, as an object of grasping. Nature appears everywhere as an object of technique. Even the nature of subjectivity itself becomes an object for man. This is the reason why subjectivity becomes the being-est entity.

What is going on in the era of the struggle for the earth? In other words: what is the ground upon which subjectivity determines the being of entities? According to Heidegger, being has become a value which blocks every experience of being. If being is a value given by man, then being in and of itself is nothing; it only gets its value from a value-founding will to power.

Nietzsche's understanding of the completion of nihilism, in the value foundation of the will to power, merely intensifies nihilism as Heidegger understands it — namely, that being itself is nothing. The worst stroke against god and the supernatural world is not that he is conceived as unknowable or that his existence is shown to be improvable, but rather the devaluation of god to the status of highest value. This stroke comes from theologians and philosophers in particular: they are the ones who primarily see god as a value.

The story of the Madman urges the question of how human beings can kill god. It is obviously Nietzsche's point of view that human beings do it. The text of the story emphasizes this point by putting into italics the following sentences: "*We have killed him,*" and, further on, "*and yet they have done it themselves.*" Human beings killed god, even though they are not aware of it.[51]

The announcement in Nietzsche's story that god is dead is not just a mere message that there is no god. For Nietzsche emphasizes that god is killed, murdered, that it is an act of human beings; he has not just disappeared. The message that is pronounced by the madman appears for the first time in a note from the fall of 1881,[52] which says that we have to bear the loss of god.[53]

The loss of god is understood as something that must come from a specific act of human beings. God's death is 'indeed actual' (*tatsächlich*); this means it is a reality that is the consequence of an act. This is the terminology with which the death of god is articulated in the story.[54] Many of Nietzsche's fragments confirm that this death of god, this lack of purpose and orientation that has befallen us, must be understood as a specific act. We have created this complete world in which we really are involved, in which all possibilities of our life are rooted. But because we forget this after creating the world, we invent a creator.[55]

When the retroactively created inventor of this world dies, then man has to remind himself of his creative power. It is a recollection of his own power to act, and not just of a simple fact. Nothing else than the actuality of their own acts has been left to humans; there is no other compass and orientation than their own deeds. God's death becomes real only when there is a perpetrator. Only then it can be asked whether man must become an almighty and holy poet.[56]

Indeed, man has to become the almighty and holy poet, but the individual human being is still too weak to take on this gigantic act. This poet appears initially in the figure of Zarathustra.[57] Obviously Nietzsche hesitated over who should announce this gigantic act. The message says that an event in the past must become an act of man. What took place without man's knowledge must be transformed into "I wanted it that way."

Nietzsche evaluates this act: "There has never been a greater deed; and whoever will be born after us — for the sake of this deed he will be part of a higher history than all history hitherto."[58] From now on, history is the result of the acts of human being; in this it is "indeed actual" (*tatsächlich*). It is a new history, not only because it results from the older, but because it destroyed the bottom of the older history by making human beings the actors of history.

That human beings kill god is almost unthinkable, even for Nietzsche. We see this in the story of the Madman, when he announces, "We have killed him — you and I. All of us are his murderers." Then the Madman asks rhetorically, "But how have we done this?" Nietzsche adds three questions to this: "How were we able to drink up the sea? Who gave us the sponge to wipe away the entire horizon? What did we do when we unchained this earth from its sun?" The last image refers to Plato's allegory of the cave, in which the sun is the place from where entities can appear. The sun shapes and limits the field of vision, the horizon, in which entities show themselves and become visible.

The horizon is the supersensible world. It is both the highest and most real entity and time the whole that encompasses everything and gathers as the sea does. The earth as the abode of human beings is released from the sun. The domain of the supersensible is no longer a normative light above them. This horizon is wiped out. The whole of entities, the sea, is emptied by human beings because man has become the 'I' of the *ego cogito*. With this, every entity becomes an object. Entities are, as the objective, absorbed in the immanence of subjectivity. The horizon no longer shines. All that remains is the perspective that arises from the value foundation of the will to power. The idea that *we* are the ones who killed god belongs exactly to the same subjectivism from which the will to power controls the earth. The killing of god has its home in the philosophy of value, in which values are given and assigned from subjectivity. In the foundation of value, the final stroke is inflicted on the being of entities. Everyone in that time thinks from the framework of value-foundation; therefore Nietzsche can say: "We have killed him — you and I." From this perspective Nietzsche understands the will to power as nihilism, because the transvaluation of all values in which god is devaluated is realized.

According to Heidegger, the foundation of value is the radical destruction of the question concerning the being of entities.

Being itself is radically removed; at most it can count as a value for the value-founding human being. Philosophy of value is destructive because it does not allow being to appear. The death of god is seen within a framework of value-giving, as though human subjectivity were able to call god out of being. This presupposition is characteristic of nihilism, in which the will to power is the absolute point of departure and the Overman becomes the norm for all sense and value-giving. So in Heidegger's analysis, Nietzsche appears within the paradigm of the metaphysics of modernity. It is the metaphysics of subjectivity as *causa sui*.

But, Heidegger asks, where does being in its truth appear, and where is it brought up? Nowhere, since the history of being starts — necessarily, according to Heidegger — with the forgetting of Being.[59] Philosophy as philosophy does not succeed in bringing up the truth of being, because being as difference withdraws from identification.

In this analysis of and reflection on Nietzsche some aspects of nihilism have become clear. Nietzsche does not see the essence of nihilism; he does not see that entities within the framework of the will to power are nothing in themselves. Through his doctrine of value he is not able to see the nothingness of entities, which, as a presupposition of his doctrine of the being of entities, affects his thinking. This presupposition is the ground of his thought. He has to think of god and the gods as human products. The basic experience or mood from which he thinks is the godlessness and wordlessness of modern man.[60] Heidegger interprets Nietzsche as a child of his time, in line with modern subjectivism in a way that he himself was not aware.

The Madman, however, persists in seeking: probably Nietzsche's Madman sensed something of being amidst the desert of all entities. Since the madman unceasingly cries, "I seek God, I seek God," in what sense is this man mad? He is torn away (Heidegger alludes here the German *verrückt*) from the old domain of human beings, for whom the reality of the ideals is enfeebled and does not count any longer. This torn-away human being has nothing in common with those who were standing around and who do not believe in god. These onlookers are not unbelieving because god became incredible to them, but because they gave up the possibility of faith since they cannot seek god anymore. They cannot seek anymore because they cannot think anymore, Heidegger concludes. For Heidegger, thinking is a questioning and seeking movement, which does not preclude the notion of god. The public onlookers abolished thinking and replaced it with chatter and gossip about nihilism, because they see nihilism everywhere where they consider their own opinion to be in danger. This is also blindness for nihilism, because they chat in response to being anxious about thinking. The madman, however, is clearly seeking god. He cries out to him. Heidegger interprets this as follows: "Has a thinking man perhaps here really cried out *de profundis?*"[61]

THE DEATH OF GOD AND THE LACK OF GOD

Speaking of the death of god in the way that Nietzsche preaches it, does not refer to faith. It names the experience of an event in Western philosophy, in which the divine lost its normative control over entities and the destiny of human beings.[62] The Christian God is the primary referent for the supernatural in general and all that is connected to it: the ideals, norms, principles, rules, aims and values. It implies all that is established above entities to give to entities as a whole an aim, an order, and a sense: god is the name for the supersensible domain of the ideas and the ideals. Since Plato, this supersensible world has been seen as the true and real world, but it is now without effective power.[63] The god of morality, the god who determines good and evil — that god is dead. And with the death of god, guilt also disappears as a phenomenon that divides the whole of entities.[64] And yet, when the name of god disappears, then new values replace it. The position of the supersensible is maintained and the ideals are kept. The empty place demands filling and new gods take the old positions; new ideals are presented.[65]

The position for the metaphysical god is the position of the causing creator and maintainer of entities. The ground of the supersensible world is seen as the effective reality of the whole. This supersensible reality has become unreal. Together with the death of god, the powerlessness of the supersensible has come to light, and this powerlessness means the loss of the established order. Against this background it would be a mistake to think that the assertion "God is dead" is a plea for atheism. Insofar as metaphysics receives a specific theological interpretation by Christianity, the downfall of the highest values has to be expressed theologically by this claim. Here, god stands for the supersensible, which positions itself as the eternal world across from the earth as its real and eternal aim. The position of god disappears, as well as the authority of conscience, reason, and progress.[66]

The connection between theology and ontology in the essence of metaphysics becomes especially visible where metaphysics indicates its basic movement: transcendence. The word 'transcendence' names the surpassing of an entity into what that entity is in its essence. Transcendence, however, also means the transcendent, in the sense of a first existing ground of entities that surpasses the entity and, as surpassing, exceeds the entity. "Ontology represents transcendence as the transcendental. Theology represents transcendence as the transcendent."[67] One always sees this movement in theology, which presents itself, generally without reflection, as theistic; it presupposes a god as a transcendent entity.

As indicated in the previous paragraph, Heidegger considers Nietzsche, just like all great thinkers in philosophy since Plato, to be a theologian. Entities are only entities out of the will to power, according to Nietzsche. Furthermore, Nietzsche's metaphysics is an ontology, and, at the same time, a theology. The ontology of entities as such understands the essence of entities as will to power. However, this metaphysical theology is, as I have already mentioned, a specific kind of negative theology, shown in the pronouncement: "God is dead."[68] Nevertheless it remains metaphysics, be the god living or dead.[69]

Where god is dead, he is absent. This is something different from the denial of god in atheism, which remains tributary to ontotheology. The loss of god, however, is not thought within metaphysics, that is, as ontotheology. Heidegger thinks of this experience of the absence of god as an experience of the poets. Metaphysics cannot experience the loss of god because it is theologically structured. For the poet, on the other hand, the absence of god is not a lack; it is not an empty space that needs completion.[70] Nor is it necessary to appeal to the god that one is used to. It is about presenting and holding out the absence of god. The poet can live in a domain of decision where ontology is not necessarily theologically structured, since in poetry the poet has to seek; but not into the divine. In poetry there is no a priori divine. It is the poet's care to face up to the lack of god without fear. With the appearance of godlessness, "he must remain near to the god's absence."[71] The poet has to stay in this no man's land until an original word is offered from the nearness of the missing god, which is capable of naming the high one.

The notion of the absent god means that there is no god visible for man; there is nothing that gathers man and things together. The world has become groundless.[72] No trace is left of the holy. Because the experience of the unconcealment of being remains withdrawn, the disappearance of the hale drags along the holy; it hides every trace of a godhead. This concealment is so strong that the absence of god is not experienced. The absence of god and the divine must lead to the appropriation of the hidden fullness of that which has been. What happens there has to be put into words.[73]

The god of metaphysics, which is assimilated with the Christian God, is also a god. This god is shown to be historical by his mortality. The god of metaphysics, and everything that is implied with that name, is dead. In Heidegger's view, Nietzsche is not the preacher of atheism. Nietzsche's understanding of being implies that a historical *Dasein* could not be possible without god and the gods. But a god is only a god when he comes and has to come. The sentence "God is dead" is not a negation of god or the divine, but the most intimate affirmation with regard to the coming god.[74]

Therefore, Heidegger can say that the gods and the godhead are assimilated into the destinies of the temple as formed historically. But in Heidegger's view the ontotheological temple of metaphysics is crumbling. According to Heidegger and Nietzsche, the death of god is a historical event, which means a history (*Geschichte*), a story. It is an event that makes history. The nature of this history can be continued, be it the history of a god or a hero, but it is a history next to other histories. This history is the history of the bereavement of a god. This does not mean that this history itself has a god, for god is also subjected to the destinies of history (*Geschick*).[75] It is a history that makes history. In Heidegger's view, historicity is connected with the historicality of Dasein. This historicality is still there when god is dead, and even when the human being, as *causa sui,* is dead. The death and coming of the gods are expressions of the historicality of Dasein.

SEVEN

The Provisionality of a Passing Last God

I have already mentioned the notion of the last god at the end of the previous chapter. In this chapter, I will investigate more explicitly what Heidegger means by this. This phrase is particularly important in Heidegger's so-called 'second magnum opus', namely: *Beiträge zur Philosophie (Vom Ereignis),* translated as *Contributions to Philosophy (From Enowning).*[1] This work, published in 1989 in commemoration of Heidegger's hundredth birthday, was written between 1936 and 1938. It is a private text in which Heidegger introduces, among others, the notion of 'the last god.' This book does not present a systematic and clearly developed theme, but is, rather, a compilation of fragments and contains a great deal of repetition. Even by Heidegger's standards it is a difficult book.[2] This seems to have been intentional on Heidegger's part, for he writes: "Making itself intelligible is suicide for philosophy."[3] Intelligibility seems for Heidegger to be connected to an ontic approach to being. Using entities where being is supposed to be thought is like confirming philosophy with facts. Those who idolize facts never notice that their idols shine is borrowed.

We find in the *Beiträge* that the notion of the last god is tied to understanding being as the event of enowning (*Ereignis*). The word *Ereignis* is, according to Heidegger, a polysemy with eight different meanings: "Enowning always means enowning as en-ownment, de-cision, countering, setting-free, withdrawal, simpleness, uniqueness, aloneness."⁴ At this point it should be fairly obvious that this polysemy does not render the notion of the last god clearer. Because the notion of a last god appears in a private text, one could ask whether it was ready for publication. In that case the danger of the text not being understood is obvious. The thinker who is in danger of not being understood and, even worse, of being misunderstood, is lonely, as he writes to Jaspers on June 22, 1949.⁵

Heidegger describes the structure (*Gefüge*) of the *Beiträge* as a fugue consisting of six sections (*Fügungen*).⁶ These six sections are framed by a further two sections, namely, section I, Preview (*Vorblick*) and section VIII, Being (*das Seyn*). The theme of the last god is present from the beginning in the *Beiträge*. The fragments that are gathered in the first section of the book function as a preface, and are a look forward (*Vorblick*). There is no foreword *per se*, but rather a look taken at, or into, something by which one gets an impression of what is offered. Heidegger summarizes the content and the plan of the book in the following words: "And here this inceptual thinking can only say little 'from enowning' (*Vom Ereignis*). What is said is inquired after and thought in the 'playing-forth' (*Zuspiel*) unto each other of the first and the other beginning, accordingly to the 'echo' (*Anklang*) of be-ing in the distress of being's abandonment, for the 'leap' (*Sprung*) into be-ing, in order to 'ground' (*Gründung*) its truth, as a preparation for the 'ones to come' (*Zukünftigen*) and for 'the last god' (*der Letzte*

Gott).[7] Although the notion of the last god is present in all six sections, Heidegger gives it particular attention in the last.

As its name indicates, the *"Vorblick"* is a preview of the issues Heidegger wants to address in the *Beiträge.* The second section, *"der Anklang,"* is concerned with the first beginning, which is Heidegger's term for Western philosophy from Plato to Nietzsche. The first beginning of Western philosophy has been dominated by what Heidegger calls the *"Leitfrage,"* the 'leading' or 'guiding question,' namely, what are entities? Heidegger holds that Western metaphysics arrives at a conception of being by searching for a common substance underlying all individual entities. Western metaphysics is the metaphysics of presence, that is, an understanding of being as a suprahistorical and enduring presence, undergirding all that is. For Heidegger, this concern with the underlying, enduring substance of entities means that Western philosophy has been concerned, not — as it has erroneously supposed — with being, but with an abstract form of entities. The consequence of this identification of being with entities is that Western thought has now forgotten being. Nevertheless, there remains a dim resonance, an *"Anklang"* or echo of the question of being in Western philosophy, which Heidegger sees as his task to recover.

The third section is concerned with the transition from the first beginning to 'the other beginning.' This transition accounts for the title *Zuspiel,* which is a sports term denoting the passing of the ball from one player to another: the question of being is, as it were, passed from the first beginning to the other beginning. A new beginning is being made, a beginning that takes up the first beginning but transforms it. Thinking the question of being from the other beginning means dispensing with thinking about being in terms of entities or substance. It means not interrogating entities, but rather posing what Heidegger calls the *"Grundfrage"*: the ground or fundamental question. This fundamental question asks the question of the truth of being, namely, '*Wie west das Seyn*?' (How does Being essence?), as opposed to "What is Being?"

This transformation of the question of being is the theme of the remaining sections of the *Beiträge*. The transition from the first to the other beginning is achieved by means of a leap (*Sprung*) in which the realization dawns that being has been forgotten. This marks the beginning of a new positing of the question of being. This new beginning, however, is not a direct transition, but a leap in which being is understood not in metaphysical terms but as an event of appropriation, an event of enowning (*Ereignis*). By means of this leap into the event of enowning of being, the grounding of the place of the moment (*Augenblicksstätte*) becomes possible. This grounding is to be undertaken by the ones to come, the future ones (*die Zu-künftigen*). The task of the ones to come is to prepare for what Heidegger calls the passing-by (*Vorbeigang*) of the last god.[8]

Because of the mystifying aspects of this text, it is not always clear what Heidegger means by 'the last god.' I understand this notion as an indication of the passing moment, in which a decision about being and the coming of god takes place. This moment has always already passed when human being (Dasein) has opened itself to the coming of the last god, and thus it is only visible as a trace and a hint. In passing, the last god effects a change in the understanding of being to the perspective of the other beginning. The last god is always a god who has passed, because it is not graspable in its presence. The notion of the last god is an expression of the historicality of Dasein and being.

This chapter contains four sections. The first section deals with Heidegger's view of the Christian God; the second is about the need for being of the gods; the third treats the notion of 'the last god'; and the fourth deals with the notion of 'the few forerunners.'

THE CHRISTIAN GOD

The Christian God, according to Heidegger, hinders the experience of the last god. The long period of Christianization has undermined the possibilities for experiencing the coming of the last god. Seen within a Christian point of view, God is understood in terms of a transcendent reality; he is thought of within a theistic paradigm, as something that goes beyond being and man. This way of thinking is present even where it is denied since it determines secularized visions of life, as was shown in the previous chapter. The last god has nothing to do with the Christian God, because the last god cannot be found from within the forgetfulness-of-being.[9] However, Christianity, with its own particular concept of God, has contributed to this forgetfulness-of-being.

For Heidegger, the idea that entities are created originates in Christianity since, according to it, everything — including being as such — is understood this way.[10] All being is originally understood as '*ens creatum,*' with the 'Creator' as the highest, most certain entity, and the first cause. Every entity is an effect of this cause, which is itself the most real entity.[11] Even when the idea of creation is omitted, the understanding of entities as caused, made, and produced still remains. The relation of cause and effect becomes completely dominant, perfected in the idea of god as '*causa sui.*' This idea marks an essential difference from the original concept of '*physis,*' and at the same time introduces the concept of making as the essence of being in modern history. Mechanical and biological ways of thinking are always merely the result of the dominant explanation of entities as makeable.[12] Heidegger sees in this the forgottenness-of-being and nihilism.

Forgetfulness-of-being is strongest where it hides itself most, and this happens particularly in Christianity. In modern history, entities, which were once created by god, become products of man — objects to be understood and mastered. From this perspective of mastery and control, man speaks of increase and progress. But it is a progress without future, because it promotes an endless repetition of the same.[13] In the concept and practice of progress, openness to the other beginning does not arise; in fact, it hides it. This is why Christianity and its secular descendants hide and deny the forgetfulness-of-being most of all.

Heidegger also sees the nihilistic consequences of Christianity in the domain of historical thinking. According to him, the Christian apologetics of history, learned and mastered since Augustine's *Civitas Dei,* intensify Christianity's nihilistic effects. Almost all secular, modern historical thought, which wants to subsume everything under the concept of progress, is subject to this Christian view of history and thereby hinders every essential decision.[14] The idea of progress will, to an immense extent, result in the exploitation and consumption of the earth and in breeding and training people as human specimens. The emergence of the ideal of progress is not to be impeded by a romantic memory of the past.

Heidegger focuses on the concept of machination (*Machenshaft*), sometimes called Jesuitism, in his struggle against Christianity and the Church.[15] The concept of the last god also plays a part in this polemic, because it is "the totally other over against gods who have been, especially over against the Christian God."[16] Therefore, one of the purposes of the *Beiträge* is to regain a new concept of transcendence and a new space for the divine in opposition to the long-since Christianized concept of God. So the fight against nihilism is at one and the same time a fight against Christianity: "The preparation for the overcoming of nihilism begins with the fundamental experience that man as founder of Da-sein is *used* by the godhood of the other god. But what is most imperative and most difficult regarding this overcoming is the *awareness* of nihilism."[17]

Heidegger is quite extreme in his determination of Christianity as a precursor to nihilisim. The demolition of churches and monasteries and the slaughtering of people is not the essential characteristic of nihilism, "rather, what is crucial is whether one knows and wants to know that precisely this tolerating of Christianity and Christianity itself — the general talk of 'providence' and 'the Lord God,' however sincere individuals may be — are merely pretexts and perplexities in that domain which one does not want to acknowledge and to allow to count as the domain of decision about be-ing or not-be-ing. The most disastrous nihilism consists in passing oneself off as protector of Christianity and even claiming for oneself the most Christian Christianity on the basis of social accomplishments."[18] Against this background it is clear that Heidegger does not expect any salvation from Christianity.

In a way that is reminiscent of Nietzsche (and Heidegger wrote this text during the years that he was lecturing on Nietzsche), Heidegger sketches the consequence of Western thinking as it is formed under the influence of Christianity. In Western thinking, the beyond-being as the beginning of being has the character of the divine and of god.[19] Ontology, the theory of being as such, is therefore inevitably ontotheology. This means that the first beginning in Platonic-Aristotelian philosophy also provides the framework for the Judeo-Christian faith and all secular forms of the Christian and Western understanding of being and man. In the Platonic understanding of the beyond-being as the good, Heidegger sees a fundamental negation of the question of being because the idea of the good is the organizing principle of all understanding of being in relation to its destination and shape.[20] This Platonism has continued in Christianity until today. It was Nietzsche who identified Platonism in its hidden form: "Christianity and its secularisations are generally 'Platonism for the people.'"[21] Christianity is also present in the determination of truth as certainty, correspondence, and similarity: this theory of truth is required for those who look upwards from beneath, but not for those with the opposite point of view.[22] One can find analyses of this kind in Nietzsche and in Heidegger's lectures on Nietzsche, as was shown in the previous chapter.

The insight into the connections between Christianity and the understanding of being is important because these connections remain the same in the metaphysics of the modern age. They remain the same even where the medieval form of the creed of the Church has long since been abandoned. In particular, the frequently changing forms of Christian thinking that dominate the secularized world complicate every attempt to get away from this soil or ground and to consider the relation of being and truth from a more original experience.[23] Christianity, with its implicit opinion that being is makeable, with its unspoken ideal of progress and its concept of history, hinders the experience of being as an event of enowning.

THE GODS AND BEING

To Heidegger, the notion of the gods involves a domain of questions: "The talk of 'gods' here does not indicate the decided assertion on the extantness of a plurality over against a singular but is rather meant as the allusion to the undecidability of the being of gods, whether of one single god or of many gods. This undecidability holds within itself what is question-worthy, namely, whether anything at all like being dare be attributed to gods without destroying everything that is divine. The undecidability concerning which god and whether a god can, in utmost distress, once again arise, from which way of being of man and in what way — this is what is named with the name 'gods.'"[24] For Heidegger the question is whether there will be gods, not whether there will be one or more. He asks if it is possible to grant being to the gods without destroying divinity as such. In metaphysics, god is represented as the most real being, as the first ground and cause of being. These determinations, however, do not arise from the divinity of god. They arise from a doctrine of being insofar as this being is represented as a presence, as an object and as subsistent.[25]

In what sense is there a relation between the gods and being? Heidegger says that the gods need being. This means that being is not equated with the godhead and that being is not situated above the gods, nor the gods above being. The gods do not need it as their property. Nevertheless, the gods need being in order to belong to themselves. This being is something that is wanted by the gods, but is never caused or determined by them. It is a very unclear and dark concept of divinity because the characterization of the gods as those who need being does not belong to a domain of foundations and proofs but is rather a first thing to hold on to.[26]

With regard to the relation of being and god, being is never a determination of god himself, but is that which god needs in order to become itself. In this way, god is completely distinguished from being. Being is not, as the concept of being in metaphysics, the highest and purest determination of the divine: neither is it the most common or emptiest roof for all that 'is.' Being gets its specific determination and magnitude when it is acknowledged as something that is necessary to god, the gods, and the entire realm of the divine.[27] What is this being that the gods need? Further on I will interpret this being as the possible.[28]

The gods need being, understood as an event of enowning. The gods do not need determinations that are taken from entities, such as the cause, foundation, absolute, unconditional, and infinite; nor is it a question of identification with being, not even with being as an event of enowning.

The passing-by of the last god is the movement that opens the space for a new birth of the gods; it is a true godding (*götterung*) of the gods. The gods 'god' (*göttern*). This plural indicates the undecidedness of the being of the gods, of whether there will be one or many.[29] With regard to the gods, nothing can be decided, because one cannot decide on being. As a thinker one does best to remain in this undecidedness, without representing it as a realization or a completion. "If we knew the law of the arrival and the flight of gods, then we would get a first glimpse of the onset and staying away of truth and thus of the essential swaying of be-ing."[30] The law of the gods is that they need being as that which withdraws because they are no longer or they are not yet. For its part, being gets its greatness "when it is recognized as that which the god of gods and all godding need."[31] God does not need being in order to become an entity. "Gods do not need be-ing as their ownhood, wherein they themselves take a stance." Rather, god completely exists in the need for being. "Be-ing is needed by gods: it is their need. And the needfulness of be-ing names its essential swaying — what is needed by 'gods' but is never causable and conditionable."[32] This is contrary to the metaphysical meaning of god as the highest being.

Withdrawal and need belong together; otherwise the relation would be based on a negative moment of entities or on a regulative idea. The withdrawal of being, more original than transcendence, is a departure from metaphysics, an entry into another history. By this departure the saving of the West can be realized.[33] But what does saving mean here? Since the danger has grown to the extreme and since everything is being uprooted and — what is even more disastrous — since the uprooting is already engaged in hiding itself, the beginning of the lack of history is already here.[34] It is the uprooting itself that has to be understood in such a way that the West can begin to be our history. The turn in the history of being (or of the West) is the beginning of an era in which the existential finitude of Dasein reveals the historical finitude of being. This is not only done by the destruction of ontotheology or by the overcoming metaphysics, but also by an openness to this historical finitude.

Later in 1966, in the well-known "*Der Spiegel* Interview,"[35] Heidegger talks about gods: "Only a god can save us," is his exclamation. Heidegger does not say "only god can save us," or reason, or science, or the experts. He was talking about *a* god, a finite mortal god who inspires the actions of man in such a way that dedication is possible, not to abstract ideals and the idea of progress, but to other possibilities which are situated beyond and before the origin of metaphysical nihilism. The question is whether there are enough individuals who are open to another possibility of the history of being and to perceiving being as an event of enowning.

When gods and man meet each other, then man is knocked over from his Western place as rational animal; he is located and understood from a different point of view or another horizon. In such a place, there is no essential room for both the animality and rationality of man.[36] The strongest hindrance to arriving at being as an event of enowning is not only found in Christianity, but also in the self-concept that present-day man has of himself. Man understands himself as a member of the human species. Where this interpretation of man prevails, every place and call for an arrival of a god is absent; there is not even an experience of the flight of the gods which would indicate man's consciousness that the truth of being has disappeared.

Heidegger locates man as '*animal rationale*' standing in opposition to man as 'Dasein.' As Dasein, man does not count the number of the gods, nor does he count on them, particularly not on a special god, as one counts on the one and only God of Christianity, who governs everything. 'Dasein' does not count but is attuned to unexpectedness, though this does not mean being indifferent to everything. This not-calculating is already the result of a more original Dasein, which is open to and concentrated on being as an event of enowning.[37] As Dasein, man is open to what happens and understands that he does not know the rules of the god.

With the turn from man as *animal rationale* to Dasein as a historical being, space is created for the experience of another history. It is the room and the place where decisions are made about the advent or abeyance of the gods for man. In this sense the gods need the place for being in order for the gods to be able to be. The place for being is the realm of possibilities that man can see only if he returns from the metaphysical project with its one and only actual god. But from the perspective of this realm of possibilities, the metaphysical god has become *a* god, one among others. This god needs being as possibility; otherwise, there would only be the eternal god of ontotheology and its eternal presence. And this would mean that there are no gods at all.

The absence of the gods, however, is not a simple forget-fulness-of-being. It is also an indication, just as total control and makability is an indication or a trace of the flight of the gods. Furthermore, when the one and only god as '*causa sui*' is discussed in metaphysics, the gods as a plurality have fled. These indications are only meaningful if we are able to bear the desolation-of-being and are open to the decision concerning the absence or the advent of the gods. Heidegger pleads for openness to this advent, which is outside the sphere of make-ability.[38] A trace of the gods, and an indication that could silence and bring reflection, is nowhere to be found: nature has become a desolate object.

According to Heidegger, nature was the place of the coming and the dwelling of the gods when it was still understood as *physis,* the essence of being. Now nature has become an object, and as such is the opposite of grace. After this demotion, nature is completely at the mercy of calculative making and thinking.[39] In the original understanding of *physis,* grace and nature were united. Similarly, in the original event of being, the *Ereignis,* and in the learning of the truth of being, insight and understanding happen to man as a gift; grace is not opposed to natural knowledge. This means that the modern understanding of grace, if it is understood as separate from nature and calculative thinking, is a result of the forgetfulness-of-being. The cleavage between knowledge and grace in this sense is a symptom of nihilism and even stimulates it.

With this paradigm we can understand what the conditions are for grace as separated from nature. Grace, as a concept opposite to natural and philosophical knowledge, is made possible by the forgottenness of being. And is it not true that the mastering of nature by science and technology has turned grace into something obscure and dark? In that case, both the mastering of nature by technology and the obscurity of grace are symptoms of nihilism as well.

We have seen more of these separations in the history of philosophy with regard to religion. When Kant made knowledge of things-in-themselves impossible by his *Critique of Pure Reason* (1781), he broke with the classical claim of metaphysics to offer knowledge of the nature of things which denies that the things we know and see are already schematized or interpreted by our understanding. But after Kant, our mind is not merely passive in the act of knowledge; it is active to the point of imposing on nature its own laws of logic. The idea that the world we know in a sense depends on the conceptual projection of our categories is a revolutionary idea that indicates a shift to pure subjective knowledge, where we do not have access to the things-in-themselves, but only to interpretations of things such as they appear to us and after they have been subjected to our conceptual apparatus.[40]

This has led to different developments, for example to the position of Jacobi (1743–1819). He finds a notorious contradiction in Kant's doctrine of the thing-in-itself: Kant excludes any notion of the thing-in-itself from his system, since it is essentially unknowable, yet he needed some objective base in reality in order to avoid a form of absolute idealism. Jacobi, following indications he found in Kant, comes to fideism. If reason cannot bring us to reality, the only thing that can give us any sense of an objective and stable world is faith in an authority higher than our limited reason. By faith, and by faith alone, we can get access to the true foundation of being. From Heidegger's perspective, this is a symptom of nihilism. This fideistic reading had some appeal at the time of Jacobi and one can observe that it still manifests itself today. Many forms of religious fundamentalism clearly stem from the fear or anxiety produced by the subjective and perspectival nature of our knowledge. It is only through the leap of faith that one gets reacquainted with, and thus reconciled to, reality.

In Jacobi we see the connectedness of a call for faith and the nihilistic situation of natural and philosophical knowledge. Both go together as a result of the impossibility of knowing things-in-themselves. This leads us to the heart of Heidegger's 'philosophy of grace.' It seems to me that, according to Heidegger, when presented as opposite to natural and philosophical knowledge, grace is itself a symptom of the desolation-of-being. This would mean that, with the passing of the last god, something other than grace as opposite to calculative and natural knowledge could be possible.

THE LAST GOD

The subject of the last god runs like a thread through the *Beiträge,* and it may be the most fascinating theme in it.[41] There is no other text in which Heidegger talks about it. Is this a new mythology, with which Heidegger tries to conquer the god that is determined as *causa sui* — a figure to whom one can neither pray nor sacrifice? Is it necessary that the other thinking or the thinking of the other beginning reinterprets the divine? Is it necessary to carry out this task by the invention of a new god or a new mythology? Is the idea of a last god a myth in Heidegger's thinking? Is it connected with Heidegger's project to think being as historical?

So the question of this notion of the last god presses upon us. How does the last god enter into the question of being, or into the truth of being, or even more into the historicity of being? This concept of the last god is undoubtedly connected with thinking being as an event of enowning; it has to do with the emphasis on the eventuality and the critical rejection of an essentializing or hypostasising history of being. The last god has its main character in passing-by (*Vorbeigang*).

When Heidegger talks about the passing or passing-by of the last god, it is not the first reference to a passing god in Judeo-Christian or Western literature. It is a term that one can find in the Old Testament, in Exodus 33.22–23: "and while my glory passes by I will put you in a cleft of the rock, and I will cover you with my hand until I have passed by; then I will take away my hand, and you shall see my back; but my face shall not be seen." At Marburg in 1924, Heidegger commented on this biblical text in a seminar led by Bultmann.[42] Moses is allowed to see God passing by and to see just a glimpse of Him. Also the first book of Kings 19.11 mentions that the Lord passed by. In this passing-by of the Lord almost nothing happens: no storm, no big transformations; only a quiet small voice can be heard, and then silence.

Nevertheless, it is important to find the origin of this notion against the background of Heidegger's specific philosophical development, from *The Phenomenology of the Religious Life* and to the experience of godlessness as it is worked out in the *Beiträge*. The experience of godlessness, the darkening of the earth that leads to a complete subjectivistic immanentism, together with the withdrawal of the godhead, are the moments in which Heidegger decisively draws upon Hölderlin.[43] It is well known that Hölderlin was greatly important for Heidegger. In the next chapters this will be worked out in more detail. Heidegger writes in 1941 that Hölderlin's words became his destiny at the moment in which he rejected the last misinterpretations of metaphysics.[44] Thus Heidegger's notion of the last god has its origin partly in Hölderlin.

The idea of the last god's passing is already foregrounded in the first Hölderlin lecture course from winter semester 1934/35 on the hymn *"Friedensfeier,"* in which the heavenly is called "quick-transient" (*schnellvergänglich*). Only for a moment does god touch the dwelling of man. Thus Heidegger finds with Hölderlin the place of the heavenly or the godlike in the fleetingness of a hardly understandable hint. This place is not *aeternitas* (the gathering of the temporal out of its dispersion into a remaining order), nor is it *sempiternitas* (the endless continuity). Rather it is a passing-by that happens in a moment.[45]

It is difficult to trace from where exactly Heidegger gets the notion of 'the last god.' In addition to Hölderlin, one may also think of Nietzsche's idea of the 'last human.' Heidegger associates the last god, which is essentially passage, transition, and passing-by, with the problems of Aristotle and Paul, *kairos* and crisis, the decisive moment, our moment: it is the moment in which the gods pass by and visit us. It is also in the moment of our death. Nietzsche and Hölderlin are thus each in their own way present in Heidegger's *Beiträge*.

As I said at the beginning of this chapter, the moment of transition from the first beginning to the other beginning plays a dominant role in the *Beiträge*. The concept of transition is connected to the question of the passing-by of the godhead. The unfolding of the truth of being as *Ereignis* (event of enowning) shows the other beginning, or at least its trace. Only if one has left metaphysics, is it possible to see this: "With this knowing-awareness of be-ing, thinking attains for the first time the trace of the other beginning in crossing out of metaphysics."[46]

Nevertheless, it is important to question how it is possible that, in the question of being or its deepening in the history of being, something like a passing god can arise. As I have already mentioned, Heidegger's reading of Nietzsche is operative in the background of the *Beiträge,* especially in the analysis of nihilism. The gods have fled; words like '*Not*' (need), '*Notwendigkeit*' (necessity), '*Nötigen*' (necessitate), and '*Notlage*' (distress) dominate the diagnosis of the present juncture. There is unrootedness, godlessness, darkening of the earth, humiliation. The world is controlled by machination and calculation. After the death of god discussed in the previous chapter comes the situation of godlessness. Heidegger begins his winter semester 1936/37 lecture course on Nietzsche rather grandly with: "Almost two thousand years and not even one new god!" ("*Der Antichrist,*" 1888).[47]

The coming of the passing god is not for Heidegger neopaganism or a return to German Romanticism, which also speak of a coming god.[48] It is, rather, as in *Being and Time,* an effort to think transcendence as temporality. Therefore it concerns the possibility of knowing a god in a postmetaphysical era. "Coming from a posture toward beings that is determined by 'metaphysics,' we will only slowly and with difficulty be able to know the other, namely that god no longer appears either in the 'personal' or in the 'lived-experience' of the masses but solely in the 'space' of be-ing itself — a space which is held to abground."[49] Heidegger is involved in a post-metaphysical theology of god. This is at first formally indicated, and is, like all formal indications, nameless and without content. Because of this it is foreign to every institutional church. The most appropriate attitude towards a god in the era of technology is refusal (*Verweigerung*), which is why Heidegger prefers to remain silent with respect to it.

The question, "What or who is the last god?" engenders a lot of negative answers, for it is not the last in the sense of the most recent, as one speaks of the recent fashion or the last of a countable series. Gods are not objects of calculation in which only one is calculated; that would be blasphemous. Nor does the last god, who is unique, know the calculation of monotheism, pantheism or atheism: "The multitude of gods cannot be quantified but rather is subjected to the inner richness of the grounds and abgrounds in the site for the moment of the shining and sheltering-concealing of the hint of the last god."[50]

The last god essentially is as passing-by, and as passing-by, the question of quantity is irrrelevant. The last god is not an end but rather a beginning, and thereby has a temporal meaning. This god *is* only as the decisive moment of its future passing-by.[51] For this reason the last god does not manifest itself as something present, but is only there as a hint.[52]

The last god is connected to the experience of being as an event of enowning, that is, with the unfolding of the truth of being. This bears on the finitude of being,[53] which Heidegger thematizes in *Being and Time* in the existential analysis of being-toward-death. Just as we understand the passing-by of being in death, so too does the radical finitude of being manifest itself in the hint of the last god. With this, Heidegger continues the polemic against the Christian idea of God, who is seen as infinite in contrast to the finitude of His creation. To the question of what or who god is, Heidegger answers, in the context of understanding being as an event of enowning, that god is a hint, and nothing but a hint.

A hint is something that gives the possibility of meaning.[54] Heidegger explicates this notion of understanding in *Being and Time,* where he writes: "Meaning is that wherein the intelligibility (*Verständlichkeit*) of something maintains itself."[55] So the image of the last god is an image that provides a hint or a clue in order to understand something. "The image is never intended to stand for itself alone, but indicates *that* something is to be *understood*, providing a *clue* as to *what* this is. The image provides a hint — it leads into the intelligible, into a region of intelligibility (the dimension within which something is understood), into a *sense* (hence sensory image). However, it is important to bear in mind: *what* is to be understood is not a sense, but rather an *occurrence*. 'Sense' (*Sinn*) says only: it is a matter of something intelligible. What is understood is never *itself* sense; we do not understand something *as* sense, but always only 'in the sense of.' Sense is never the *topic* of the understanding."[56] The hint of the last god refers to the historicality of Dasein and being, to the paradigm or horizon within which Dasein is to be understood.

Thus, in talking about the last god, we do not mean the last of a series of gods or a final synthesis.[57] The notion of the last god refers to a moment of decision in which the experience of the last god's passing-by opens the room for other possibilities of being. Out of this experience, man could learn to be open and to look forward to another beginning. However, people do not know what this means, and they are not able to know as long as they are imprisoned, just like the people in Plato's cave, in a method of calculative knowing through which they understand things, circumstances, and themselves.

In the experience of the total objectivity and makeability of being and truth, there is a moment of decision. On the one hand, one is far away from the last god; on the other hand, paradoxically, this means that one is in the presence of the god, since it is in the distress of the desolation of being that the last god is near.[58] Heidegger thinks the desolation of being and the possible advent of the gods together in the event of the enowning of being. They are two sides of one coin.

The word 'last' has no ontic meaning. It indicates something that anticipates very far into the future towards the deepest beginning, that reaches out the farthest and cannot be outstripped. The last god therefore withdraws from every calculation and has to bear the burden of the loudest and most

frequent misinterpretations.[59] The hint of the last god springs
from a moment that is beyond calculative thinking, "Given that
as yet we barely grasp 'death' in its utmost, how are we then
ever going to be primed for the rare hint of the last god?"[60]
With the last god we arrive in a domain of decision that is
more difficult to reach than death. But just as in *Being and
Time* death opens the appearance of being as possibility, so
does the passing of the last god.[61] Likewise, both are difficult
to understand authentically. Because of this difficulty, the
domain of decision is perceptible to only a few people. After
all, everything has been made convenient to the planned control and the correctness of a safe and successful outcome. If we
calculate towards the last god out of this background and
regard the 'last' as conclusion and outcome, then all understanding
of it is misunderstanding.

The image of the last or the extreme limit is an essential
aspect of Heidegger's concept of the enowning of the event of
being. This event is marked by a turn that takes place at the
limit. It is in such an extreme situation that Dasein becomes
conscious of the potential for a change, a turn towards another
possibility or another beginning. In this turn, enowning needs
Dasein and, needing it, must place it into the call and so bring
it before the passing of the last god.[62] The turn is the moment
of decision in which another beginning can come to pass.
Dasein must be brought out of the desolate situation of metaphysics into the understanding of the other beginning.

Because of this 'transitional' meaning, the last god has its
own uniqueness and stands beyond the calculating determinations indicated by terms such as monotheism, pantheism, and
atheism. Monotheism and all other kinds of theism have only
existed since Judeo-Christian apologetics, which have metaphysics, or objectifying calculation, as their philosophical
presupposition. With the death of this metaphysical god, all
kinds of theism disappear. The multitude of gods cannot be

quantified, but are, rather, subjected to the inner wealth of the grounds and the abysses that appear at the moment in which the hint of the last god lights up.

Therefore, "the last god is not the end but the other beginning of immeasurable possibilities for our history."[63] This stands in contrast to the history of progress, in which everything is a repetition of what went before. In the openness to these other possibilities and in the mood of reservedness, a hint of the last god can be understood. A permanent seeking is necessary in order to be ready for the event of the enowning of being and to not turn away from being, as happens in the metaphysical concept of truth and being.[64]

The passing of the last god as historical moment is not an ideal situation, because an ideal situation moves against the essence of history as a realm of possibilities; an ideal situation stops history by a repetition of the everlasting same.[65] But there will be a long and very relapsing and exceedingly hidden history until this unpredictable moment arrives. The beginning of this event of enowning of being is not to be visualized as a goal, which is a superficial phenomenon compared to what happens historically.[66] Nor is the passing-by of the last god a goal that realizes itself or that one can wait for. One can only acquire a reserved susceptibility to it, in which one is open to the other beginning. Concepts like 'goal,' 'aim' and 'end' imply the continuity of metaphysical nihilism.

As a moment of transition, the passing of the last god is not an end but a beginning. The end is only where being has been separated from the truth of being. There, every question, which means every ontological difference, is denied: everything is endlessly repeated and multiplied. The end is the endless and-so-forth; the notion of the last has nothing to do with this. 'The end' never sees its own end, but understands itself as a completion. Therefore it is not prepared to expect and to experience 'the last,' because the last is only to be experienced in the fore-running (*Vor-laufen*). This fore-running is pro-visional (*vor-läufig*), and so it is only understandable as having passed-by. This moment of provisional forerunning is the moment of the experience of the hint of the last god.

The passing of the last god opens the perspective of the possible. Only in be-ing as an event of enowning does the possible hold sway, as be-ing's deepest cleavage. It is in the shape of the possible that be-ing must first be thought in the thinking of the other beginning. In metaphysics the 'actual' as entity has been taken as the starting point and goal for the determination of being.[67] But in opposition to the metaphysical understanding of being as actuality, Heidegger's offers his counterparadigm of the possible: "The possible — and even the possible pure and simple — opens out only in the attempt. The attempt must be totally governed by a fore-grasping will . . . That being is and therefore does not become a being; this is expressed most sharply thus: Being is possibility, what is never extant and yet through en-ownment is always what grants and refuses in not-granting."[68] Being, as a place for the godhead and man, is a wealth of possibilities.[69]

To understand this, one has to leave metaphysics, and get away from objectifying calculative thinking. From a metaphysical position it is difficult to understand the other; namely, that god no longer appears either in the personal or in the lived experience of the masses but solely "in the space of be-ing itself . . ."[70] No heretofore existing 'cults' and 'churches' and the like can provide the essential preparation for the colliding of god and man at the midpoint of be-ing. For the truth of be-ing itself must at first be grounded, and for this assignment all creating must take on another beginning.[71]

With the phrase the last god, Heidegger thinks the possible appearance of a god that depends on being as the event of enowning. This last god is not itself this event but needs it because it is that to which human being as Dasein, belongs.[72]

The unfolding of the truth of being as an event of enowning indicates the other beginning or a trace of the other beginning. One sees these traces of the other beginning only if one has abandoned metaphysics: "With this knowing awareness of being, thinking attains for the first time the trace of the other beginning in crossing out of metaphysics."[73] The transcendence is always a transcendence from . . . towards . . .; from metaphysics towards the other beginning. This transition can only take place when human being is understood as Dasein.[74]

ONLY A FEW FORERUNNERS

As Dasein human beings are open to the possible; indeed, their task is to take care of the possibility of the possible. This does not happen as long as man is understood as *animal rationale*. Against this background, Heidegger introduces the notion of a "few forerunners." There are only a few who understand Dasein from out of and within its historicality, which implies understanding Dasein in its provisional anticipation.

Understanding being as an event of enowning is only possible when Dasein is open to the moment of the passing-by of the god. Every moment of the passing-by of the god is a moment to see something new, a different possibility, one that is other to the realized and actualized possibility of the first beginning. Only a few can experience the moment of the last god's passing and see another beginning because, at the moment of the passing of the last god, the highest motivation of man is gone and burned out and shown to have been mortal. Those who have this openness are the 'ones to come' or the 'future ones' (*die Zukünftigen*): they are the stillest witnesses to the stillness in which an inaudible gust moves the truth towards its origin out of the confusion of all calculated correctness. The 'ones to come' are those who understand the hint of the coming of the last god.[75] They are the ones who can bear and endure the passing-by of a god whose arrival is at the same time a farewell. The arrival of the last god is seen in the same event as the end of calculating and technical thinking.

As we have said, there are only a few who are able to experience the inessential character of the ontology of the present-at-hand, and who are able in this experience to make way reservedly and distantly for the passing-by of the last god. One is lonely in the awareness of this problem, if one perceives the nearness of the last god. From that moment on, one sees the gods as mortal and as plural, which in turn implies the mortality of the metaphysical project as *a* project. But on the other hand, the mortality of the metaphysical project opens up space for possibilities that are beyond and before metaphysics. Being close to a god is not a matter of fortune or misfortune; it depends on the event of being. Those who question here are lonely and without help.[76] They give up all curiosity and inquisitiveness: their seeking loves the abyss, in which they know the deepest ground. They have to bear this loneliness in the highest hour, the hour in which one is open to another beginning.[77]

The encounter with the last god is especially tuned to "restraint" (*Verhaltenheit*).[78] Restraint stands midway between fear and diffidence; in this mood *Dasein* tunes itself to the stillness of the passing of the last god.[79] This concept of reservedness turns up again in Heidegger's later works as 'letting-be' (*Gelassenheit*). If man wants to be delivered from the desolation of being and wants to exist historically, then this can only happen in the hidden history of the stillness in which the reign of the last god opens and gives shape to being. Therefore, stillness must come over the world. This stillness originates in keeping silent, and this keeping silent arises from reservedness.[80] This again is connected with the refusal (*Verweigerung*).[81] In the refusal, one prefers to keep silent about the metaphysical idea of god. The reservedness has to be discerned from wondering; wondering used to be the basic mood from which the Greeks started to philosophise.[82] Wonder is the mood of the first beginning of philosophy, not of the other beginning.

To understand Heidegger's interpretation of those who have the experience of a passing god and are in the mood of reservedness, the notion of provisonality or temporarity is very important.[83] In *Zur Sache des Denkens,* Heidegger emphazises this once again. For thinking that is understood from being as an event of enowning it is provisional (*Vorläufig*). It is a preparing thinking, but in its deepest sense it is a fore-running. This provisional character of the forerunning concerns the finitude of thinking and that which must be thought. The more adequate the step backwards, the more adequate the provisional forerunning or anticipating thinking.[84] This provisionality is also mentioned at the end of his *Letter on Humanism*: "Thinking is on the descent to the poverty of its provisional essence."[85]

Because of the dominance of the calculating culture there are only a few of these 'ones to come'; their guessing and seeking is hardly recognizable, even to themselves. However, this seeking bears a certainty that is touched by the shiest and remotest hint of the last god.[86] Hölderlin is their poet who comes from farthest away and is therefore the poet most futural of the ones to come. And, coming from so far away, he traverses and transforms that which is greatest.[87] So Hölderlin is for Heidegger a true foregoer (*Vorgänger*). A foregoer creates the space in which man can live by finding words and ways of understanding that are different from the 'realistic and actual' paths of the current culture. But the foregoer is also someone who reaches out to the future by guessing and seeking a human destiny that is other than the continuing progress of a planned history. Only those who stand outside the borders of the first beginning are capable of experiencing both the monotony of this history and at the same moment the possibility of an alternative history. But this experience is only weak and provisional.

Because of this dual experience of the beyond of the first beginning, the arrival of the last god exists also in the flight of the gods and their hidden transformation.[88] Those who experience the monotony of Western history are trying to find the way back (*die Rückwegigen*) out of the desolation of being. In doing this, they prepare the ones to come, who have the experience of the last god. Without those who are on the way back, there would not even be the dawning of the possibility of the hinting of the last god. "Those who are on the way back are the true forerunners (*Vorläufer*) of those who are to come."[89]

The connection of those on the way back and those to come makes clear that the passing of the last god is only understandable after it has taken place. In the provisional forerunning of the foregoers, what is anticipated is so weak and silent that it can only be understood afterward. What is anticipated is so indeterminate and far away that the last god cannot be objectified or planned, but can only be experienced on the way back, and only in such a way that the last god has passed-by. So the last god can only be understood as a god who has come and gone. The farthest anticipation (*vorlaufen*) can therefore only be understood as already gone-by (*vorlaüfig*): what remains is a trace or a hint.

A long period of preparation is needed for the great moment of the passing of the last god, for this turn in the understanding of being from the perspective of the other beginning. Once we understand Hölderlin as the forerunner, Heidegger's next passage becomes understandable. "With the question of be-ing, which has overcome the question of beings and thus all 'metaphysics,' the torch is lit and the first attempt is made for the long run. Where is the runner who takes up the torch and carries it to the forerunner? All runners must be *fore*-runners; and the later they come, the stronger fore-runners they must be — no followers, who at most only 'correct' and refute what is first-attempted. The fore-runners must be *inceptual,* more and more originarily inceptual than the ones who run 'ahead' (i.e., who run behind them) and must more simply, more richly, and unconditionally and uniquely think the one and the same of what is to be questioned. What they take over by taking hold of the torch cannot be what is said as 'doctrine' and 'system' and the like, but rather what obliges (*das Gemüßte*), as that which opens itself only to those whose origin is in the abground and who are one of the compelled."[90] Those who are forerunners feel obliged and compelled to seek and to guess and to reach for the farthest future and with that for the deepest past to find another origin. So, therefore Heidegger writes about the 'last' of the last god: "The last is that which not only needs the longest fore-runnership but also itself *is*: not the ceasing, but the deepest beginning, which reaches out the furthest and catches up with itself with the greatest difficulty."[91]

The last god is the horizon that is farthest away, which surrounds as the uttermost possibility which cannot be overtaken and which must anticipated in provisionality, because as such it cannot be outstripped.[92] This recalls the discussion of death in *Being and Time*. Since death cannot be outstripped, its anticipation must be provisional: "Being-toward-death is the anticipation of a potentiality-for-Being of that entity whose kind of being is anticipation itself."[93] So it is contradictory to the structure of '*Vorlaufen*' as an essential characteristic of Dasein's historicality that it could be outstripped or objectified; it only can be provisional (*Vorlaüfig*). For this experience of the historicality of being, only the ones to come — the few — are called up. Only the great and unrevealed individuals will provide the stillness for the passing of the god and, among themselves, for the reticent accord of those who are prepared.[94]

It is a matter of stepping backwards into the direction of the other beginning. The first beginning has to be freed from its unspoken understanding of being as eternal presence so as to see itself as a possibility together with the possibility of another beginning. This is a task of those who are to come. They take over and preserve belongingness to the event of enowning, and they come to stand before the hints of the last god.[95]

We have seen that the last god has a temporal meaning.[96] This temporality is not understood from the perspective of Dasein as is developed in *Being and Time,* but here it is understood from the perspective of being as an event of enowning, which presupposes Heidegger's explication of Dasein. To radicalise this notion of temporality, Heidegger calls upon the services of a god who is characterized as passing-by. As an essentially momentary and historical transition, the passing of the last god is not an end, but offers the possibility of a beginning. This god is only in the decisive moment of passing by, because passing-by is the way of presence of this god. It is the fleetingness of a hardly understandable hint that can show all happiness and fear in the moment of going-by. This god has its own measures. It is only (for) a moment, hardly touching the dwellings of humans, and those do not really know what it is. And they cannot know, as long as they are caught in that way of knowledge according to which they understand things and situations and themselves. Passing-by — and not presence, nor arrival — is the being of the last god. This means that the last god does not manifest himself, he is present only as a hint. The innermost finitude of be-ing reveals itself in the hint of a last god.[97]

For Heidegger, the gods are an expression of human finitude, just as death is. The gods are involved in the historicality of humans: they do not appear after death, but through it. 'Through death' means that they appear not in the process of deceasing, but by the fact that death inheres in Dasein.[98] Anticipating god is even more difficult than anticipating death. Just as death is not to be outstripped, a god cannot be outstripped either.

The god who enters into its history of being — by passing-by — is not the last god in a metaphysical sense, which would imply a transcendental foundation, but is god insofar as it is pure withdrawal that cannot be outstripped. The finitude of being is the true issue in the lastness of the god. This last god is marked by death. It is not the death of Christ, because Christianity is over, but death as the possibility that cannot be outstripped. "Only man 'has' the distinction of standing before death, because man inabides in be-ing: death is the utmost testimonial for be-ing."[99] Thus the last god is not a god that became human. Rather, human beings receive their historical essence in the passing-by of the god, which means in its not being present.[100]

Metaphysical theology understands the 'last' as the highest by comparing the one with the other. Heidegger wants to free the divine from this comparison by referring it to the experience of temporarinessty just as *Dasein* has in the anticipating (*vorlaufen*) of death.[101] The adjective 'last' in the word 'the last god' has to keep open how to speak about the divine. What *Being and Time* says about the anticipation of death counts for the ones to come: in this anticipating and forerunning every orientation gets lost with regard to the given. The future ones, or the ones to come, do not anticipate something real or present, but 'something' possible that has yet to be decided.

The divine that has its essence in passing-by gives itself to *Dasein* in a hint; that means in something that is to be interpreted, in which one is uncertain and provisional. The hint is something that disappears in the distance in such a way that the divine withdraws when it gives itself to man — suddenly and briefly, as ungraspable and unavailable.[102] Those originally in a relation to being determined by metaphysics will slowly understand the other beginning, which does not appear in a personal or in a massive experience of the godhead, but only in the abyss of being. All worship and churches together are not able to assist the essential preparation of the meeting of god and man in the centre of being.[103] The last sentences of the *Beiträge* suggest that man is waiting for god, but only a few know that god waits for the change in the foundation of the truth of being and the corresponding change of man into Dasein. Philosophy pretends to prepare the site of moment for the hint of the gods, without wanting to decide about whether man and god will historically answer each other. Only a few know that the god-head is waiting for the foundation of the truth of being as an event of enowning and thus await man's leaping-into Dasein. "Instead it seems as if man might have to and would await god."[104] However, Heidegger suggests that this is the most insidious form of the most acute godlessness.

That the last god is totally other to the Christian God, pre-supposing that this god is not explicable from the perspective of entities, whether the entity be anthropological or ontological. Understanding the divine from a perspective or framework in which god is in the end the fulfilment of a maladjusted human need for certainty goes against the possibility of experiencing the last god. This leads, for example, to the philosophy of reli-gion understanding religion from the perspective of a func-tional social need.[105]

Is it possible to see any theology here in this historizing of the godhead? It only could be a hermeneutical theology with-out reference or presupposition of 'something' eternal and unchange-able. This would be a theology that is completely historical, because its subject is historical: a passing god. It is therefore not a question of whether these gods are pagan or Christian.[106] What is at issue is the historicity of being, which implies the historicity of the gods. Therefore any talk of theology here is not to be taken seriously. Heidegger would never call this 'the-ology,' because all theology presupposes the *theos,* the god as an entity; and it does this so certainly that everywhere where theology arises, the god already flies.[107]

In thinking from the perspective of the ontological differ-ence, from the difference of being and entities, the last god is not an entity, not even the highest one. Nor is it being itself, nor the truth of being in its being as an event of enowning. The god that is thought within ontological difference is different from being. Nevertheless, this god appears within being as an event of enowning and within its truth. This could be called the 'theological difference' of god and the truth of being.[108] But it is too simple to see in the other beginning a task for theology.[109] That would turn the whole project of a provisional passing god into a theistic theology.

The true future points to an event that can never really begin, because we always already are it.[110] It is not sufficient to say in the era of nihilism that god is dead or that transcendental values pass away; rather, one must learn to think a god's being, as well as its truth, as passing-by. Who or what is this god? It is no longer the god of metaphysics or the theistic God of Christianity.

EIGHT

Subjectivism or Humanism

T he "Letter on 'Humanism'" (1947) plays a crucial role with regard to Heidegger's position toward the gods and the holy. The *Gesamtausgabe* edition of the essay includes a marginal comment by Heidegger which explains that the "Letter on 'Humanism'" was first conceived long before it was written. It is based on a path of thinking whose course Heidegger began in 1936, in the moment of an attempt to say the truth of being in a simple manner.[1]

In the "Letter on 'Humanism,'" Heidegger asks how the thinking of being makes possible the thinking of the divine. It is important to follow this because it may be that in Heidegger's philosophy something like an ontotheological structure appears. It is no accident that Heidegger rejects the reproach of atheism with regard to his thinking: "With the existential determination of the essence of the human being, therefore, nothing is decided about the 'existence of God' or his 'non-being' no more than about the possibility or impossibility of gods."[2] Heidegger rejects the charge of atheism because it is not a reproach in which he recognizes himself. He does not speak out about the existence of a god or godhead, but this is because he thinks about the possibility and framework within which something like a god has to be thought. To stress this, Heidegger refers expressly to an earlier footnote in "On the Essence of Ground." Philosophy as the analysis of Dasein and facticity does not speak to the human relationship with god. "Through the ontological interpretation of Dasein as being-in-the-world no decision, whether positive or negative, is made concerning a possible being toward God. It is, however, the case that through an illumination of transcendence we first achieve an adequate concept of Dasein, with respect to which it can now be asked how the relationship of Dasein to God is ontologically ordered."[3] This is not a plea for a kind of indifference. He wants to keep the question of Dasein's relation to god undecided. It is important not to make a decision, because the gods themselves are a domain of decision.

Heidegger does not show himself to be an atheist or an agnostic. He wants to avoid every prematurity with regard to the divine. Before one decides about god or the gods, one has to think of being. We do not know what we ask for as long as we do not know what being is, and how the divine is related to being. Does this imply that every thinking about and of being is also a thinking of the divine? In what way does this relationship have to be thought? If it has to be thought as ontotheology, Heidegger will not see the divine in it.

Because being is normally understood as an objective thing, this is all the more reason not to see the divine in it. The dominant understanding of being is blamed for the fact that in Western philosophy something like the divine cannot be thought. God is understood as the highest being, the highest thing. The highest and first thing in ontotheology is seen as the foundation and explanation for all that is. In the chapter on the idea of *causa sui* we saw this kind of thinking in the overwhelmingly technological approach to the world. The hypertrophy of causal thinking rules the whole world.

Heidegger sees the highest moment of nihilism in the total dominance of technology. He finds a kinship between Nietzsche's philosophy, technology, and nihilism. Everything that exists is taken up by a process of progress, in which it is understood as material for production. And this production, understood as progress, is a goal in itself.

Against this background the question arises to what extent a relation to god can be thought in Heidegger's thinking. Where metaphysics as philosophical theology traditionally thinks the philosophical relation to god, nowadays it has become a nihilism, in which one cannot, according to Heidegger, be related to a god. In the "Letter on 'Humanism,'" he expressly speaks out about this. A god cannot be thought in its own terms, because thinking is not able to dispose of the ontotheological framework; therefore it does not succeed in thinking the divine. This situation recalls Nietzsche's preaching that god is dead. In particular, the cry "I seek God, I seek God" means for Heidegger a possible relation to god. Heidegger comments on this with the question: "Has a thinking man perhaps here really cried out *de profundis*?"[4] This does not imply that Heidegger sees a possibility for a relation to a god, but that thinking reaches its bottom when it has lost the metaphysical god. A new way to a godhead has to be found from this bottom.

HOW TO THINK THE DIVINE

In the "Letter on 'Humanism'" Heidegger describes some of the steps required to reach that kind of thinking of the divine. He resists the indifference that is attributed to him. For him it is about indicating that the thinking of being, which thinks from the perspective of the truth of being, thinks more originally than the ontotheology of metaphysics: "Only from the truth of being can the essence of the holy be thought. Only from the essence of the holy is the essence of divinity to be thought. Only in the light of the essence of divinity can it be thought or said what the word 'God' is to signify."[5] Some authors see this as a place to introduce the notion of "theological difference" in Heidegger, because the truth as the openness of being is not god itself, but the space in which the holy, the divine, and god can appear or withdraw.[6] God is not being, but nevertheless there is a relation between the truth of being and god, for instance in the insight that gods need being. There is, however, no immediate relation and implication between being and god, as is the case in ontotheology, where the truth of being is related to the holy. So it is important to make clear what the truth of being is.[7] Therefore it is important to find a trace of the holy in the truth of being.

How is the holy found in the truth of being? The truth of being can be found in what appears, in the unveiled, as well as in what withdraws: in the phenomenon that, in unveiling, something withdraws. The being-there of appearing is the first beginning of Western philosophy. From there, the philosophy of presence spreads optimally in technology. The reference to the holy has to be sought on the other side. Truth has a relation with concealment, and in this concealment, that is, in the forgottenness, or *lēthē*, the holy has to be found. The holy is that dimension of truth in which the phenomenon of the withdrawal would appear. This is clarified in Heidegger's essay on Trakl, "Language in the Poem." There Heidegger discusses how Trakl's poem brings to language the tension in twilight between light and dark. In twilight, the dark appears: "Ghostly the twilight dusk / Bluing above the mishewn forest." The poet talks about "Clarity sheltered in the dark" as blueness.[8] The interplay of light and dark in the blueness corresponds philosophically to the interplay of lighting and concealment in the event of truth, of *alētheia* and *lēthē*. The holy shines out of the blueness, even while veiling itself in the dark of that blueness. Blue is not an image indicating the sense of the holy. Blueness itself is the holy, in virtue of its gathering depth which shines forth only as it veils itself.

The holy is not only that which appears, the unveiled. The holy is, rather, in the dimension where the truth of being tends to hide, where the lighting disappears in the dark, where lighting is experienced as lighting of the hidden, as unconcealed, as *a-lētheia*. The depth that shines in the concealed, which appears as concealment, opens the dimension of the holy. The trace of the holy leads to the origin of the truth of being. This origin has its twilight in the dimension of the holy; it is the twilight of the sun that sets, which calls deeper into the setting, calls deeper into the withdrawing.[9] The holy gleams in the dark. It calls back in the silence, completely different from what appears, and the wondrous, which asks for an ever-more-intense mastery. This withdrawing asks for a step backwards, it asks for reservedness, that silently accepts what withdrawing offers to understand.

This kind of appearing of the divine is the appearing of the withdrawal within the truth of being in the sense of lightning. The appearing of god happens thus within the truth of being from the dimension of the godhead. With this, the theological difference is guaranteed. Being and god are different. Heidegger clearly says that the godhead as essencing (*Wesendes*) receives its origin from the truth of being.[10] Therefore the god needs being. This is emphasized again: "the admission by god that it needs be-ing, an admission that does not relinquish god or its greatness."[11]

What does the word "need" (*brauchen*) mean here? It does not mean that something of the godhead's greatness is given away. It is not a lack or a shortage. It does not mean something absent or a negative. Therefore, Heidegger can write: "Proper use (*brauchen*) is neither a mere utilizing, nor a mere needing. What we merely need, we utilize from the necessity of a need. Utilizing and needing always fall short of proper use. Proper use is nearly manifest, and in general is not the business of mortals."[12] With regard to the original meaning of the word "*brauchen*" Heidegger writes, "So understood, use (*brauchen*) itself is the summons which demands that a thing be admitted to its own essence and nature, and that the use keep to it. To use (*brauchen*) something is to let it enter into its essential nature, to keep it safe in its essence."[13] In the "Anaximander Fragment," the interpretation is as follows: *Brauchen* means "to place in someone's hands or hand over, thus to deliver, to let something belong to someone. But such delivery is of a kind which keeps this transfer in hand, and with it what is transferred."[14]

By this *brauchen* of being, the godhead gets its essence. This kind of *brauchen* does not need something but gives and grants something. In this way god (as the essence of the godhead) gets its origin from the event of the truth of being, that is, from the lighting of being. Therefore, Heidegger can say that god is waiting for human beings and for the foundation of the truth of being, and not the opposite. "How few know that god awaits the grounding of the truth of be-ing and thus awaits man's leaping-into Da-sein. Instead it seems as if man might have to and would await god."[15]

So it is important to raise the question of god where it belongs — in the dimension of the holy. Heidegger raises the question of the holy especially with regard to and in dialogue with Hölderlin. One needs a certain sense of the holy to raise the question of god in an appropriate way. In the technological era and world, human beings have lost their sense of the holy. Therefore it remains fixed as a specific dimension for human beings: "But this is the dimension of the holy, which indeed remains closed as a dimension if the open region of being is not cleared and in its clearing is near to humans. Perhaps what is distinctive about this world-epoch consists in the closure of the dimension of the hale (*des Heilen*). Perhaps that is the sole malignancy (*Unheil*)."[16] As long as the ontotheological framework rules, the holy cannot reach into the nearness of human beings. The god of ontotheology is in the end a very godless god. For instance, a proof for the existence of god can be constructed by means of the most rigorous formal logic and yet prove nothing, since a god who must permit his existence to be proved in the first place is ultimately a very ungodly god. The best that such proofs of existence can yield is blasphemy.[17]

Precisely because technological thinking always implies a highest god, Heidegger introduces a godless thinking. This is a move that we also saw in the earlier Heidegger. He pleads for thinking that gives up the ontotheological structure of philosophy. Such a godless thinking is closer to the divine, according to Heidegger. It is more free for god.[18]

Heidegger wants to separate the certainty of faith and the questions of philosophy. He rejects the certainty of faith when this certainty is the result of philosophical reasoning. He does not resist a god of faith; he resists a god that is a part of a necessary conclusion of thinking. Consequently, he resists a metaphysical approach within a theology that understands itself as explication of faith. God as a necessary philosophical moment has no message for the believer. "Man can neither pray nor sacrifice to this god. Before the *causa sui*, man can neither fall to his knees in awe nor can he play music and dance before this god."[19]

THE LOSS OF THE GODS AND THEOLOGY

The feeling for the holy has disappeared because man is unable to experience it. Ontotheology is a symptom of the absence of the holy: every possibility of relating to the holy in a thinking way seems to be absent. Human beings in this period of time are condemned to seeing the holy and the divine as meaningless. As Heidegger explains in his essay "What are Poets For?" "The era is defined by the god's failure to arrive,

by the 'default of God.' But the default of God which Hölderlin experienced does not deny that the Christian relationship
with God lives on in individuals and in churches; still less does
it assess this relationship negatively. The default of God means
that no god any longer gathers men and things unto himself,
visibly and unequivocally, and by such gathering disposes the
world's history and man's sojourn in it. The default of God
forebodes something even grimmer, however. Not only have
the gods and the god fled, but the divine radiance has become
extinguished in the world's history. The time of the world's
night is the destitute time, because it becomes ever more destitute. It has already grown so destitute, it can no longer discern the default of God as a default."[20]

Here it is clear that Heidegger, as a philosopher, does not
speak out about the faith of the believer. The disappearance of
the gods does not depend on believers but is a symptomatic
characteristic of the modern age. Heidegger describes this
clearly in his essay, "The Age of the World Picture," when he
says that, "A fifth phenomenon of the modern age is the loss
of the gods (*Entgötterung*). This expression does not mean the
mere doing away with the gods, a gross a-theism. The loss of
the gods is a twofold process. On the one hand, the world picture is Christianized inasmuch as the cause of the world is
posited as infinite, unconditional, absolute. On the other hand,
Christendom transforms Christian doctrine into a worldview
(the Christian worldview), and in that way makes itself modern and up to date. The loss of the gods is the situation of
indecision regarding God and the gods. Christendom has the greatest share in bringing it about. But the loss of the gods is so far
from excluding religiosity that rather only through that loss is
the relation to the gods changed into mere 'religious experience.' When this occurs, then the gods have fled. The resultant
void is compensated for by means of historiographical and psychological investigation of myth."[21]

When Heidegger enumerates the characteristics of modernity in "The Age of the World Picture," and sees the objectification of being as predominate, he not only refers to the positive sciences but also the humanities, including theology.[22] Another feature of modernity that applies to theology is the idea that something is only known and understood when it has been given an anthropological explanation. Modern man finds his certainty by liberation from the revelational certainty of salvation. This applies to Bultmann, who thinks concepts like self-understanding, care, and anxiety not from the perspective of being, but from the perspective of the 'I' of the person.[23] Because Bultmann mainly understood Heidegger's analysis of Dasein as an anthropological analysis of basic structures of the human being, he could use this basic structure for his demythologising of religion.[24] When Bultmann speaks in his theology about the human being, he understands the human being as it appears in Heidegger's analysis in *Being and Time,* which he knew from contacts and conversations at Marburg.[25] He saw in Heidegger's analysis liberation from revelation, by understanding it as a human project. But to this liberation from revelation Heidegger answers: "Hence liberation from the revelational certainty of salvation had to be intrinsically a freeing to a certainty (*Gewissheit*) in which man makes secure for himself the true as the known of his own knowing (*Wissens*). That was possible only through self-liberating man's guaranteeing for himself the certainty of the knowable."[26]

Through this anthropological certainty two domains of questions arose in the center of theology.[27] First, the questions: What really happened? What is historically fixable? What is really true? And second, the questions: How is that which really happened historically verifiable? And how can what cannot happen historically be understandable and explainable? What is the meaning of the historical and the unhistorical for faith?

The first domain is supported by historical-critical methodology/research. There human beings try to ascertain objectively the truth and reality of past history through source criticism, criticism of sources and questions; consequently, this applies also for the questions that are posed in the sources. This second domain of questions is therefore decisive. Man as subject has a certain projection of reality which applies for both science and history. What does not fit into the projection, is therefore unreal or is at best an exception. But whoever thinks historico-critically does not permit the facts that are exceptions. The *Leben-Jesu-Forschung,* for example, has as its basis the anthropological project of reality. In an effort to avoid dogmatic thinking, it describes several images of Jesus; however, it stems from the idea that reality has to have a human measure. In the rational explanation, in the cult mystery, in the teacher of ethical attitudes, in the preacher of the *eschaton,* in every case the inquiring man, as a human subject, looks for truth and ascertains truth by giving an account of himself in what can be seen.

The second domain of questions is also anthropologically motivated. To assert that everything is a lie and a fantasy, and that nothing has really happened, still remains within a paradigm in which human reality is most indicative of truth. The historical is unimportant; only the meaning of the message matters for the believer. A rupture between the historically possible and real and the historically impossible and unreal generally arises from the modern concept of reality. Against this background it is possible to gather what is important for faith by reduction to the historic, and to point out the historically impossible as something meaningless for faith. Or one does the opposite: the unhistoric and unreal is interpreted as important for faith. Idealistic, psychological and existential interpretations are three names for the same process in which the historically impossible has been made important for anthropological thinking. The historical Jesus is here in one line with the idea of demythologizing. Only what fits within contemporary man's concept of reality is acceptable and real in the interpretation of the historically impossible. Therefore, the current philosophy of that moment has to help and to support the interpretation.[28] Moreover, it is especially striking that theologians understand hermeneutics as a process of actualization of the message to the current understanding of reality.

This anthropological orientation in theology is, in Heidegger's view, a symptom of the absence of the gods. But in its turn, the absence of the gods reflects a moment of undecidedness with respect to them. As we have mentioned before, the situation of undecidedness is what Heidegger indicates as the absence of the gods: "The loss of the gods is the situation of indecision regarding God and the gods."[29] This statement requires special attention, along with the statement in the Contributions that the gods are a domain of decision. As a philosopher, Heidegger indicates this problem of the absence or arrival of the gods without taking a position. He does not want to decide; for him, the gods are present as philosophical items, and never as something or someone to worship. Heidegger's philosophy remains parasitic with regard to this 'degodization' and the situation of undecision that is given with it. It is the undecidedness of a neutral philosophical subject. If he had to worship a god, he is afraid that he would have to close the workplace, because gods would then have an identity.

The phenomenon of 'degodization,' according to Heidegger has nothing to do with the relation between belief and unbelief. Christendom is encompassed by and stimulates the process of degodization. It is a process by which the current forms of belief are also encompassed. The degodization is not an atheism; it is not the same as the disappearance of Christianity out of Western culture. It is connected with the centralization of feeling as subjective religious feeling. Further on, I will pay attention to this phenomenon, in which Christendom plays an important role.

The process of degodization has two important characteristics. At first degodization is characterized by a Christianizing of the world picture where the metaphysical systems of modernity understand the ultimate ground of reality from the perspective of God and the Bible. The ultimate cause is understood as the infinite, the unconditional, and the absolute. This happens in Descartes, Kant, and Hegel. Degodization is supported by the ontotheological structure of metaphysics. This is what Heidegger calls nihilism. Being is understood as value, and in ontotheology, as the highest value. "When one proclaims 'God' the altogether 'highest value' this is a degradation of God's essence."[30] The god of the philosophers is, as the highest value, connected with the God of Christianity. But with this the godhead is downgraded at the same time. Philosophy thinks god only because of the specific structure of Western ontotheology. God enters into philosophy because philosophy as ontotheology thinks a necessary, highest entity. Especially insofar as Chrsistendom connects itself with this ontotheology, the Christianizing of the world implies a degodization and gives support to and promotes this degodization.

Initially Christian theology adopted a lot of elements from Greek philosophy. However, god does not appear in philosophy because of theology or Christianity. Because of the specific structure of metaphysics as ontotheology, Greek philosophy could be used within the framework of a Christian theology. Therefore, degodization has its origin in metaphysics.

The second characteristic of the Christianizing of the world is that Christendom itself becomes secularized. Christianity wants to be current. Degodization implies that Christendom becomes a worldview. Faith gives its life in order to be well adapted to the spirit of the new time. As we have seen before, Heidegger marks the difference between Christendom and

Christianity. Christendom and Christianness are not the same. Christianness is located in the original faith of the New Testament. Christendom is the historic and political appearance of the Christian church. This church has social power and a great influence on the education of Western man; therefore it also has significant cultural influence. Christendom refers, according to Heidegger, to the socio-cultural and political incorporation of Christian faith. Christianness refers to the original Christian experience. It alludes to the time of the early Christians, the time in which the gospels were not yet redacted and in which Paul did his missionary work.

As we have seen, Heidegger presents pure Christianness as an attitude that lives on the faithful expectation of the coming of Christ. It is a way of living that is directed towards an open future, and does not count on a guaranteed reality to come. The god that is involved here is not one that lives in another world or is a highest entity. Heidegger also does not understand what is believed in faith to be a project of Dasein. It is a message that is revealed, and whose content man does not determine. It is a move that cannot be made by philosophy, but that has to find its possibility in Dasein. The attitude of faith can find its justification only in faith. It is not something that can be made or projected by man.

This is completely different from a metaphysics in which god is calcified into a highest entity. Faith is dragged along by metaphysics to become a worldview that functions as an explanation for the world. This worldview offers a guideline to understand man's place in the world. It is also used as ideology to bring political control. The original Christianness is no longer recognizable here. This means that a relativization of Christendom does not imply a rejection of Christianness. Here Heidegger recognizes his position in Nietzsche: "Christendom for Nietzsche is the historical, world-political phenomenon of the Church and its claim to power within the shaping of

Western humanity and its modern culture. Christendom in this sense and the Christianity of New Testament faith are not the same. Even a non-Christian Life can affirm Christendom and use it as means of power, just as, conversely, a Christian life does not necessarily require Christendom. Therefore, a confrontation with Christendom is absolutely not in any way an attack against what is Christian, any more than a critique of theology is necessarily a critique of faith, whose interpretation theology is said to be. We move in the flatlands of the conflicts between world views so long as we disregard these essential distinctions."[31] Because Christianity becomes a worldview, it receives an ontotheological structure and functions as a principle of explanation for reality. That is the place of the degodization implied by metaphysics, which ends in technology as nihilism.

The fact that thinking becomes something proper to the human subject also plays an important role. In this process of subjectification, degodization introduces another phenomenon: namely, religious feeling. Metaphysics in modernity goes along with religious experience. The relation to the divine becomes a subjective-affective mood in man. Religion loses the framework in which the religious can be thought as an objective reality. As the objective system of metaphysics disappears in the subjectification of the modern age, so too does the relation to the divine become a purely subjective matter. God is no longer seen as something that is present in reality. Reality itself loses its sacral dimension. The last place for the divine is the subjectivity of the believer. The domain of the divine is indicated as feeling, personal experience, individual conviction, and existential pathos.[32]

Therefore, the gods are fled once religion has become religious feeling. Because religion withdraws in subjectivity, it is withdrawn from the world. Even though the religion of subjectivity protests against the degodization of the world, degodization is actually a symptom of the very religion that protests against it. The logic of subjectivity rules in both degodization and modern metaphysics. Christendom itself stimulated the subjectification of metaphysics. "The fact that the transformation of reality to the self-certainty of the ego cogito is determined directly by Christianity, and the fact that the narrowing of the concept of existence is indirectly determined by Christian factors only proves how Christian faith adopted the fundamental trait of metaphysics and brought metaphysics to Western dominance in this form."[33] Thus Heidegger identifies Kierkegaard and Hegel within the same perspective.[34] Kierkegaard is called a religious writer who corresponds to the destiny of his era. He writes during the same time in which Hegel's metaphysics and Marx's system rule. It is the era in which we still are: the era in which subjectivity rules in Western thinking. Although Kierkegaard as a religious writer and Hegel as a thinker are deeply different from each other, both belong to the same paradigm of Western philosophy: in one giving rise to a religious subjectivity and in the other a rational subjectivity. Both are located in the degodization of the world. Even though the subjective feeling resists the increasing degodization, in the end it is a symptom of it.

So the process of degodization appears in two forms. It appears in the figure of rational subjectivity by way of Descartes, Kant and Hegel. And we find the figure of passionate subjectivity in the line that includes Pascal, Jacobi, and Kierkegaard. The essence of modern religion and modern metaphysics are connected. Both lines express a deeper process: degodization, which is the result of the ontotheological structure of metaphysics, and the modern thinking of subjectivity that is connected with it.

The disappearance of the divine from the world has as a consequence the commencement of historical and psychological research of myth and religious phenomena. By the sociological and historical study of religion, one can indicate in what way religion still exists, but this is nevertheless a symptom of degodization. The modern scientific analysis of religious representation, both individual and collective, is also connected to the culture of subjectivity, because the question of being of the gods is no longer raised. The scientific and the philosophical approaches to religion are highly reductionistic.[35] Mostly the religious is understood from the perspective of nonreligious phenomena using words like projection, ideology. However, the scientific approach to religion is not, according to Heidegger, the cause of degodization. The emptiness in which degodization arises creates space for the reductionistic approach. The relation with the divine is replaced by a scientific explanation of the history of religion. This becomes obvious in biblical research and the psychological and sociological research of what historically is understood as mythical. As myth, religion is neutralized and degodded. Such an approach is only possible when the gods are fled. This flight, however, has its grounds in what is called the essence of metaphysics.

This also offers some insight into what Heidegger means in his essay "The Age of the World Picture," when he says that "The loss of the gods is the situation of indecision regarding God and the gods."[36] The time of degodization is a time in which thinking cannot understand the divine and the relation to the divine as mortal. There is no dedication to a question; dedication, devotion, and deepening are left behind, for everything has become an objectifiable and calculable value. Because man has to give meaning to everything, devotion and dedication become an impossibility.

Heidegger wants to conquer this indecisive subjectivism by not making man responsible for it. It is not man that fails. If this were the case, then it would be caused by man, and would imply a continuation of the subjectivism. Indecisiveness is something that happens to man. It is connected with the essence of metaphysics, understood here not in the sense of essential, but in the sense of being about and wandering. This wandering and the destiny of metaphysics are wanted or caused by human thinking. Nobody decided about the meaning of the word 'subject' in modernity. Nevertheless, it happens in human thinking. It originates from the historicality of being; it is a disposition of being: "Whether the god lives or remains dead is not decided by the religiosity of men and even less by the theological aspirations of philosophy and natural science. Whether or not God is God comes disclosingly to pass from out of and within the constellation of Being."[37]

Against this background Heidegger can say that it is too early to speak about the divine. We have to prepare a non-metaphysical speaking of the god. For this it is necessary that the thinker learns to open his mind for the word of the poet. This word is, according to Heidegger, that of Hölderlin, the pre-eminent poet. The poets can prepare us for a new openness for the holy, the place within which the divine can be spoken about and make possible a speaking of a nonmetaphysical god outside ontotheology. To make this possible, man has to learn to stay in the nearness of being: "In such nearness, if at all, a decision may be made as to whether and how God and the gods withhold their presence and the night remains, whether and how the day of the holy dawns, whether and how in the upsurgence of the holy an epiphany of God and the gods can begin anew. But the holy, which alone is the essential sphere of divinity, which in turn alone affords a dimension for the gods and for God, comes to radiate only when being itself beforehand and after extensive preparation has been cleared and is experienced in its truth."[38] This passage clearly indicates that Heidegger's thinking of being has an openness for the holy, the divine, and the godhead.

IN THE NEARNESS OF BEING

Only from the nearness to being may an openness for the holy be accessible. Heidegger defines being as the nearest and the human being as the neighbor of being. The relation of being to human beings is the truth of being, as the nearness itself.[39] In the metaphysical approach, human beings are understood as created, as finite in relation to the absolute. We have seen this already in the *Beiträge,* where human beings have to become Dasein to be able to have a historical relation to the gods. The translation of the Greek *zōion logon echon* defines human being as a combination of animality and rationality for the rest of Western history.[40] This animal rationale is determined as subject and it actualizes the presentation of the reality that is understood as object. Moreover, man as rational, presenting subject is understood as willing. This determination also unifies the Platonic metaphysical determination and the theological. The philosophical determines the human being as presenting subject, while the theological doctrine of man determines the human being as person.

The anthropomorphic approach is also dominant nowadays in the interpretation of the ancient Greek world: "The 'anthropomorphic' conception of the Greek gods and the 'theomorphic' conception of Greek men, who have neither humanized nor anthropomorphized god nor divinized themselves into gods, are equally groundless answers to deficient questions. To ask whether the Greeks anthropomorphized the 'divine persons' or divinized human personalities into divine persons is to inquire into the 'person' and 'personalities' — without having determined in advance, even provisionally, the essence of man and of the divinities as experienced by the Greeks and without giving a thought to what is in fact first, namely that for the Greeks no more than there are 'subjects' are there 'persons' and 'personalities.'"[41]

The fundamental essence of the Greek divinities, in distinction from the Christian God, consists in their origination out of the presence of present being. This essential characteristic is the reason the Greek gods, just like men, are powerless before destiny and against it. By contrast, in Christian thought, all destiny is the work of the divine providence of the Creator and Redeemer, who as creator also dominates and calculates all beings as the created. And so Leibniz can still say: *cum Deus calculat, fit mundus.*[42]

Human beings in the era of the forgottenness of being speak of the worth and dignity of man, but they always understand their humanity at an anthropocentric and ontic level. Man is therefore alienated from his ontological essence, which leads to an understanding of the human being as subject and king of entities, not as the shepherd and neighbor of being which is authentic humanism. As a consequence of the forgottenness of being and the alienation of the human essence that is connected with it, human beings roam about in an endless nothing, finding no place for their dwelling. The roaming about is attributed to the forgottenness of being; Nietzsche attributes it to the death of god. People need gods to be able to dwell, but the ontotheological god is burnt out and is not able to give human beings a place on earth. Human beings have to find a place to dwell after ontotheology in the nearness of being. "The homeland of this historical dwelling is nearness to being. In such nearness, if at all, a decision may be made as to whether and how God and the gods withhold their presence and the night remains, whether and how the day of the holy dawns, whether and how in the upsurgence of the holy an epiphany of God and the gods can begin anew. But the holy, which alone is the essential sphere of divinity, which in turn alone affords a dimension for the gods and for God, comes to radiate only when being itself beforehand and after extensive preparation has been cleared and is experienced in its truth. Only thus does the overcoming of homelessness begin from being, a homelessness in which not only human beings but the essence of the human being stumbles aimlessly about."[43]

The order that is presented here would be: being (nearness), the holy, godhead, gods or god. The dimension of the holy will remain closed as long as being does not lighten and draw near to human being in this lightening. Perhaps the particularity of our current time is that the whole (Heile) is cut off; perhaps this is the only threat. The question of the holy together with the arrival or the flight of the gods is secondary with regard to the question of being. The trace of the holy is tied to this nearness of being as the time-space play in which the holy can appear. If this nearness remains closed then the holy cannot appear, then there is no place for the godhead, and then god and gods cannot be experienced, not even as distant or fled gods.

The forgottenness of being is not a forgetfulness of human being, but arises from the given that being itself withdraws. This is especially the experience of Hölderlin. In the poem "Bread and Wine" Hölderling calls his time a "destitute time" (dürftige Zeit), which is defined by the gods' failure to arrive, by the default of god. This is, however, connected with Hölderlin's experience of the holy. Hölderlin does not understand the night as opposite to the day, but as the place in which the gods stay away and withdraw. On the other hand the night is also the time-space in which the godlike withdraws, and from which a new day of the holy, a new arrival of the gods or of the god, can be handed. Therefore the night is called the mother of the day.[44] The default of god and the divinities is absence. But absence is not nothing; rather it is precisely the presence, which first must be appropriated, of the hidden fullness and wealth of what has been.[45] This turns the night into a holy night. Heidegger situates the night as a place of decision: the absence is the 'no more' of the fled gods and the 'not yet' of the arriving gods.

The default of god means: "that no God any longer gathers men and things unto himself, visibly and unequivocally, and by such gathering disposes the world's history and man's sojourn in it."[46] This is precisely what the god of ontotheology did. The default of god also means in a more radical sense that the divine radiance in the world's history has been extinguished. With this a place for the presence of a god is closed. The world becomes groundless: it hangs in the abyss.[47] However, "The turning of the age does not take place by some new god, or the old one renewed, bursting into the world from ambush at some time or other. Where would he turn on his return if men had not first prepared an abode for him? How could there ever be for the god an abode fit for a god, if a divine radiance did not first begin to shine in everything that is?"[48] The god only has an abode when there is a divine radiance in which he can dwell.

That the holy does not manifest the divine, may become evident wherever the holy appears but the divine stays away, as Heidegger writes in his interpretation of "Homecoming" (*Heimkunft*).[49] The holy is not an attribute of the divine; it is the dimension in which the godlike can appear. Not only the trace of the divine but also the trace of the holy has become unrecognizable.[50] The expression 'the trace of the holy' is ambiguous by virtue of the genitive that is used. It is the trace that brings us to the holy, in the sense of a trace into the holy, and at the same time it is a trace that is owned by the holy, in the sense of a remnant or a radiance of the holy. Those remnants or radiances lead to the holy. This means that the experience of the divine becomes more difficult when the trace of the holy becomes more unclear.

It was not unclear in the Greek experience. Man as Greek Dasein, and only he, was in his essence and according to the essence of *alētheia* the god-sayer. This can only be understood insofar as the essence of *alētheia* prevails in advance throughout the essence of Being itself, throughout the essence of divinity and the essence of humanity, and throughout the essence of the relation of Being to man and of man to beings. If the originary divinity emerges from the essence of Being, should not the oblivion of Being be the ground for the fact that the origin of the truth of Being has withdrawn itself into concealedness ever since, and no god could then appear emerging out of Being itself? Atheism — correctly understood as the absence of the gods — has been, since the decline of the Greek world, the oblivion of Being that has overpowered the history of the West as its basic feature. "Atheism," understood in the sense of essential history, is by no means (as people like to think) a product of freethinkers gone berserk or the proud posturing of philosophers. "Atheists of such a kind are themselves already the last dregs of the absence of the gods."[51]

As long as the night of the world lasts, the intact and unharmed whole of being remains in darkness. "The wholesome and sound withdraws. The world becomes without healing, unholy. Not only does the holy, as the track to the godhead, thereby remain concealed; even to track to the holy, the hale and whole, seems to be effaced. That is, unless there are still some mortals capable of seeing the threat of the unhale, the unholy, as such."[52] The hale of the holy remains unmarked; that is the biggest threat for human being. Only when the danger is recognized as danger can the saving arrive, as reflected in Hölderlin's hymn, "*Mnemosyne.*" It is important to experience in the forgottenness of being the disaster and the godlessness as such, the danger as danger, and the threatening doom. This experience leads us to the trace of the nearness of being and lays a trace to the trace of the whole of the holy. Heidegger expresses this at the end of "What are Poets For?": "The unholy, as unholy, traces the sound for us. What is sound beckons to the holy, calling it. The holy binds the divine. The divine draws the god near."[53] Being a poet in this

destitute time means being on the way to the trace of the fugi-
tive gods.

The gods disappear because being withdraws, nor can they
arrive on their own. As the hymn "*Mnemosyne*" says, the heavenly are not capable of everything. For this it is necessary that
human beings prepare a place for the gods. The divine and the
mortals depend on each other; they need each other to arrive
at their essence. This is only possible when human beings and
gods enter into a pact with each other and celebrate the wedding about which Hölderlin's hymn "The Rhine" speaks. This
wedding, as a pact of human beings and gods, has its ground
in the holy. In the wedding the holy brings gods and human
beings to their essence and settles them into what is convenient
to them, that is, in what they properly are in their togetherness.[54] The wedding festival is not something in history among
other events, but is itself the ground and essence of history. It
is the historic event of the holy. In the wedding festival of
human beings and gods, Hölderlin founds a new beginning of
a new history.[55]

HUMANISM IN THE NEARNESS IN THE FOURFOLD

The subjectivistic interpretation of humanity is most radically rejected in Heidegger's notion of the fourfold (*Geviert*).
This idea intensifies the notion of the nearness of being; an
idea that apparently goes back to Hölderlin.[56] The fourfold indicates the unity of earth and sky, divinities and mortals. The
earth is the building bearer, nourishing with its fruits, tending
water and rock, plant and animal. The sky is marked by the
sun path, the course of the moon, the glitter of the stars,
the seasons of the year and the light and dusk of the day. The
divinities are the beckoning messengers of the godhead. Out of
the hidden sway of the divinities, the god emerges as what he
is, which removes him from any comparison with beings that

are present. The mortals are the human beings. But human beings are not mortal because of the finitude of life; they are mortals because they can die. To die means to be capable of death as death.[57] And this means to experience death as the shrine of Nothing. As the shrine of Nothing, death harbors within itself the presencing of Being. But this is something of which man as *causa sui* is not capable. Therefore, Heidegger writes at the end of his address, "The Principle of Reason": "It depends on us, so it is said. But not on whether we live from atoms, rather whether we can be the mortals that we are, namely, those to whom being appeals. Only such beings are capable of dying, that means, to take on death as death."[58]

The four are so deeply connected that each automatically indicates the other three. All four are dependent on each other; there is no sky without earth, no divinities without mortals, etc. An intervention into one of them always has consequences for the other three: they are related as a mirror-play.[59] In the fourfold, things are at their place; the thing gathers itself as thing. Then human beings dwell in the nearness of being. Heidegger expresses this with words like nearness, dwelling, and neighbor. This is the reason why Heidegger can say that the human being dwells poetically.

Against this background, Heidegger uses words like homelessness (*Heimatlosigkeit*) and home (*Heimat*) in his "Letter on 'Humanism.'" He connects this with the poetical experience of Hölderlin, understood from the perspective of the historicality of being. The experience of the distance of being becomes an experience of nearness insofar as this distance is expressed in Hölderlin's poetry.

Almost at the same time in which Heidegger writes the "Letter on 'Humanism,'" he writes his essay "What are Poets For? (1946). There he writes that the time remains destitute not only because god is dead, but because mortals are hardly aware and capable even of their own nature. Death withdraws into the enigmatic. The mystery of pain remains veiled. Love has not been learned. But the mortals are. They are, in that there is language. Song still lingers over their destitute land. The singer's word still keeps to the trace of the holy.[60]

Heidegger will always resist a kind of thinking in which human beings become the measure of things. He rejects every anthropocentrism and subjectivism. This also has consequences for the understanding of religion. In Heidegger's approach, religion has to be understood from the perspective of the historicality of being and not from the perspective of a human anthropocentrism or subjective anthropology.[61] Heidegger stresses the difference of these approaches, presenting his approach from the perspective of the historicality of being as opposite to the modern approach from the perspective of the human subject.[62] The question arises what the difference is between a religion that is understood from the perspective of the historicality of being as opposed to Aristotelian-scholastic-Hegelian metaphysics. Are not both evidence of unbelief with regard to belief? Is this not an effort to give faith a support and a crutch? Is faith not in Heidegger's own understanding an act of god? Why use concepts like "understanding of being," "history of being," and "ontological difference"? One might object that there is no doctrine of being in the Bible. Whoever sees an ontology in the Old Testament words "I am who I am" does not know what he is doing. Is not this use of philosophy a way of little faith? Heidegger believes that modern theology is looking to make Christianity contemporary, but what about Kierkegaard?

From the perspective of man in the nearness of the fourfold, Heidegger prefers to keep silent with regard to theology insofar as it is dominated by a subjectivistic anthropology: "Someone who has experienced theology in his own roots, both the theology of the Christian faith and that of philosophy, would today rather remain silent about God when he is speaking in the realm of thinking."[63] With these words, Heidegger points out that keeping silent is not always due to a lack of knowledge. He dissociates himself from ontotheology and its fusion with Christian theology. Whether there is a place here for negative theology is very doubtful, because negative theology remains paradigmatically connected with ontotheology. It is premature to look for a kinship between Heidegger and negative theology.[64]

NINE

A Phenomenology of the Holy

*H*aving examined the tension between humanism and sub-jectivism, it is clear that the notion of the holy plays an important role in Heidegger's view of the divine. Nevertheless, it seems that there is no direct connection between naming the holy and thinking of being. In the Postscript to "What is Metaphysics?" Heidegger writes that thinking, obedient to the voice of being, seeks from being the word through which the truth of being comes to language. "The saying of the thinker comes from a long-protected speechlessness and from the care-ful clarifying of the realm thus cleared. Of like provenance is the naming of the poet. Yet because that which is like is so only as difference allows, and because poetizing and thinking are most purely alike in their care of the word, they are at the same time farthest separated in their essence. The thinker says being. The poet names the holy."[1] This kinship and difference make further examination of the relation between being and the holy more urgent.

It is important to notice that references to the holy only begin to appear in Heidegger's work in 1934.[2] In particular, the holy appears in conjunction with the words of the poet who names god: Hölderlin.[3] In the later Heidegger, the most important texts that mention the holy are found in the *Elucidations,* especially in the essay, "Hölderlin and the Essence of Poetry."[4]

Heidegger finds that Hölderlin's poetry articulates the essence of poetry itself. "Hölderlin is for us in a preeminent sense the poet's poet. And for that reason he forces a decision upon us."[5] When we read further, we see what Heidegger means by the essence of poetry: "Human existence is poetic in its ground. But we now understand poetry as a founding — through the naming of gods and of the essence of things. 'To dwell poetically' means to stand in the presence of the gods and to be struck by the essential nearness of things. Existence is 'poetic' in its ground — which means, at the same time, as founded (grounded), it is not something earned, but is rather a gift."[6] Hölderlin's expression of the essence of poetry is not as a timelessly valid concept. This essence of poetry belongs to a definite time, and yet it does not merely conform to that time as something already existing. Rather, by providing anew the essence of poetry, Hölderlin determines a new time. It is the time of the gods who have fled and of the god who is coming. It is the time of need because it stands in a double lack and a double not: in the no-longer of the gods who have fled and in the not-yet of the god who is coming.[7] This is the importance of Hölderlin for Heidegger.

But what is the meaning of the holy according to Heidegger's interpretation? And what is the relation between the holy and being? This last question is important because the thinker is focused on being. In Heidegger's interpretation of Hölderlin's "As When On a Holiday . . ." we read that Hölderlin connects the notions of nature and the holy. "The poetic naming says what the called itself, from its essence, compels the poet to say."[8] Why should the holy be the word of the poet? Because the poet has to name all that to which he listens as a divination. What he listens to is nature, which in awakening unveils its own essence as the holy.[9]

Heidegger understands nature as earlier than the era we live in. It is older than the ages (Zeiten), it is more original than time, and yet it is not supertemporal in the metaphysical sense.[10] Nature is more primordial, earlier, and more temporal than the time with which man reckons and calculates because it clears and opens everything that can appear in it. It is not the eternity of Christian metaphysics. It is above the gods, not in the sense of an isolated domain of reality, but because in nature as lightening all things can be present. Hölderlin names this nature the 'holy' because it is older than time and higher than the gods. "Thus 'holiness' is in no way a property borrowed from a determinate god. The holy is not holy because it is divine; rather the divine is divine because in its way it is holy . . . The holy is the essence of nature."[11] The gods are not on a higher level than the holy.[12] Even god and the gods are subjected to the law of the holy. A god is not the legislator or the cause of all order; the holy is the law. This makes it clear that it is not about a metaphysical god because here the holy is not a property of god; it is rather the opposite. In its awakening, nature awakes as the holy, and there is no reality that is earlier than the openness of nature.

The holy (*Heilige*) is what is always earlier. It is the primordial, and it remains in itself unbroken and "whole" (*heil*). This originary "wholeness" gives a gift to everything that is real by virtue of its pervasiveness: it confers the grace of its own abiding presence. But the primordial wholeness, which thus grants holiness, still enshrouds all fullness in itself as the immediate. It holds in itself the fabric of the essence of all — thus it is unapproachable by any individual, be it god or man. "The holy, as the unapproachable, renders every immediate intrusion of the mediated in vain. The holy confronts all experience with something to which it is unaccustomed, and so deprives it of its ground."[13] One cannot approach the holy by the mediate and the familiar. It deranges or displaces one from any ground. "Deranging in this way, the holy is the awesome itself. But its awesomeness remains concealed in the mildness of its light embrace. Because this light embrace educates the future poets, they as the initiated ones, know the holy. Their knowledge is divination. Divining concerns what is coming and what is rising, that is, the dawn."[14] But is knowledge of the holy not lost as nature is forgotten and misunderstood? For man subjects the earth and nature to his will, and with this pervasive nature is placed in bondage. And yet, Heidegger replies, nature has allowed this: she left it to men to misconstrue the holy.[15]

The holy expressed by the poet concerns what is coming, which is expressed with the words, "But now day breaks." The holy itself comes. Hölderlin's poem says: "But now day breaks! I awaited and saw it come, And what I saw, may the holy be my word."[16]

However, the poet does not have the power to name the holy immediately, for this the poet needs something that is higher than what is nearer to the holy, and is nevertheless different from it: a god must throw the kindling lightning-flash into the poet's soul. Since neither men nor gods by themselves can ever achieve an immediate relation to the holy, men need the gods and the heavenly ones need mortals.[17] They cannot exist without each other. In spite of the fact that the gods are not the holy, they are needed for man in order to name it.

This lightning flash is not the result of the poet's creativity or power. It strikes the poet suddenly. "So 'struck,' he would be tempted to follow only the good fortune and to lose himself in the sole possession of the god. But that would be misfortune, because it would signify the loss of his poetic being; for the essential condition of the poet is grounded not in the reception of the god, but in the embrace of the holy."[18] The holy encompasses the poet. When the holy ray strikes him, he is not carried away into the blaze of the ray but is fully turned toward the holy. The poet quakes and is shocked by the opening up of the holy that takes place. What happens in the opening up of the holy? "The shaking breaks the peace of silence. The word comes to be."[19] This is what happens in the hymn. Here the togetherness of god and man appears. Mediated by god and men, the song bears witness to the holy. In the hymn the holy becomes word, and appears.

When does this coming happen? The appearing of the holy is not the empty continuation of current affairs. It is the coming of the beginning. As coming, the primordiality of the beginning is the abiding before which nothing else can be thought.[20] It is important to hear what is said at the end of the poem: "But now day breaks! I awaited and saw it come, And what I saw, may the holy be my word."[21] This "now" is not 1800, the year in which the poem was written. It is Hölderlin's time as the time whose tone is set by his words. The "now" names the coming of the holy, which indicates the time in which history decides essentially. One cannot date such a time, and it is not measurable by historical dates and periods. Historical dates are merely a peg for human calculations. They happen at the sur-face of history, which is an object of research. This history, however, is not the event of occurring itself. The event of occurring is only there when there is a primordial decision on the essence of truth.

The holy, which is older than time and higher than the gods, is founded in its coming from another beginning and another, more primordial history. The holy takes a decision from its beginning in the matter of men and gods: whether they are and who they are, how they are and when they are. The coming is named in its coming through a calling. Hölderlin's word is now a calling word. This gives another meaning to the Greek word *hymnos*, normally translated by the words 'praise' and 'cele-brate.' But now the poetic word is a foundational saying. The word of this song is no longer a hymn to something, to the poet, to nature; it is the hymn of the holy. The holy bestows the word, and itself comes into word. "This word is the primal event of the holy. Hölderlin's poetry is now a primordial call-ing which, called by what is coming, says this and only this as the holy. The hymnal word is now "compelled by the holy," and because compelled by the holy, also sobered by the holy."[22] This sobriety is the basic mood that is always ready for the holy. Hölderlin's word conveys the holy, thereby naming the space of time that is only once: the time of primordial decision for the essential order of the future history of gods and humans.

THE FOURFOLD AS A COUNTERPARADIGM

The holy, as the fourfold of gods and mortals of heaven and earth, encompasses the speaking about god, the gods, and the godlike. Since god is always a god in relation to mortals, the flight of the gods is a dissonance of the fourfold. The fourfold functions as a counterparadigm to ontotheological thinking and its anthropocentric and subjectivistic forms.[23] As I have said before, the different positions of the fourfold are understood from the perspective of their counterparts.[24] Each of the four mirrors and is mirrored in the others.[25] In these mirror-relations, things come to their essence in losing themselves. "Their interplay is the span that man traverses at every moment insofar as he is as an earthly being."[26] The things which man has to meet do not lead to the earth. Indeed, the earth is no longer land and bottom but refers to a relation between earth and heaven, in which one is turned to the other and in which the one mirrors in the other. "The ringing out of the earth is the echo of heaven. In resounding, the earth by its own movement replies to heaven."[27] Likewise, the water in the river, which is spanned by the bridge, comes from heaven and raises back to heaven. Both enter into a play in which they belong to and differ from one another.

The godlike and the mortals also relate to each other in a mirror-play. In this way, the godhead appears in its presence and withdraws in its concealment.[28] Its absence is as present as its arrival. The mortals are capable of death as death, whereas so long as man is oriented to and focused on metaphysics, he is not capable of death as death. "Metaphysics, by contrast, thinks of man as animal, as a living being. Even when ratio pervades animalitas, man's being remains defined by life and life-experience. Rational living beings must first become mortals."[29] Man has to learn to die in order to become the mortal who he is. This image functions as a counterimage that has to strive against the classical images of metaphysics. Mortals are brought to the nothingness that becomes clear as the secret of being itself, since death is never an entity yet nevertheless presences.[30]

The four of the fourfold are in a certain sense equal to each other. There is no subordination of higher and lower. However, there seems to be more kinship between heaven and the godlike, on the one hand, and the earth and mortals on the other. Nevertheless, no two couples are against each other and each finds itself from the coming together of the four. In this way they are connected to each other. "Each of the four mirrors in its own way the presence of the others. Each therewith reflects itself in its own way into its own, within the simpleness of the four."[31] Above and under are no longer placed statically in front of each other; rather, they mirror each other in an 'in-finite' circular relation. "In-finite means that the ends and the sides, the regions of the relation, do not stand by themselves cut-off and one-sidedly; rather, freed of onesidedness and finitude, they belong *in*-finitely to one another in the relation which "thoroughly" holds them together from its center. The center, so called because it centers, that is, mediates, is neither earth nor heaven, God nor man. The in-finity that is to be thought here is abysmally different from that which is merely without end, which, because of its uniformity, allows no growth."[32] Yet none of the four stays and goes one-sidedly by itself. In this sense, none is finite. None is without the others. They hold themselves to each other, they are what they are from the in-finite relation; they are this whole relation itself. Consequently, earth and heaven and their connection belong in the richer relation of the four.[33]

With the in-finite movement of the fourfold this figure gets a specific form. But I do not understand this as Heidegger's eschatology, since this notion is too strongly connected with classical theology. In my view, it is better to understand it as a counterparadigm with regard to ontotheology and the doctrine of two worlds, which we saw explicitly in the chapter on the death of god. But it is also a counterparadigm to the notion of the technical "enframing" (*Gestell*). There is no longer a division between this life and the other world. The fourfold is that situation in which being is understood as historic event and man as Dasein. In this situation the gods are also seen from the perspective of being as historic event. "For even the god still stands under destiny. The god is one of the voices of destiny."[34] What is coming is not a god as an isolated element. "But what comes is not the god by himself alone. What comes is the whole in-finite relation in which, along with god and mankind, earth and heaven belong."[35] Is it still possible that this god comes especially now that technical-industrial domination has already covered the entire earth? The earth and heaven of Hölderlin's poem have vanished. The in-finite relation of earth and heaven, man and god, seems to have been destroyed. Or has it never yet appeared within our history as this in-finite relation, purely joined together by the gathering of the voices of destiny, never yet become present, never yet been founded as a whole?[36] The appearing of the infinite relation as a unified whole remains denied to us. This is why we are hardly able to hear the "voices of fate" from their unity.[37] Heidegger does not say that it is impossible for the god of the fourfold to come, but that we hardly hear the voices of fate. And it is not the god to come but the fourfold as a whole that has to arrive.

This whole is thought as a coming kairological moment. It is not to be understood as the coming of Christ, but as a coming of a world in which mortals, the godlike, heaven, and earth are connected as fourfold. If this kairological moment is to be compared with what was mentioned in the early Heidegger as the coming of Christ, then the coming of Christ has to be understood as the arrival of the fourfold. "We only half-think what is historical in history, that is, we do not think it at all, if we calculate history and its magnitude in terms of the length of duration of what has been, rather than awaiting that which is coming and futural in what has first been as the commencement."[38] This coming is not the arrival of something that has never been before; it is the coming of something that is concealed in the beginning. This double structure of presence and absence enfeebles the idea of hope, because the idea of hope presupposes an absence that has to be filled.

Sometimes it seems that the divine has a special position. It seems as if the godhead ducks out of the notion of the fourfold, exempting itself from destiny by being the element that rules it. This is suggested, for example, in the *Der Spiegel* interview, "Only a God Can Save Us," and where Heidegger says that "the divinities are the beckoning messengers of the godhead. Out of the holy sway of the godhead, the god appears in his presence or withdraws into his concealment."[39] Here the divinities, the godhead, and god are spoken of without any explanation of their relation in the fourfold. Yet a certain order is discernable. The godhead seems to be the first by its holy sway. Its beckoning messengers are the divinities, and the god who appears and withdraws, appears only out of the holy sway of the godhead. It seems as though the godhead steps out of the whole of the fourfold, and is not to be found in it, but in the holy. The holy does not inhere in the fourfold, nor in the divinities or the mortals. Rather, the holy is the whole relation that comes as the fourfold.[40] Only in the lightning of the holy can the whole be present. "The holy primordially decides in advance concerning men and gods, whether they are, and who they are, and how they are, and when they are."[41] The holy is not holy because it is divine; rather, the divine is divine because it is holy in its way.[42] The divine is holy because it participates in the holy, which is the whole of the fourfold.

From the perspective of the notion of the fourfold that arises from the later interpretations of Hölderlin, it is strictly speaking inconsequent to say that the god is nearer to the holy. What is said here is that the god is placed under the holy and that the relation to the holy can only be held in common with man.[43] With this, the mortals as well as the divinities are placed in the fourfold under the holy. The holy indicates the whole of this relation.

The fourfold is not a counterparadigm like an eschatological moment that has to be fulfilled in the future; it is a counterparadigm of ontotheology in the way of a concealed beginning that still has to come. The fourfold is already; as beginning it precedes everything that is present.[44] Yet it is not a priori and formal. Just as Dasein is what it already was, so is the fourfold already in its concealment. Dasein is a counterparadigm for the *animal rationale*. The fourfold becomes the counterparadigm for ontotheology. Even though the four of the fourfold belong together, this togetherness nevertheless has to be guarded. To guard and to save is a task for the mortals.[45] This saving is a counterparadigm to the mastering and subjugating of the earth. In this way, human beings dwell like a guard and save the earth. Human beings as mortals dwell, insofar as they are capable of death as death, so as to lead their nature into the use and practice of this capacity so that there may be a good death. This does not mean making death the goal.[46] In short, the notion of the fourfold is the counterparadigm to the make-able world (*Macherei*).

The counterparadigm of the fourfold no longer implies a subjectivistic relation to the divine and the holy. Human beings dwell insofar as they await the divinities as divinities. In hope, they hold up to the divinities what is unhoped for. They wait for intimations of their coming and do not mistake the signs of their absence. They do not make their gods for themselves and do not worship idols. In misfortune they wait for the salvation that has been withdrawn.[47] Under certain conditions one can speak here of theology, but only in a non-ontotheological way. It is impossible to define the holy here ontotheologically, since all ontotheology presupposes a *theos,* or god, as an entity. It does this so certainly that wherever ontotheology arises, the god has already fled.[48] In the next chapter, I will show in what sense one can speak of theology here.

THE POETICAL DWELLING OF MAN

As was shown in the former chapter, the poet has a place in the fourfold.[49] It is within the fourfold that the poet can name the holy. When a human being lives in the fourfold, he dwells on earth poetically.[50] What is meant by "... poetically man dwells ..."? This question presents another aspect of Heidegger's concept of man.[51] The words are taken from a late poem by Hölderlin. It is a statement on the essence of man, not of something accidental. When Hölderlin speaks of dwelling, he is focused on the basic character of human existence. What is more, he sees the poetic by way of its relation to this dwelling, thus understood in its essence. The poetical is not a decoration of, or ancillary to, the dwelling. It is poetry itself that first causes dwelling to be dwelling; it is poetry that lets us dwell. We are now faced with a double task: first, we are to conceive of man's being through the nature of dwelling; second, we are to think of the nature of poetry as a letting dwell, as a kind of building.

Man gets his insight into the nature of dwelling and poetry from language, if language is respected in its own nature. This does not mean that man is master over language, as it is usually understood. Language is not the means of expression: "For strictly, it is language that speaks."[52] Man can only speak when he responds to language by listening to it presenting itself. It is this ability to listen to the appeal of language that determines the poet and his poetry. A poet is more poetic when he listens to the words spoken in language. Obeying and submitting, the poet tunes into the words to come, which makes him prepared for the unforeseen. Only then can he be far away from merely propositional statements that are considered as correct or incorrect.[53]

To explain the broader context of Hölderlin's words, Heidegger listens to the whole phrase from which the words are taken: "Full of merit, yet poetically, man dwells on this earth."[54] The words 'Full of merit' are not to be explained as referring to man's cultivating, caring and building, activities that can be meritorious, because building and erecting are not meritorious activities in themselves. The farmer's growing things, the erecting of edifices and works are already a consequence of the nature of dwelling. This dwelling significantly takes place on this earth. Merit for building can never fill in the nature of dwelling, because the essence of dwelling is dwelling on this earth. Dwelling indicates the way the mortals are related to the earth.

This does not mean that poetry, as something fantastic and nonrealistic should be 'down-to-earth.' Poetry does not fly above and scale the earth in order to escape from it and hover over it. "Poetry is what first brings man onto the earth, making him belong to it, and thus brings him into dwelling."[55] Heidegger, however, is concerned with rethinking what Hölderlin says in poetic words. He wants to know to what extent and when man dwells poetically.

Heidegger finishes the quotation of Hölderlin's poem with the words: "Is there a measure on earth? There is none."[56] Man is a being looking for a measure, and this is done in poetry. Taking measure is what is poetic in dwelling. But what is the meaning of measuring here? Obviously we must not subsume it under just any idea of measuring and measure. What takes place in poetry lies at the basis of the very essence of all measuring; to write poetry is to take measure, and through this measure, the breadth of man's being unfolds. Man's measure is ultimately given with his death. Man is mortal, and he dies so long as he stays on this earth, so long as he dwells. His dwelling, however, rests in the poetic.

In listening for the words to come, the poet waits for the unknown. "For Hölderlin, God, being who he is, is unknown and it is precisely as this Unknown One that he is the measure for the poet."[57] But the unknown can be a measure only insofar as it manifests itself. God's manifesting himself is mysterious: he is manifest like the sky. Thus, the unknown god appears as the unknown in the sky's manifestness. This appearance is the measure against which man measures himself. The godhead is the measure with which man measures out his dwelling, his stay on the earth beneath the sky. Insofar as man takes the measure of his dwelling in this way he is able to be commensurately with his nature. "Man's dwelling depends on an upward-looking measure-taking of the dimension, in which the sky belongs just as much as the earth."[58]

As long as man is, his being must now and again be measured out. This requires a measure, which involves at once the entire dimension. To discern this measure, to gauge it as the measure, and to accept it as the measure is for the poet to make poetry. Poetry is this measure-taking for the dwelling of man. The distinctive measure taking of poetry has nothing to do with numbers; measure and numbers are mostly understood as quantitative. The measure of the poetry, is not something tangible; it is the experience of something issuing forth from what has been dealt out.[59]

Poetically dwelling on this earth means that the sky is the measure, not the earth. But the sky is an appearance of the unknown god. Dwelling occurs only when poetry happens and is present, and indeed in a way whose nature we now have some idea of, as taking a measure for all measuring. There is no a priori, given measure from which man knows how to dwell. Dwelling as poetry is itself an authentic measure-taking since in poetry, man finds his most fundamental way of dwelling. It happens through listening for the words to come, to present themselves to the mind. In this poetical dwelling, man is looking for a measure, a point of orientation that cannot be found on earth. The measure for poetical dwelling is found in the unknown coming. This means that there is no a priori measure on earth. In poetical dwelling, the poet awaits and reaches out for that which comes. This makes dwelling something historical.

In Heidegger's comment on Hölderlin's poem "Remembrance," it becomes clear that poetical dwelling is connected with man as a poet who lives on earth. The poet dwells near to the origin so that he shows what draws near in the coming of the holy. The poet can discern this coming. The poet is open for divinity and humanity; his gaze shows the opening in which gods first come as guests and men can build a housing for the true, where they may be able to secure themselves. "The poet shows this open realm of the between in which he himself must dwell in such a manner that his saying, showing, follows the origin, and thus is that which endures, securing itself in the holy which is to come into words . . . A dwelling which founds in this way is the original dwelling of the sons of the earth, who at the same time are the children of heaven. Those are the poets."[60] Writing poetry means fastening the origin. With this, the holy is understood as making fast and grounding everything in the groundless abyss, in the sight of an unknown god.[61]

It is important to understand that the holy is not related to religion as confession. Faith has no place in thinking.[62] The thinker is focused on being, the poet on the holy. In this way, Heidegger's "theology" is not an offshoot of his thinking of being, but of his interpretation of the poet. It has no origin in faith.[63] The suggestion that Heidegger's philosophy has itself theological or religious elements must be understood in the right way. Notions like "listening," "obedience," "piety," and "holy" are not introduced to give place to a Christian God; they are introduced only in the thinking of being. In this way, one could say that Heidegger makes these theological or religious notions an element of his thinking. These notions are no longer positioned in a domain that is different from philosophy — not, at least, if this philosophy is understood as the thinking of being.

A Phenomenology of the Holy?

The phenomenon of the holy is, according to Heidegger, embedded in the question of being and understood in relation to being. This refers also to the relation between the poet and the thinker. To sharpen this kinship between both, I ask: Is it possible to see in Heidegger's thought a phenomenology of the holy, and to find this meaningful for a philosophy of religion? Heidegger himself does not present an extensive phenomenology of the holy.[64] He never intended to present a phenomenology of the holy as such; nevertheless, one can ask whether it is possible to find some indications of it in his writings.

We must ask what specific problems appear in a phenomenology of the holy. And is a phenomenology of the religious possible in this context? Can one connect here the holy and the religious? Is there a specific religious domain for the thinker of being? What exactly does Heidegger say, and what are the implications of his position?

In a phenomenological approach, there is an interaction between act and intended object. This also applies for religious intentionality, as we have seen in Heidegger's analysis of early Christianity. This act is the condition of the possibility that something appears. This means that, with regard to the phenomenology of religion, one can only intend the religious reality in acts of worship. Consequently, this means that someone who wants to say something about god or the gods but does not know what worship means (and so does not know what the holy is), does not know what he is speaking about. The god that is displayed upon neutralizing the act of worship, the god of proofs or sociological analyses, is not the reality of the divine that is connected to worship. We see this in Heidegger's understanding of the onto-theological god to whom one can neither pray, sacrifice, or fall to his knees in awe, nor to whom one can play music or dance.[65] For such are the human activities that constitute worship.

However, the inverse is also important. It is impossible to worship something religiously that is not an element of religiosity. To indicate this reality one needs to use the word 'holy'. Phenomenological thinkers have always resisted this explanatory way of thinking. One can find evidence of this throughout Heidegger's body of work. The phenomenological approach to worship is never an explanation of the religious act, for instance from a psychological or a sociological perspective. It is about the quality of the act and its object. Just as one will never understand what color is merely by the description of chemical processes, one loses the quality of the religious act if one thinks one can describe the object and the act from a psychological or sociological perspective, or from an ontotheological perspective.

Moreover, the religious act as an act of faith is, especially in Christianity, understood as *gratia infusa*. The hoping and the loving one, if he believes, loves and hopes in a faithful way and knows that he has to thank for his faith the one in whom he believes, whom he loves and in whom he hopes. Heidegger formulated this very clearly in "Phenomenology and Theology." But in Heidegger this knowledge about the call of being, thanking, etc., is not a specific religious act. It is a characteristic of thinking as such. "To the most thought-provoking, we devote our thinking of what is to-be-thought. But this devoted thought is not something that we ourselves produce and bring along, to repay gift with gift. When we think what is most thought-provoking, we then give thought to what this most thought-provoking, matter itself gives us to think about."[66] He finds that what phenomenology of religion regards as characteristic of religious thinking, feeling, and acting, is a general characteristic of human thinking, especially the thinking of being. Transcendence is a transcendence that comes to meet human beings.

However, a phenomenology of religiosity is about showing and thematizing the specificity of the religious. Therefore, it is impossible to reduce the religious act to other acts with other objects. This applies also for art, science, politics, and music, etc. But is it possible to unite all these different regions? Is the identity of the thinker also at stake? What defines the unity of the 'I' of the thinker from the perspective of all these different approaches? Is it not necessary to reduce them all to the truth of one domain? Is it not possible to surpass this in an encompassing unity of a general ontology? This is the question that, in phenomenology and especially in Heidegger, generates a special interest for a general ontology. In *Being and Time,* Heidegger attempts to clarify the connectedness of phenomenology and general ontology.

Human activity originates in existence. The way in which we learn that something exists is founded in wonder, in a listening and obedient questioning attitude. What calls up those kinds of questions? The human being is claimed by being, and he tries to answer this claim. That which gives us the word to answer the claim of being, is the holy: "The Holy bestows the word, and itself comes into this word. This word is the primal event of the holy."[67] Only when the holy bestows the word is man able to answer the call of being and to verbalize this claim. In this region we remain seekers; we do not become skeptics, but remain ones who ask. This is why, for Heidegger, questioning is the piety of thinking: a philosophical piety formulated in religious words.[68]

How is this significant for a phenomenology of religion? Heidegger presupposes, together with the history of philosophy, that our thinking and speaking is in correspondence with what shows itself. This appears in Heidegger's interpretation of the word phenomenology. Phenomenology is necessary to uncover the hidden. What is hidden in an egregious sense is the being of entities.[69] In "On the Essence of Truth," we read that the hiding shows itself as the most hidden, that "concealing appears of what is first of all concealed."[70] Concealing appears as the hidden.

General phenomenology as ontology and the specific phenomenology of religion are structurally connected in Heidegger. The showing of itself appears in the way of concealing itself. What appears in religion is always in the way of concealing. In the case of god, gods and the holy, it is clear that they are concealed. For Heidegger, ontology is hermeneutics, and hermeneutics is hermeneutics of facticity. However, it is not possible to say that religion is therefore an unfolding of human life. Nor is it correct to say that Heidegger has anthropologized religion from the beginning.[71] Religion does not explicate human life; it explicates the message of god or the gods. That is why the question of the anthropological reduction is so important. It is something that always lurks, both for religion as well as for ontology. It is obvious that Heidegger sees a relation between religion and the question of being when he explicates the meaning of the word hermeneutics.[72] The expression "hermeneutic" derives from the Greek verb *hermeneuein*. It is connected with the Greek divine messenger Hermes, who brings the message of destiny. It is an exposition that brings tidings to someone who can listen to a message, an interpretation of what has been said earlier by the poets, who are messengers of the gods. Because Heidegger's thinking as a whole wants to avoid reductionism with its phenomenological approach, it can therefore function as a model or framework for a philosophical understanding of religion. The poet can name the holy only when it is not understood from an ontotheological perspective.

The holy has been an object of the philosophy of religion for a long time, as Rudolf Otto shows. Everything can become an object of worship of the holy: stones, trees, houses, persons, etc. Historical experience teaches us that specific objects do not characterize the religious world. Religiosity is constituted instead by the way the object appears. The religious object has to show itself as holy for the subject. Therefore the question arises, how is something experienced as holy? How should something be in order to show itself as holy?

For Heidegger the question would be: is an experience of the holy possible within the technical world? Entities can be dominated and made. It seems that in such a world, the experience of something that shows itself as holy is impossible because such an experience is only given to acts of worship. Religious experience as an experience of the holy has become an object of anthropological study. Its proper place is on a reservation: a private, protected area away from the cultural mainstream. Within this context, the word holy can indicate a holy tree, a holy day; it indicates the dimension from which this behavior or manner springs: one approaches and treats something as holy because it is holy. But, in Heidegger's view, the holy is not only a domain of certain protected subjects and objects. Heidegger adds a third dimension to this: the dimension that makes it possible to thematize the divine.[73] Thus, the holy indicates a condition of the possibility for the appearing of the divine. The interwovenness of contrasts, the foundation of life and the power to kill, the beginning life and its limits, all belong to the phenomenon of the holy. Therefore the holy hesitation belongs to the manner in which the holy is experienced. The rise of opposite reactions of feeling, such as fascination and fright, belongs to the presence of the holy. We see this in Heidegger in the metaphor of twilight.

Against this background religions always have a history because their external circumstances change. Whether their message will be received by new generations depends on this. They have a history because the way the holy appears (*hierophany*) is connected with the openness of the situation in which it appears. It is historical because it is taken up in the destiny and historicity of being. The systematic place of speaking about the holy in the phenomenology of religion is, on the one hand, the definition of the essence of that reality, which makes it possible that the religious can appear and, on the other hand, the showing of the historical development in which the history of religions is rooted. Religions are historic. This cannot be understood ontotheologically, because in that case the religious manifestations would be a manifestation of a highest entity that transcends every entity.

Religion and religions have to be understood from the perspective of Heidegger's understanding of being. The understanding of being is a claim, a demand from being: "Such thinking responds to the claim of being."[74] Thinking, in its saying, merely brings the unspoken word of being to language. The phrase "bring to language" employed here is now to be taken quite literally. Being comes, clearing itself, to language. It is perpetually under way to language.[75] The poetic is an answer in which being comes to language. In this the holy plays a role. "The holy bestows the word, and itself comes into this word. This word is the primal event of the holy."[76] It is important here for the thinker to listen to the poet. This relation, which is founded in the greeting of the holy and in the answering greeting of the human being, is not constituted by human acts nor commanded by human works, but is celebrated in a festival. "The festival is the primal event of the greeting, in which the holy greets, and in the greeting appears."[77] The holy celebration, the religious festival, is a remembrance of the meeting with the origin. And as remembrance, the origin is present in the celebration.

Religions are not assaulted by external powers; they free the dynamics of history. Therefore, the connection between hierophany and the history of religions is a central theme in the phenomenology of religion. In this way Heidegger connects the holy and the historicity of being. Only he who sees the twilight, sees the holy in its tension of decision. Therefore, it is important not to regard historic changes as variations of the eternal same. In that case phenomenology would misunderstand historicity as onto-theology does.

It is important in understanding religions and their gods to understand them historically. The era of the forgottenness of being is also the era of the absence of god from the perspective of the history of religions. As long as there is a forgottenness of being in ontotheology, there is also a forgottenness of the historicality of the gods. Ontotheology is an understanding of being in which god and the gods do not have a place. Such a time needs the poets to get an entrance to the holy. Therefore Heidegger can say: "Rather, by providing anew the essence of poetry, Hölderlin first determines a new time. It is the time of the gods who have fled and of the god who is coming."[78] The poets keep open the nearness of the distant god. Thus for the poet's care there is only one possibility: without fear of appearing godless, he must remain near to the god's absence, and wait long enough in this prepared nearness to the absence till out of the nearness to the absent god there is granted an originative word to name the high one. Therefore it is important to stay near to the nearness of questioning and seeking. In this the future remains open and is expected as the future of being. Thinking is tuned to such an arrival of the future. Therefore, human beings are not swept away by a greeting of the holy as an ahistoric being, but are called to account in their historic essence.

From the perspective of the question of being, all religious phenomena remain tied to the correspondence of claim and answer. With this the human being is called into the provisionality of his answer and called to account in his historicality. In other words, man is called into the unfinished course of his history. The implication of historic existence is that he is in danger of getting onto a wrong track and of being mistaken. The godhead then can lose its holiness and highness, its secret and its distance, by the way it is represented.

The holy has to appear as that in which human being can find its wholeness. The holy is not god, the godhead, the highest entity of metaphysics, or the divine grace. It is an ontological phenomenon that is expressed in the thinking of being. The holy is a phenomenon that is easily neglected and overseen by the fideistic man. Nevertheless, the religious man would not understand himself without the holy. The holy as an ontological phenomenon can be the entrance to the religious. Without understanding the holy we behave with respect to it like tourists and visitors of a museum. Further, where the understanding of the holy has withdrawn, the central place of the sacrifice is once again attributed to arbitrariness and barbarian cruelty. However, understanding it from the perspective of the historicality of being is an entrance to understanding religion and the religions, god and the gods.

TEN

A Longing for the Coming of the Gods

T heology, as part of metaphysics, is not something that has a place in the historicity of the event of being, according to Heidegger. Instead, Heidegger develops the paradigm of the fourfold. The counterparadigm of the fourfold no longer implies a subjectivistic or ontotheological relation to the divine and the holy. However, this does not mean that mortals or human beings, as understood from within the fourfold, have no relation with the gods. In a certain sense, they have a theology when they sing and praise the gods. We can see this especially in what Heidegger says about the poet, particularly Hölderlin. The poet waits for the word that comes, and with it, the poet can name the gods. Heidegger describes this situation as follows: "Mortals dwell in that they await the divinities as divinities. In hope they hold up to the divinities what is unhoped for. They wait for intimations of their coming and do not mistake the signs of their absence. They do not make their gods for themselves and do not worship idols. In the very depth of misfortune they wait for the weal that has been withdrawn."[1]

So we have two moments: first, the waiting of the poet, and next, the naming of the gods. I want to begin by examining the notions of awaiting and hope that are mentioned above. In order to do this, I show how the notion of desire can be traced through Heidegger's works, because the notion of hope and awaiting presuppose Dasein as a desiring human being. After having traced the notion of desire, I will examine the way this structure is present in the praising and naming of the gods.

LONGING FOR THE POSSIBLE

At first sight, the notion of desire would appear to be completely absent in Heidegger's thought. The question is whether there are traces in Heidegger's work that permit us to assign the issue of desire a place in his thinking about human existence.[2]

It is obvious that the "early" Heidegger interprets the notion of desire in Plato from the perspective of care. "The soul is desire (Care is the Being of Dasein!)"[3] This means that care also takes up the notion of desire. Indeed, it is not accidental that Heidegger refers to Plato's description of the soul's relation to being as an *eporeksis:* "This passage shows that we do not attain the primary kind of being-determinations through the bodily organs, but the soul itself, purely of itself, according to its intrinsic freedom, relates to being. Of itself the soul extends itself out of itself toward being, i.e., it is the soul, purely by itself, that, in the manner of *eporeksis* (stretching out towards), understands anything like being."[4] Thus the soul understands something like being in the manner of desire. Thus, although the notion of desire is almost absent in Heidegger's work, nevertheless we can find traces of it, as in the example cited above.

In *The Basic Problems of Phenomenology,*[5] a lecture course from 1927, Heidegger refers to the notion of *oreksis* in his interpretation of the feeling of respect in Kant.[6] To understand this idea, Heidegger points out that antique philosophy already understood practical behavior as *oreksis*. *Oreksis* in Aristotles' view is characterized by *diōoksis* and *phugē*.[7] *Diōoksis* concerns pursuit and following, striving for, and aspiring to something. *Phugē* means receding, fleeing from, stepping back, withdrawing, and moving away from. Kant's description of respect comes, in Heidegger's view, from these characteristics of *oreksis*. Kant uses 'inclination' for *diōoksis* and 'fear' for *phugē*. He says that the feeling of respect is analogous with both phenomena, inclination and fear, moving towards and moving away.

In his book on Kant, Heidegger writes that no further steps are necessary to see that the basic structure of respect shows the original figure of transcendental imagination.[8] Heidegger points out that transcendental imagination projects the total range of possibilities in which Dasein exists. In Heidegger's view, this imaginative capacity is not an independent given, but exists in the execution of original temporality and is as such productive.[9] Respect refers to that which, as transcendental imagination, projects possibilities and that to which Dasein subjects itself. Heidegger sees a striving in the motion of forming a project and in the subjection to the formed project. As a striving, the imagination projects images as prototypes (pre-images). In the light of these prototypes, entities can appear.

Heidegger understands the whole of possibilities projected by Dasein as 'something' towards which Dasein transcends in understanding. He talks about this whole as the 'world.' In Dasein's transcending activity, this world surpasses every real entity.[10] It is the project that precedes the entity so that the entity always appears in the light of some project. This pre-project (initial project) is effected by Dasein's transcending activity. In "On the Essence of Ground," Heidegger states: "Dasein transcends means: in the essence of its being it is worldforming, 'forming' (*bildend*) in the multiple sense that it lets world occur, and through the world gives itself an original view (form (*Bild*)) that is not explicitly grasped, yet functions precisely as a paradigmatic form (*Vorbild*) for all manifest beings, among which each respective Dasein itself belongs."[11] The whole of the essentially possible is presented to being as a pre-image, or an example, as it were.

Heidegger also uses the characterization of *oreksis* in his discussion of Kant's understanding of the will. "This surpassing that occurs 'for the sake of' does so only in a 'will' (*Willen*) that as such projects itself upon possibilities of itself."[12] This will provides Dasein with its 'for-the-sake-of,' its motive, by projecting the whole of possibilities as pre-images to which Dasein subjects itself. With the stipulation of transcendence as willing, this willing is not a normal 'act' like proposing, judging, enjoying oneself, etc. Heidegger states that will, as a surpassing and in surpassing, shapes that which wills it. This means that the whole of possibilities is projected in the willing of Dasein, in which the projection of possibilities is the motive for this will. At the same time, Dasein subjects itself to the possibilities, pre-projected by this will, which serve as the light in which the entities can appear, including Dasein itself as entity. This is a double movement similar to that indicated by Heidegger in the structure of *oreksis*.

Nevertheless, the will is not seen here as an ontic or subjective act. Heidegger, in all periods of his thinking, wrestles with a conception of being in an elusive middle voice, that is to say, being as an event that is neither objective nor subjective, neither passive nor active in the strict sense, neither independent of human existence nor grounded in the human. So far, we have seen in what direction Heidegger explores the movement of transcendence.

In Heidegger, Dasein is interpreted as motion. This means that it never finds itself at rest. That toward which the willing of Dasein is directed, namely the whole of possibilities as the

for-the-sake-of-which, never becomes a permanent, fixed possession. For Heidegger the structure of Dasein as 'being concerned with' is the only issue. This 'being concerned with'
is a 'being related to' the 'why.'[13] In this condition of not having permanent possession of the 'for-the-sake-of-which' and the
'why,' Heidegger stipulates Dasein as a persistent being-as and
being-in-relation to possibility. Projecting toward the possible is
prior to having and appropriating the actual. That is why the
projection of possibilities, by virtue of its being, is always
richer than the possession already appropriated by the projector
(the one projecting).[14]

   This aspect of the primacy of the possible runs through
Heidegger's entire work.[15] The entire analysis of temporality is
written from this insight into the persistence of the possible. It
is not the content of the projects that makes projecting so
important.[16] Heidegger maintains that the richness of Dasein
lies in the projection of possibilities, not in their actualization.
This concept of possibility must be distinguished from the logical concept of possibility and the concept of possibility as accident. Heidegger's characterization of the possible is such that
the realized entity is insufficient by comparison. For him, the
possible is always higher than the actual.

A DESIRE OF THE MORTALS

   The 'original will' that projects of preceding possibilities is
focused on the persistence of the possible because of its priority over the actual. This insistence on the primacy of the possible distinguishes Heidegger from the Western metaphysical
tradition, which is primarily concerned with the actual and the
possession of the real. In the phenomena of seeing, observation, *theoria,* idea, and intuition, Heidegger sees no possibility
of thematizing transcendence adequately. Instead, he sees the
possibility for thematizing transcendence in the will.

In this context, we need to introduce an aspect of striving that is understood by Heidegger from the preference for seeing in the Western constellation of knowledge. This preference for seeing brings about an ontology of its own. Heidegger starts his analysis of seeing and the ontology belonging to it with the beginning of Aristotle's *Metaphysics*: '*pantes anthropoi tou oidonai orogontai phusoi.*' He translates this as, "The care for seeing is essential to man's Being."[17] The result of this beginning is that Western philosophy holds to the thesis that primordial and genuine truth lies in pure observation. Heidegger calls this phenomenon 'curiosity.' The notion of curiosity in *Being and Time* is a further elaboration of curiosity in Augustine, as we saw in chapter two. In *Being and Time* it is interpreted from the perspective of the possible and the actual. This curiosity seeks novelty only in order to leap from it anew to another novelty. Curiosity wants to make things present: it cannot endure — it cannot stand — absence. Heidegger connects curiosity to 'falling,' which means that it is related to presence. It cannot leave a possibility alone without trying to actualize it.[18] In this knowledge constellation, things are thus made present for the sake of having them present.

When Dasein is essentially regarded as a projector of possibilities, as is also the case in Heidegger's analysis of the possibility of death, then, Dasein which is essentially being-possible, in the 'curiosity-structure,' in which all that counts is the actual, must always, without delay, look for and actualize new things.[19] In this ontology of the present-at-hand, which is connected to the primacy of seeing, the structure of the possible in Dasein is neglected, though it certainly remains active. This is not so because of the greed (*Neu-gier*) that lies in curiosity, but simply because in Dasein's 'curiosity-constellation' there is an ontology operative that leads Dasein and entities to be absorbed (submerged) in an actualization by neglecting the possibility-character of Dasein. Therefore, it is not the endless immensity of what has not yet been seen, by which curiosity or eagerness for knowledge is instituted as a basic structure of the Western knowledge-constellation; rather, it is the structure of temporalization of the present in which being-possible has lost its primacy. Against this background, only the present is important for Western knowledge. The curiosity-constellation neglects the primordial temporalization of Dasein. Because Dasein is standing in the temporalization, and because the overall view, the panorama, to which it is striving in this constellation suspends things, it has to look for new entities to actualize again and again. Insofar as theoretical observation stands in this tradition, human beings in this ontology will keep searching, without delay, always eager to move on to that which is not yet seen.

Heidegger conceives of seeing as an offshoot of projecting understanding. He thereby points out the primacy of seeing in Western philosophy and its knowledge-structure. This corresponds to an ontology of the present-at-hand.[20] Insofar as Western thinking is characterized as 'intuition,' and intuition is regarded as the goal of desire, desire is also directed towards the actualization and imagining (visualizing) of entities. A desire that is structured in this way is not able to hold on to the possible as such. Therefore, such a desire cannot abide with entities and is pushed into an unceasing further searching. The actualization of the possible makes desire a restless moving, in which the possible has always fled toward a present made ever anew. The dominance of seeing has structured desire to be focused on a present-at-hand goal. Desire has become the desire to see the real, supremely represented in the human desire directed towards the "*visio beatifica Dei,*" the ultimate realization of desire in the ontotheology of metaphysics and anthropology. However, in Heidegger's stipulation of transcending as willing, the persistence of the possible is the main goal.

Just as Heidegger subsumes an 'original will' in understanding, he likewise designates thinking in particular as that which is desired. When he asks: "What is called thinking?" he points to the following meanings of 'calling': "instruct, demand, allow to reach, get on the way, convey, provide with a way."[21] The call implies an anticipatory reaching out for something that is reached by our call, through our calling. It means: what desires that we think? What calls us to thinking? Authentic thinking comes about as a desire that is aware of its being desired. That which in the early Heidegger appears from the retention of the possible as the projection towards possibility, is not, in the later Heidegger, treated as a project initiated by Dasein, but as something to which it is called and empowered from being and made possible from there. It returns in the notion of desire, seen as something that does not want a well-defined object, but is rather attuned to that which will come. This attunement to that which will come and into the possible comes about when we desire 'being' authentically. We desire 'being' authentically when this 'being' itself desires us. From this desire, man can think authentically. Against this background Heidegger can affirm that "Who the deepest has thought, loves what is most alive."[22] Heidegger intends a kinship between thinking and loving. This love makes authentic thinking possible.

Precisely because this desire is a mutual event, Dasein is not always capable of it. On the one hand, we desire authentic thinking too little; on the other, that which we desire authentically has to desire us first. This temporalization does not lead to a present-at-hand-actuality that is to be made present and to be made into a possession. As a source of possibility it is not absorbed in the actual, but withdraws from human control and always remains higher than all actual things. Thus being as 'the quiet force of the possible' is always retreating from actual reality. Nevertheless, it is not completely absent for human beings; as a source of possibility it attracts us. Accordingly, Heidegger outlines the relation of Dasein to being in terms of attracting and withdrawing. Being attracts Dasein precisely because it is withdrawing: what attracts us has already expressed its coming. Heidegger writes, "What withdraws from us, draws us along by its very withdrawal, whether or not we become aware of it immediately, or at all. Once we are drawn into the withdrawal, we are drawing toward what draws, attracts us by its withdrawal. And once we, being so attracted, are drawing toward what draws us, our essential nature already bears the stamp of 'drawing toward.' As we are drawing toward what withdraws, we ourselves are pointers pointing toward it. We are who we are by pointing in that direction — not like an incidental adjunct, but as follows: this 'drawing toward' is in itself an essential and therefore constant pointing toward what withdraws. To say 'drawing toward' is to say 'pointing toward what withdraws.'"[23] What is withdrawing here, in Heidegger's perspective, is the coming and the possible, in that it can never be presented as real. It remains, as persistent coming and as persistent possibility, unovertakeable. In this way, it is preserved for man in its own nature.

The ontology of the present-at-hand is inclined to change the possible into the actual without holding on to the possible. The essential structure of desire, on the other hand, is such that the possible remains standing above the actual. With this explanation of desire Heidegger positions himself in opposition to Western ontology, which, he claims, is ever concerned with dominance of the actual over the possible. From Greek philosophy on, being-in-act, the actual, has been placed above the possible. Heidegger, in contrast, wants to define the actual from the measure of the possible.

THE POETIC THEOLOGIA

As I mentioned before, openness for the possible is something that is present throughout Heidegger's work. In his interpretation of Hölderlin's poem, "Remembrance," Heidegger mentions this priority of the possible and sees a special task here for the poet.[24] The possible in Heidegger is situated in the dream; it is the 'place' where the possible appears. Instead of reducing the dream to something unreal, and measuring the dream by actual reality, Heidegger suggests the opposite: the dream determines the perspective in which the actual appears. The unreal is given priority over the actual. Heidegger confirms the place of the possible in the dream when he writes that the dream brings about the not-yet-appropriated fullness of the possible.[25] "Their nonreality must be thought according to the meaning of the poet. However the nonreal is for that reason never a mere nullity because it can be either the no-longer actual or the not-yet-real . . . This dream shows itself to the poet because the dream, as this divinely terrible nonreality, is the poem of the holy that cannot be composed in advance . . . The becoming-real of the possible, as the becoming-ideal of the actual, in the realm of the free imagination of poetry, has the essential character of a dream . . . But the poets can compose that which is in advance of their poem only if they utter that which precedes everything real: what is coming . . . The holy which is foretold poetically merely opens the time for an appearing of the gods, and points into the location of the dwelling of historical man upon this earth."[26] In Heidegger's view it is the poet who can wait and long for the coming; he is, based on this longing, capable of naming the holy. In naming the holy, the poet creates a holy place to prepare an abode for gods and mortals.

The traditional interpretation of poetic thinking and speaking, from the perspective of the power of imagination, stems from representational thinking.[27] Heidegger says that language speaks in order to reject representing thinking. To understand this, one has to listen to the speaking of language; this means that the poet does not have to look for the image but has to listen to what is already said. When we understand language in this way, then we do not understand it as founded in something that is no longer language. Language is not an entity that can be founded in another entity, for the being of entity is not an entity itself.[28] If we consider poetic activity as depicting an exemplary image, then this explication is completely tied to representational thinking.[29]

Heidegger places the theological element of thinking in the work of the poet. Heidegger's philosophy thus has its own theology within the thinking of being. How this is connected is the second point I want to work out in this chapter. For this, it is necessary to analyze what Heidegger writes about theology as poetry. This is something especially present in Heidegger's later work and in his interpretations of Hölderlin.

Heidegger not only uses the word theology with regard to poetry, but also with regard to a hermeneutics of faith as we saw in chapter three. The second meaning of theology is the metaphysical meaning, which I discussed in the chapters on the *causa sui*. Theology also has poetic meaning: "*Theologos, theologia* mean at this point the mytho-poetic utterance about the gods, with no reference to any creed or ecclesiastical doctrine."[30] Heidegger's use of the word 'theology' therefore has three meanings: theology as a hermeneutic of faith, theology as ontotheology, and theology as the poetic naming of the gods.

Heidegger understands this concept of *theologia* as a *logos* from and about the gods, a mythical and poetical naming of the gods. In poetry something is named. What is this naming? This naming does not hand out titles, it does not apply terms, it calls into words. Calling brings closer what it calls.[31] Such a calling is an original naming, which calls into presence something out of the hidden. This naming is a glorifying. Glory in Greek is *doxa. Dokeō* means: I show myself, appear, enter into the light. Here the emphasis is on sight and aspect, the regard in which a man stands. To glorify, to attribute regard to and to disclose regard, means in Greek to place in the light and thus endow with permanence, being. Heidegger wants to show that for the Greeks, appearing belonged to being, or more precisely that the essence of being lay partly in appearing. In the other Greek word for glory, *kleos,* the emphasis is on hearing and calling. Thus glory is the fame (call, reputation) in which one stands.[32] For the Greeks, glory was not something additional that one might or might not obtain; rather, it was the mode of the highest being. For the moderns, glory has long been nothing more than celebrity and is as such a highly dubious affair, an acquisition tossed about and distributed by the newspapers and the radio — almost the opposite of being.

Logos as Gathering, Presencing, and Keeping

Heidegger understands theology as the utterance of a logos about the gods. To understand this, it is important to explicate Heidegger's concept of logos more precisely. Generally we tend to define the Greek word *logos* as *ratio:* as thinking about and judging about reality, sometimes even as the calculating of reality. This has developed within onto-theology. But Heidegger wants to point out the original meaning of the word. *Logos* originally means 'word,' 'language'; it is connected with the word *legein. Logos* has nothing to do originally with speaking. *Legeō, legein, legere* is the same as the German word *lesen* (to gather, collect, read): "*Ähren lesen, Holz lesen, die Weinlese, die Auslese*" (to glean, to gather wood, the vintage, the cream of crop); "*ein Buch lesen*" (to read a book) is only a variant of *lesen* in the strict sense, which is to put one thing with another, to bring together, in short, to gather. It is a selective gathering in which the pros and cons are weighed.[33]

Logos is that which executes the activity of gathering. Thus *logos* does not mean in the first place something like word or doctrine; rather it indicates that gathering takes place.[34] *Logos* means the gathering which is in itself permanently dominant.

Gathering is never a mere driving-together and heaping up, nor is it the neutralizing of differences. The *logos* as gathering activity does not let what it holds in its power dissolve into an empty freedom from opposition, but by uniting the opposites maintains the full sharpness of their tension.[35] It is an activity in which the extremes are gathered and yet stay apart.[36] The activity of *logos* is more subjectively indicated by what we mean by the word synthesis. The *logos* gathers together in such a way that the differences in reality are not equalized; there is meaningfulness and harmony together with the maintaining of the differences. "It is proper to every gathering that the gatherers assemble to coordinate their work to the sheltering, and — gathered together with that end in view — first begin to gather. The gathering (*die Lese*) requires and demands this assembly. This original coordination governs their collective gathering."[37]

The original gathering still can be heard, in a very faded way, in indicating judgment as combination of subject and predicate.[38] So when we hear today the words being and unity we do not immediately think of uniting and gathering from the *logos*. This gathering of the *logos* pervades and is earlier than all judging reasoning, meaning and being convinced. Only within the gathering of the *logos* can man exist in the world as a domain of meaning.

But *logos* is not only a gathering. *Legein* indicates gathering as well as laying, in the sense of bringing to lie. Thus to lay is also at the same time to place one thing beside another, to lay them together. To lay means to gather (*lesen*). The *lesen* better known to us, namely the reading of something written, remains but one sort of gathering, namely as letting-lie-together-before.[39] For the Greeks, saying is especially lying-before and lying open. Saying is thought in a Greek way as bringing out, as showing something as it appears. What is laid-before becomes visible in lying-before, and is therefore presented. The *logos* presents the presence of what is laid-before and shows it in its presence. Saying means, when thought in a Greek manner, "to bring to light," "to let something appear in its look," "to show the way in which it regards us," which is why a saying clarifies things for us.[40] Speaking does not mean the transmission of what someone has in his head. For a long time, speaking has been considered as the expression of inner thoughts or as the giving of meaning to external entities. Saying and speaking are now determined as what let things and entities lie-before; they are gathered into entities by speaking and saying and so become visible in their presence. This is what Heidegger calls the being of entities: in the logos the being of entities is shown and made visible.[41] Heidegger himself expresses this concisely when he interprets a poetical experience of Stefan George: "Where word breaks off no thing may be." Heidegger connects *logos* and being: "The word is *logos*. It speaks simultaneously as the name for Being and for Saying."[42]

Thus in order to work out the concept of *theologia* as it appears in the later Heidegger, I must explicate the concept of *logos*. From the preceding it should be clear that this word indicates the presencing of entities. *Theologia* can then be understood as the language of the gods. What happens in language? The *logos* in language is that which evokes the presence of something around and before man. Especially insofar as man is, and is related or is able to relate to entities, man needs word and language. "In the Greek definition of the essence of human being, *legein* and *logos* mean the relation on the basis of which what is present gathers itself for the first time as such around and for human beings. And only because human beings are insofar as they relate to beings as beings, unconcealing and concealing them, can they and must they have the "word," i.e., speak of the being of beings."[43] Human being is a being that has *logos*. Language shows, lets appear, and lets hear. The wording lets appear. In language an unconcealing happens — in Greek, *a-letheia.* "Because the logos lets lie before us what lies before us as such, it discloses what is present in its presencing. But disclosure is aletheia."[44] The unconcealing draws the present out of the hidden and the dark.

In speaking out the word, the gathering happens in such a way that the present is presented in its presence. Saying and being, word and thing belong together in an inscrutable way because this relation is prior to the searching thinker. To indicate this, Heidegger uses the aforementioned poem by Stefan George: "Where word breaks off no thing may be."[45] Things are only in word and in language: "In the word, in language, things first come to be and are."[46] The searching thinker only investigates questions that are already there, because the relation between word and thing is earlier than scientific research. Therefore, speaking as Heidegger sees it cannot be considered as something in which meaning is given afterwards, or another mark given to an already familiar or present thing.

When mortals speak language, the world and things get their place and difference.[47] The saving in the word happens simultaneously with the opening of being: language happens and there is putting-into-words. Language starts where man awakes in being. Language as a mortal, poetical work is a proto-poetizing. However, it is not only the bringing into light of entities, but also the safekeeping of the entities in the light. What awakens arrives in the word, is gathered in it, and is kept saved in it. Especially with regard to the safekeeping function that language has, there is the possibility of dissoluteness, recklessness and loss. Language comes not only as an unconcealing poem, but also as chatter and talk. Instead of the opening of the being of entities, it functions as the concealing of them. Instead of selecting, gathering, and synthesis, there is dispersion into unfittingness.[48]

THE A PRIORI CHARACTER OF THE LOGOS, LISTENING AND BEING ATTUNED

When we employ the usual understanding of language, namely that it is man as subject who speaks, then we assume that it is man who is the maker and master of language. This is why man can see language as a mere means of expression of his inner thoughts.[49] Heidegger problematizes this position, and asserts that on the contrary it is language that dominates man.[50] "Language speaks" is a well-known and amazing statement by Heidegger.[51] In the tradition of language in which man is situated and in the environment in which he grows up, language has always already spoken. It is earlier and prior, a priori.

Man would be indifferent to the priority of language were he not attuned to what is said there.[52] The addressed is itself that which lies before us as gathered. In order to really understand what is said, man must concentrate. Hearing is actually this gathering of oneself which composes itself on hearing the pronouncement and its claim. What is heard comes to presence in hearkening.[53] Here it is not so much a matter for research, but rather of paying thoughtful attention to simple things; man can hear wrongly insofar as he does not catch what is essential. It is not about a physiological process in the ears; we hear, not the ear.[54] When we listen, we are in the room of the spoken word. In this room, the words spoken in the addressed open up. Heidegger says that words are a wellspring, not terms, and thus are not like buckets and kegs from which we scoop a content that is there. Words are wellsprings that are found and dug up in the telling, wellsprings that must be found and dug up again and again, that easily cave in, but that at times also well up when least expected. If we do not go to the spring again and again, the buckets and kegs stay empty, or their content gets stale.[55] This going to the spring means listening to what is said in the tradition and its words.

Listening to the words is something different from a mere activity or investigation of words, as happens in philology. Listening to the words in this way is difficult because we tend to direct ourselves to the commonplace. When we hear something, we are immediately directed to that about which something is said, the thing or the object that is there, without hearing what is said in the word itself.

In words very akin to Heidegger, W. F. Otto describes this process.[56] Otto points out that the poets, however they appear to us as the ones who create and make, experience themselves as those who receive and listen to something that precedes them. What the poet says was addressed to him; he has listened to the mythical word. Myth is a truth that is not examined. It immediately interferes with life and determines man as a whole.[57] The language of the poet is originally not a means to make something understandable. The language of the poet is the open figure of truth in the myth. This truth is not found by an investigating subject or by the research of man; this truth reveals out of itself. Furthermore, the god reveals itself and is revealed by its word.[58] Because the unconcealment of the word precedes all speaking, it is said that in poetry man himself does not speak, but the godhead. It is the muse who sings, whereas the poet only echoes the tune. Therefore it is not man who finds the words to speak out reality and the divine character of reality. The muses indicate the divine wonder that being speaks out from itself. Heidegger expresses this as follows: "The writing of poetry is the fundamental naming of the gods. But the poetic word only acquires its power of naming, when the gods themselves bring us to language."[59]

Myth, poetry, and music are experienced as being executed without reason. They let truth appear from themselves. Because they happen by and from themselves, their disclosing is attributed to the gods; only when man has received from the gods is he able to speak.

Nietzsche also pointed out the importance of music, rhythm, and myth. Poetry to him means the rhythmicising of language.[60] The rhythmic prayer is more understandable and better heard by the gods. Rhythm is a compulsion; it provokes assent and surrender in which the whole soul is involved. Earlier than philosophy, music has the power to cleanse the soul. According to Nietzsche, there is a kinship between myth and music. This is the reason why he speaks of the myth-building spirit of music.[61]

The myth, the original word that is said because of itself, is related to the rhythm of music insofar as it evokes assent and surrender for its own sake. Therefore, the word was spoken originally with rhythmic song. Rhythm and music are not placed in the service of something else; they are said and done because of themselves. That is why the work of the poets and singers is claimed by the gods. Wherever people sing, the human singer is primarily someone who listens; he attunes his voice before he starts to sing. In this phenomenon a knowledge appears that something precedes human speaking, something that has to be received and to be heard, before a mouth can say it for an ear.[62]

Therefore language appears as something without any object because it existed at first musically and as singing. This is because singing is self-sufficient and does not want to produce something. The music-making man has to speak sounds without an object and without being heard by others. What applies for music in general has to apply for language as well, because language is a kind of music, even though it is deprived of every melody.

Spoken, everyday language does not flow anymore; it is stopped by a tendency toward the static. The melodic sentence is divided into independent words. Once the word has become a specific sound combination and has become a calcified element, then it appears as a thing and an object. Where there is no language, there are no things, and there is no thinking of things. Only in language are things present as things. In myth and music, conversely, the being of the world appears not like an object or representation. Myth is the primal phenomenon of human thinking and knowing. Gods and myth are not invented; they appear and show themselves because of themselves. They appear with singing speaking, which does not stem from a self-willed power, but is experienced as something to receive and to hear. Rhythm and music that originally belong to language show the basic tone of human speaking.

Modern theories of language generally locate the origin of language in the need for communication. With that one passes easily to other linguistic expressions that do not fit into this category. The idea that language is communication presupposes that there are things in themselves and that these things receive a meaning from language in order to remember them and to inform others. However a thing really exists only in language-thinking. Language does not give meaning to the things, but lets them appear.[63]

Poetic speaking, therefore is not at first a communication of something, but exists, like music, for its own sake. The poet and the original speaker speak because language itself speaks through them. Therefore, every verbal expression can be considered as a living organism and as a melodic whole. This originary speaking is prior to communication, just as singing is primarily a singing for its own sake and is not in service to something else.

Both rhythm and speaking provoke assent from their own accord.[64] Poetic speaking is attuned to what is said in the *logos* in order to correspond to it. This correspondence is a listening, by which an original speaking is made possible, as the musician listens to the possibilities that are handed down to him and that come over him in making music. The musician is in the first place in service to the music, not the opposite. Similarly, language is not at the service of human beings but the reverse; human beings are at the service of language.[65] So the human being only speaks when he corresponds to language, and when he listens to what language says and addresses to him. This corresponding to language occurs, according to Heidegger, in the saying and speaking that is pronounced in poetry. The more poetic a poet is, the more his saying is at the service of listening. But by the same token his speaking is distanced from statements about which one can only say that they are true or false.[66]

Therefore, speaking itself is already a listening, which means listening to the language we speak. Listening to and hearing language is prior to every other kind of listening. To be able to listen to a language, the human being has to be attuned to what is said in language. We not only speak a language, we speak by way of it. We can do so solely because we have always already listened to the language.[67]

When we turn back now to Heidegger's concept of *theologia,* then we have to conclude that it has all the characteristics of *logos.* In this case, it is a *logos* of the gods. To speak the *logos* of the gods, the poet has to be attuned and to listen to what is said in the *theologia.* With this reference to the *logos* of *theo*-logia, we try to clarify its original meaning. At first, we saw that the *logos* of *theo-logia* presents the appearing of the gods and gathers them in their presence. In theological speaking, the gods come into their being; they are unconcealed and saved in it. Secondly, it is not the subjective will of the human being that calls up the gods like a kind of magic or by an independent action of the human being. In speaking the language, the gods appear. When the human being listens to the language, he or she listens to what language says about the gods. After this rather formal characterization of *theo-logia* as the poetic presentation of the being of the gods, we need to ask who, according to Heidegger, is a *theo-logos.* Who names and praises the gods and offers them presence?

THE POET AS A THEOLOGOS, LONGING FOR THE RIGHT WORD

The concept of poetry has a broader meaning than verbal poetry, from Heidegger's perspective. All art, as the letting happen of the advent of the truth of what is, is essentially poetry.[68] Linguistic poetry is only one way of the lightning project of truth, of poetry in the broader sense. Nevertheless, poetry in its narrow sense as a work of language has a special place in the domain of art. Language alone brings what is, as something that is, into the open for the first time. Where there is no language, there is also no openness of what is. Language first brings entities to word and to appearance. Only this naming nominates beings to their being from out of their being. Such saying is a projecting of the clearing, in which the entities that come into the open are first announced. Entities like water, stone, and god are called forward by naming them. That which is gathered and laid down in the name, by means of such laying, comes to light and comes to lie before us.[69] The poet knows about the relation between word and thing. The relation between word and thing is not such that the word is situated on one side and the thing on the other side: "The word itself is the relation which in each instance retains the thing within itself in such a manner that it "is" a thing."[70] The verb "is" has here a transitive meaning. The word is involved with the thing in such a way that it "is" the thing that it means, as it presents the thing. Hölderlin especially writes poetry from the perspective of the relation between word and thing. Through Hölderlin, Heidegger invites language itself to speak, in contrast to considering language as a sign of something else, as has been the case since Aristotle.

Because man has to listen to what is said in language, not-hearing and being mute are also possible. Therefore language also gives the possibility of the loss of being.[71] Because the openness of entities has to be saved in language by listening to what language says to us, the openness of entities can get lost. That the poet has to listen to language means also that he has to stay in its track; he has to listen to what is announced, he has to be attuned in the right way, but therefore he is also exposed to error.

The requirement of listening is at first present in conversation. A conversation has as a condition that one be able to listen and be attuned to the word that comes from elsewhere. This means being directed towards what is said and announced in a word. Being able to talk and being able to hear are co-originary. Only then is a conversation possible.[72]

Against this background, Heidegger brings up the appearing and the arrival of the gods in Hölderlin's words. Gods are not constituted out of or with the help of language. The words in which they are named are not experienced as an act of man, but as an answer to a call of the gods. But the gods can come to expression only if they themselves address us and place us under their claim. A word that names the gods is always an answer to such a claim.[73] Myth and *logos,* which are prior, and to which the poet listens and is attuned, call for naming and praising the gods.

The naming of the gods is executed as poetry. What is expressed by the poet attuned to the word of the *logos,* is experienced as a gift, a gift of the gods. Now it becomes clear that poetry is a founding: a naming of being and of the essence of all things — not just any saying, but that whereby everything first steps into the open, which we then discuss and talk about in everyday language. "Poetry is the sustaining ground of history, and therefore not just an appearance of culture."[74] Poetry proper is never merely a higher mode of everyday language; everyday language is a forgotten and therefore used-up poem, from which there hardly resounds a call any longer.[75] In language as poetry, human existence gets a ground, a ground that is experienced as a bestowed gift. It is a gift that is handed down to man and that comes over to and is sent to him. Wherever language provokes mortals to listen, it is the gods who call and commit to the right word. The poet experiences himself as compelled by the claim of the gods, and as called up to answer this claim and to be attuned to it. The listening of the poet to this claim is both a reception and a hearing. The poet is placed in an intermediate area between the man to whom the poet offers a ground and the gods who call the poet up to say the right word and to express it.

Heidegger's explication of the naming of the gods is connected with his question of the destiny of being. Being is not an all-controlling agency; that would not correspond to the idea that it happens as an overcoming destiny. Nor should the naming of the gods be considered as a level still to be transgressed in order to reach a complete understanding of being. It lies in the destiny of being whether the right word will appear to name the gods. Only when words are addressed to the gods and offered to name them, only then will the poet be able, by listening to the language, to find the right names.

Consequently the poet is only able to say a poem when the poet is able to put into words the coming and what is offered to the poet as a gift. Then the poet's word is the foretelling word. In that sense the poet breaks new ground and is prophetic, not in the Judeo-Christian sense of the word but from the essence of poetical foretelling.[76] In going out and reaching out to the unknown and strange, and in the listening to the coming, the shining light of the holy rises. The holy has to be caught by the poet in the right word. Only then can the appearing show itself as it complies with and saves itself in the right word. The poet listens to what is said in the offered address; expecting and listening (not planning or calculating) he realizes the real saying.

The poet would not be able to say the right word and be open to it if he or she were not attuned to the gods. That the poet is attuned means that the poet is in a mood. Man is already in a mood before being able to think and to choose. Because human beings are fundamentally in an attuned mood, they can be moved: the things that happen can play on them. So humans can be played upon and can assent to the words that call them, entering into the play and the mood in such a way that he is attuned to the play. The poet is the one who hopes for and longs for the corresponding attunement. Thus attuned to the words of the gods and directed towards an expression of them, he is in a mood of desire with respect to the gods, looking for a corresponding word in answer to this desire.

The poet is the one who, in his outreaching search, is on the way. The longing of the poet realizes itself as being on the way. Heidegger expresses this as follows: "To a thinking so inclined that reaches out sufficiently, the way is that by which we reach — which lets us reach what reaches out for us by touching us, by being our concern. The way is such, it lets us reach what concerns and summons us."[77] The longing for the corresponding attunement in the claim of the gods is realized as being on a way. There we long for what concerns us. What we long for reaches out to us, claims us and demands us, and lets us come in that place where we are at home. The way is what brings us to our concern. It is the poet's concern to be attuned to the claim of the gods and to find his home there.

The saying and naming of the gods is not an arbitrary process. The gods are only put into words when there is an authentic speaking. In poetry the authentic conversation takes place. The poet names the gods when the words are handed down, and the gods are confirmed in their being. When the poet speaks the essential word, then by this naming the entity is named as what it is; thus is the entity known as an entity, and the god as god.

The poetic naming of the gods is more than just pointing out the holy. The holy is the place where gods can appear; when this place fails, gods cannot be named. Naming the gods means letting them appear. "To name poetically means to let the high one himself appear in words."[78] The poets have to prepare a shelter for the gods in the holy. In explicating the holy, the poet is called to name it as holy by listening to it. "The poet's word is the pure calling of what those poets who are always divining wait and long for. The poetic naming says what the called itself, from its essence, compels the poet to say."[79] The gods need the word of the poet in order to appear, so that they can be as gods in their appearing. As we have already mentioned, Heidegger sees Hölderlin here as the poet *par excellence*. "Hölderlin's poem gathers *poesis* under a holy compulsion: naming the present gods, gathering them into a saying which is needed by the heavenly ones and ordained by them. Since Hölderlin spoke it, it speaks in our language, whether or not it is heard."[80]

Heidegger describes theology as the poetical naming of the gods; but to make this possible, the holy names fail. It is a time in which the gods are fled. The poetical desire looks for a right attunement to say the right word, but the right word is difficult to find.

Humans are never able to speak on their own, because as mortals they are always the addressed one. This is the important difference between Heidegger and all philosophy of intentionality and will. He rejects a transcendental and constituting conscience, as is there for Husserl and the German Idealists, because of the given that man is always already addressed. According to Hegel, language is neutralized into a pure, immaterial concept; in Heidegger, on the other hand, entities would not appear in their being without language. Not only language and temporality are earlier than human being, but also the longing attuning that looks for its right attunement and destiny. Humans are always already situated in language and addressed by language; they are always in a certain mood when they look for attuning.

Especially because Hölderlin experiences language as something given and as already spoken before him, he is able to be
open for the word that is able to name the high. Longing for
attuning and being in the language in which one looks for the
right word are inseparably connected in Heidegger. The word
is not constituted by acts of conscience, but it falls to man's lot
and comes over to him. From the desire for attunement, the
word that does not come over can be experienced as failing.
Whether that word will come or not disposes the destiny of
being.

The gods who appear get respect and esteem upon their
appearance. The Greek word *doxa* means regard, the regard in
which someone is held and the standing he has. Therefore *doxa*
means splendour and praise. Praising means showing that
someone is held in high regard; it means giving regard to
someone. The poet says the praise and in praising, the gods
become what they are. The praise turns into a song and
announces someone's name; the song celebrates the advent of
the gods. Song is not the opposite of a discourse, but rather the
most intimate kinship with it.[81] Singing in particular cannot be
understood on the basis of human intentionality. Singing and
praising are motivated and called by the overcoming.

The poet knows that he or she is called by the gods in order
to praise their name. This implies that the poet at first has to
be a listener to know how to receive and to get the word like
a gift and an endowment. *Theologia* in this respect is at first
instance a praising that springs from the knowledge that he is
called, without a connection to a dogma or a church. This poetical *theologia* does not ask for the first cause or the totality of
entities. This *theologia* is the song that is sung by the poet
when he is called up by the gods for whom he longs and
whom he praises when he finds the right word.

Heidegger not only writes about theology as poetry, but also
as has been shown in the earlier chapters, about theology as a

hermeneutics of faith and as metaphysics. Theology is *logos* of and about the gods. This means that much of what Heidegger says about *logos* also applies to the *logos* of *theo-logia*. I have pointed out that the *logos* gathers together, presents, and saves entities. It has the character of something that happens prior to that in which human being is situated, and on which he or she depends to present reality. This implies that the human being has to be attuned to this prior being to be able to put something into words. One tunes into language and into what is addressed in language by listening to the words. Language is originally for its own sake. This means that it is not its aim to communicate thoughts out of someone's mind, but just as music is a goal in itself, so too is language. And just as music provokes assent and attunement, so does language; human beings responds to this demand for attunement by listening to it.

The *theologia* is a poem insofar as it longs for the right attunement with which to name the gods, so that what has to be said about the gods can be put into words in a right way. This presupposes in the poet a desire for the right word to be passed down. As far as this wording succeeds, right names will be handed down; but it can also happen that the names of the gods stay away because the space does not fit. When the attunement succeeds, then the poet is the one who finds the right word in praising and presents the gods in it.

Conclusion

*I*n deriving philosophical insights related to religion from Heidegger's work, I am myself working in the sphere of a philosophy of religion. However, one tendency of a philosophical understanding of religion is to make religion itself into a part of philosophy. This is particularly apparent where all forms of religion get absorbed into an ontotheological philosophy. In such cases religion is understood from a concept of god, which is, as a philosophical idea, the beginning and the end of philosophical rationality. Hegel's philosophy is perhaps the clearest example of this tendency. When ontotheology is taken up in this way, however, certain possibilities for understanding religion are foreclosed. Heidegger, too, speaks as a philosopher about god and the gods. Yet what is the status of his speaking? It is not, as I showed, a description of religion. Nor is it a poetry of religion or a metaphorization of religion. Nevertheless, it is a philosopher that proclaims: "Only a god can save us!"

It is my view that Heidegger's thinking on religion occupies a place between the forms of poetic and philosophical speaking. To understand the poetic aspect of Heidegger's language, one must turn to his interpretations of Hölderlin. And to give his philosophical expression its proper context one must refer his "Letter on 'Humanism,'" wherein religion is located in the neighborhood of the thinking of being. Yet religion maintains its own tension with regard to both sides: if we grasp religion completely from a (ontotheological) philosophical point of view we tend to neutralize it; on the other hand, if we conceive it simply as poetic expression, we tend to be philosophically indifferent to it. These tensions urge us to take up the question of Heidegger's position. It turns out that Heidegger's thinking is, in the end, a theological thinking of a specific kind. It is a theology in which he avoids every connection to an ontotheological concept of god. His thinking of being tends toward a poetic theology of naming the gods, which is both a praising and an invocation of them. According to Heidegger the thinking of being is a movement no longer in accordance with the thinking of faith or of divinity (*Gottheit*). Each of these is heterogeneous in relation to the other. The experience of the thinking of being manifests itself rather as a topological disposition, that is, as an indication of a place characterized by availability. It is a topological disposition for waiting for, though not expecting, the reception of being, as a place for the happening of being. Therefore Heidegger states that he does not know god; he can only describe god's absence. His atheistic philosophy (in the sense of an ontotheology) maintains an openness toward the possible reception of religious gods.

In the first chapter I looked for the roots of Heidegger's thought. I discussed the way in which Heidegger first attempted to conceptualise an ahistorical Catholicism, and how he later came to the historicity of religion through Friedrich Schleiermacher. Moreover, I discussed Heidegger's rejection of a theoretical approach to religion while nevertheless endeavouring to preserve the piety of philosophy — including the piety of the philosophy of religion. I called this the pre-historical Heidegger. The term pre-historical refers to the timeless character of scholastic and neoscholastic Catholicism, the intellectual environment out of which Heidegger emerged, and the period prior to his adoption of a historical perspective. Heidegger's persistent questioning towards the ontological and temporal as the 'earlier' and 'prior' is to be understood as piety (*Frömmigkeit*).

Heidegger's language with respect to the phenomenon of religion, however, finds itself mired in a pious atheism: where the object of phenomenology is concerned, he attempts to remain radically atheistic, yet on the other hand, he seeks to be pious and devoted when it comes to this same object. The pious person here is the devoted ascetic who understands his object as it demands to be understood, i.e., from out of its factical character. Only when philosophy has become fundamentally atheistic can it decisively choose life in its very facticity, and thereby make this an object for itself. Because philosophy is concerned with the facticity of life, the philosophy of religion must be understood from that same perspective. For Heidegger the very idea of philosophy of religion (especially if it makes no reference to the facticity of the human being) is pure nonsense. Such nonsense evolves out of a lack of piety, i.e., a merely theoretical approach that fails to attune itself to the facticity of life. Thus, Heidegger's endeavours to destruct ontotheology have their roots in his experience that theistic conceptuality is not appropriate to understand the facticity of life.

Through his explication of the notion of historicity, Heidegger was able to find a path leading out of the closed religious world in which he was raised. This rupture takes place with his encounter with Schleiermacher. Through Schleiermacher's thinking, Heidegger was offered the possibility of isolating the religious as the absolute; and in so doing, he was led away from both theology and theoretical philosophy in his thinking. Out of this engagement, Heidegger was able to conclude that the religious is none other than the historical, due to the fact that the radicality of a personal position is only to be uncovered within history.

Heidegger directed his philosophy toward the facticity of human being, which will be developed as the historicality of Dasein. The attempt to think facticity was his guiding interest during this early period, and it is from the standpoint of this interest that his approach to religion must be understood. As the winter semester approached in 1920, Heidegger announced his upcoming lecture course, entitled "Introduction to the Phenomenology of Religion." The question here, however, is how Heidegger, as a philosopher, understood this conception within the horizon of his philosophy of the facticity of life. The first answer that must be given is that he formalized the fundamental Christian experience of life. He does not choose a position with respect to the particular content of this experience, but rather limits himself to investigating the sustaining conditions of the possibility of this experience. Heidegger asks whether the kairological moment can be preserved within the history of the actualization of life and the unpredictability of the *eschaton*. It could potentially be understood as a possibility that we ourselves have or something that is under our control, so that the future that withdraws from us becomes part of our own planning. Yet, if it were to be understood thus, the specific character of the *kairos* would then be lost in a totalizing form of calculation. The future would then be conceived in the end as a horizon of consciousness out of which experiences evolve in a certain order. For Heidegger, the *kairos* has more to do with the conditions of the possibility of facticity, which it goes on to determine in a formal way. For what takes place with regard to the content in the moment of the *kairos* can itself never be deduced. If it is possible to encounter properly the suddenness of the *kairos*, it must be accomplished without the aid of deduction.

Heidegger's interpretation of Augustine is an elucidation of this. This interpretation points out that the quest for true life tends to ossify as a result of humanity's devotion to sensual preoccupations. We can see here that Heidegger's quest for truth is no longer devoted to the highest being, as was the case during his early studies in Freiburg. Rather, the historicity of religion has to be understood out of its own situation and out of the presuppositions contained within it. It should not be taken up from a philosophical framework, as if from the standpoint of some highest being, precisely because the philosophical idea of a highest being hinders our understanding of facticity, and with this, religion as an expression of facticity. In Heidegger's thinking, the orientation toward the highest is instead reformulated as a historical orientation. We see this change actualized in Heidegger's earliest writings, and it involves as well the philosophical paradigm with which he approaches religion. What we are left with, then, is a religion that is an expression of historicity.

Heidegger looks for a better philosophy, but not for a new faith that would be a faith without philosophy. In his complete devotion to philosophy, he distances himself from religious philosophical approaches, in which a religious a priori is supposed. He distances himself as well from a conciliation of faith and reason that would reduce faith to reason, as in the philosophies of Kant and Hegel. Nor does he assume the harmony of faith and reason at which Thomistic philosophy aims. Instead, the metaphysical paradigm is put into perspective, where one can see how it opposes the understanding of facticity. Heidegger seeks an atheistic philosophy, or at the very least, a philosophy without an a priori conception of god.

Heidegger understands faith as the natural enemy of philosophy. Faith appears as a possibility of existence, yet one which implies death for the possibility of the existence of philosophy. In chapter 3 we saw the fundamental opposition of two possibilities of existence, which cannot be realized by one person in one and the same moment. Yet neither excludes a factical and existentiell taking seriously of the other. This does not mean

that the scientists in each respective field must behave like enemies. The existentiell opposition between faith, on the one
hand, and philosophical self-understanding, on the other, must
be effective in its scientific design and in its explications. And
this must be done in such a way that each meets the other with
mutual respect. This can be undertaken more easily where one
sees more sharply the different points of departure. Christian
philosophy, therefore, is in Heidegger's view a "square circle."

Nevertheless, one can thoughtfully question and work
through the world of Christian experience, the world of faith.
This would be, then, theology. Heidegger sees in theology's
dependence on philosophy a lack of greatness in theology
itself. Only ages that really no longer believe in the true greatness of the task of theology arrive at the pernicious opinion
that, through a supposed refurbishment with the help of philosophy, a theology can be gained or even replaced, and can be
made more palatable to the need of the age. Philosophy for
originally Christian faith is foolishness.

If Heidegger rejects the philosophical paradigm with which
religion usually is approached, the question arises from where
stems the ontotheological philosophical approach of religion?
This ontotheological approach is at work even today. Heidegger
sees its origin in Aristotle's philosophy. For Heidegger, Greek
philosophy reaches its climax in Aristotle and is decisive for
the whole of Western philosophy. Therefore, Aristotle's thinking is a normative point from which the philosophical tradition
can be determined more precisely. The well-thought-out way in
which Aristotle follows the motive of philosophy marks at the
same time the limit of the whole tradition, which becomes visible now as a finite possibility for thinking and as a temporary
answer to the question of being.

Already, in his earliest writings, Heidegger emphasizes the
relation between ontology and theology in Aristotle's first
philosophy. Heidegger sees the metaphysical tradition as an

ontotheological tradition that follows from the tendency for philosophy to forget its original motive. This tendency is due to the fact that understanding has its concrete possibility for being actualized in being free from daily concerns, which places the possibility of theorizing against the background of the facticity of life. *Theorein* is the purest movement which life has available to it. Because of this, it is something "god-like." But for Aristotle the idea of the divine did not arise in the explication of something objective which was made accessible in a basic religious experience; the *theion* is rather the expression for the highest being-character which arises in the ontological radicalization of the idea of being.

Being is understood from a normative perspective, from the perspective of the highest way of being. Connected with this is the highest way of moving, which is pure thinking. This also determines the way Christianity speaks about the highest being of God. The question whether there is ontology without a theology for Heidegger is, however, no longer a question within the domain of philosophy and metaphysics. Rather, it is within what he calls the domain of 'thinking.' The motive of philosophy, strictly speaking, has disappeared from philosophy, but it has been preserved in the thinking of being. This domain of thinking is, in a sense, a counterparadigm to philosophy in which the question of being is not answered with an entity that represents the highest way of being, the whole of being and the cause of being. The "without why" is the counterparadigm of metaphysics with which Heidegger presents an atheological ontology.

Heidegger's criticism with regard to the metaphysical concept of god is especially directed toward the concept of god as cause. In the wake of Aristotle, being is understood as *actualitas*. The highest representation of *actualitas* is an entity, which as a determining characteristic has this *actualitas* in the purest way. This means that it is *actus purus*. Being in the first and the purest way is proper to god. Such a metaphysics does not transcend the level of entities, because it does not understand the difference between being and entity (ontological difference). On one hand, it speaks about being as a characteristic of entities and is only understood as this characteristic (*actualitas* as determination of the dominant understanding of an entity). On the other hand, it sets as the ground of entities another entity, which possesses the criterion for being an entity in the most perfect way. In a certain sense, god is an exemplary instance of being as *actualitas,* of something that actualizes completely. This idea of actualization is also present in the modern ideal of the self-actualization of the human being.

But Heidegger doesn't understand human beings from the perspective of self-actualization. The quest for meaning is a quest for the whole space in which man can exist. This whole cannot become a fixed property. In the end, we are not that which makes us possible, for it is earlier than and prior to us. Man is understood by Heidegger as an entity that cannot appropriate the whole of his conditions of possibility, because he cannot appropriate his temporality which is always earlier.

The project out of which someone experiences his or her life really anticipates a *temporary* destination or a *provisional* end. This provisional end provides the actual present with meaning and place. The whole from the perspective of which one understands one's life is not something that one can wind up and cause oneself. The future can hold a lot of possibilities, and things can develop in a completely other way than what one ever had expected. The provisional and temporary whole that we constantly anticipate mostly happens to us — it is handed down to us, which means it is not the result of planning and calculation. This temporary meaning generally appears for a living human being unexpectedly and suddenly: it is given to, approaches, or is handed down to one. This is the reason why Heidegger speaks in *Being and Time* about 'destiny' and 'inheritance.' Therefore, meaning as embedded in tradition does not belong to the kind of "things" that one can make, control, found, or bend to one's will. Meaning and sense are beyond the range of a planning and making will; they presuppose a receptive openness toward that which is handed down. It is important for human beings that they learn to be the mortals that they are. For Heidegger this means those to whom being appeals are capable of dying, that is taking on death as death.

The implications of the ontotheological structure of metaphysics, which leads to a subjectification of reality in modern times, are worked out on the basis of Heidegger's interpretation of Nietzsche. Heidegger considers Nietzsche, just like all great thinkers in philosophy since Plato, to be an ontotheological philosopher. Entities are only entities out of the unifying principle of the Will to power according to Nietzsche. Therefore, Nietzsche's metaphysics is, as ontology, at the same time a theology. This metaphysical theology is a specific kind of negative theology, its negativity shown in the pronouncement "God is dead." Nevertheless it remains metaphysics, be the god living or dead.

Where god is dead, he is absent. This is something different from the denial of god in atheism, which remains tributary to onto-theology. The loss of god, however, is not thought within metaphysics, that is, as ontotheology. Heidegger thinks this experience of the absence of god as an experience of the poets. Metaphysics cannot experience the loss of god because it is theologically structured. For the poet, on the other hand, the absence of god is not a lack; it is not an empty space that needs completion. Nor is it necessary to appeal to the god that one is used to. It is about presenting and holding out the absence of god. The poet can live in a domain of de-cision where ontology is not necessarily theologically structured, since in poetry the poet has to seek, but not into the divine. In poetry there is no a priori divine entity. It is the poet's care to face up to the lack of god without fear. With the appearance of godlessness, he must remain near to the god's absence.

In Heidegger's view the ontotheological temple of metaphysics is crumbling. According to Heidegger and Nietzsche, the death of god is a historical event, which means a history (*Geschichte*), a story. It is an event that makes history. The nature of this history can be continued, be it the history of a god or a hero, but it is a history next to other histories. This history is the history of the bereavement of a god. This does not mean that this history itself has a god, for god is also subjected to the destinies of history (*Geschick*). It is a history that makes history. In Heidegger's view, historicity is connected with the historicality of Dasein. This historicality is still there when god is dead, and even when the human being, as *causa sui*, is dead. The death and coming of the gods are expressions of the historicality of Dasein.

The difficult notion of the last god is also an expression of the historicality of Dasein and Being. That the last god is totally other to the Christian God presupposes that this god is not explicable from the perspective of entities, whether the entity be anthropological or ontological. Understanding the divine from a perspective or framework in which god is the fulfillment of a maladjusted human need for certainty goes against the possibility of experiencing the last god. The last god is historizised without a reference or presupposition of 'something' eternal and unchangeable. This points to a 'theology' that is completely historical, because its subject is historical: a passing god. It is therefore not a question of whether this god is pagan or Christian. Heidegger would never call this 'theology,' because all (metaphysical) theology presupposes the *theos*, the god as an entity; and it does this so certainly that everywhere where theology arises, the god already flies. It is not sufficient to say in the era of nihilism that god is dead or that transcendental values pass away; rather, one must learn to think a god's being, as well as its truth, as passing-by. It is no longer the god of metaphysics or the theistic God of Christianity.

The "Letter on 'Humanism'" plays a crucial role with regard to Heidegger's position toward the gods and the holy. Here he asks how the thinking of being makes possible the thinking of the divine. It is no accident that Heidegger rejects the reproach of atheism with regard to his thinking. With the existential determination of the essence of the human being, nothing is decided about the 'existence of God' or his 'non-being' any more than about the possibility or impossibility of gods. He does not speak out about the existence of a god or godhead, but this is because he thinks about the possibility and framework within which something like a god has to be thought.

With regard to the framework of the highest entity and the self-actualized human being, the subjectivistic interpretation of humanity is most radically rejected in Heidegger's notion of the fourfold (*Geviert*). The fourfold indicates the unity of earth and sky, divinities and mortals. The earth is the building bearer, nourishing with its fruits, tending water and rock, plant and animal. The sky is marked by the sun path, the course of the moon, the glitter of the stars, the seasons of the year and the light and dusk of the day. The divinities are the beckoning messengers of the godhead. Out of the hidden sway of the divinities, the god emerges as what he is, which removes him from any comparison with beings that are present. The mortals are the human beings. But human beings are not mortal because of the finitude of life; they are mortals because they can die. To die means to be capable of death as death. And this means to experience death as the shrine of Nothing. As the shrine of Nothing, death harbors within itself the presencing of Being. But this is something of which man as *causa sui* is not capable.

From the perspective of man in the nearness of the fourfold, Heidegger prefers to keep silent with regard to theology insofar as it is dominated by a subjectivistic anthropology. Someone who has experienced theology in his own roots, both the theology of the Christian faith and that of philosophy, would today rather remain silent about god when he is speaking in the realm of thinking. With these words, Heidegger points out that one keeps silent is not only due to a lack of knowledge but to dissociate oneself from ontotheology and its fusion with Christian theology. Whether there is a place here for negative theology is very doubtful, because negative theology remains paradigmatically connected with ontotheology.

After having examined the tension between humanism and subjectivism, it is important to ask which role the holy plays in Heidegger's view of the divine. It seems that there is no direct connection between naming the holy and thinking of being. In the postscript to "What is Metaphysics?" Heidegger writes that thinking, obedient to the voice of being, seeks from being the word through which the truth of being comes to language. The saying of the thinker comes from a long-protected speechlessness and from the careful clarifying of the realm thus cleared. Of like provenance is the naming of the poet. Yet because that which is like is so only as difference allows, and because poetizing and thinking are most purely alike in their care of the word, they are at the same time farthest separated in their essence. The thinker says being. The poet names the holy. This kinship and difference make further examination of the relation between being and the holy more urgent.

Heidegger links the experience of the holy to the experience of being as wholesomeness. Ontotheology is an understanding of being in which god and the gods do not have a place. As long as there is a forgottenness of being in ontotheology, there is also a forgottenness of the historicality of the gods. It is important in understanding religions and their gods to understand them historically. Such a time needs the poets to get an entrance to the holy.

The holy has to appear as that in which human being can find its wholeness. The holy is not god, the godhead, the

highest entity of metaphysics, or the divine grace. It is an ontological phenomenon, expressed in the thinking of being, that
can be the entrance to the religious. Without understanding the
holy, we behave with respect to it like tourists and visitors of
a museum. Therefore an understanding of it from the perspective of the historicality of being is an entrance to understanding religion and the religions, god and the gods.

The last chapter developed the paradigm with which Heidegger approaches the gods as historical. Theology, as part of
metaphysics, is not something that has a place in the historicity of the event of being, according to Heidegger. Counter to
this, Heidegger develops the paradigm of the fourfold. The counterparadigm of the fourfold no longer implies a subjectivistic or
ontotheological relation to the divine and the holy. However,
this does not mean that mortals or human beings, as understood
from within the fourfold, have no relation with the gods. In a
certain sense, they have a theology when they sing and praise
the gods. We can see this especially in what Heidegger says
about the poet, particularly Hölderlin. In Heidegger's view it is
the poet who can wait and long for the coming; he is, based
on this longing, capable of naming the holy. In naming the
holy, the poet creates a holy place to prepare an abode for gods
and mortals. Mortals dwell in that they await the divinities as
divinities. In hope they hold up to the divinities what is unhoped for. They wait for intimations of their coming and do
not mistake the signs of their absence.

Heidegger's interpretation of the poetic word has a theological element in it. He places the theological element of thinking in the poetical work of the poet. Heidegger's philosophy
thus has its own theology within the thinking of being. *Theologos, theologia* mean at this point the mytho-poetic utterance
about the gods.

The saying of the poet is only possible when he listens to
the word. The poet knows that he or she is called by the gods
in order to praise their name. This implies that the poet at first

has to be a listener, to know how to receive and to get the word like a gift and an endowment. *Theologia* in this respect is at first instance a praising that springs from the experience that it is called, without a connection to a dogma or a church. This poetical *theologia* does not ask for the first cause or the totality of entities. This *theologia* is the song that is sung by the poet.

Notes

NOTES TO INTRODUCTION

1. See J. O. Prudhomme, *God and Being: Heidegger's Relation to Theology* (Atlantic Highlands: Humanities Press, 1997).

2. In order to avoid the immediate identification of the word god with the concept of a highest being I lowercase the word god in almost all cases, except where I quote from authors who use uppercase. This means that I lowercase all references to the metaphysical god.

3. Pero Brkic, *Martin Heidegger und die Theologie: Ein thema in dreifacher Fragestellung* (Mainz: Matthias Grünewald, 1994), 39. Rudolf Bultmann remarks on this in a letter: "Das Seminar ist diesmal besonders lehrreich, weil unser neuer Philosoph Heidegger, ein Schüler Husserls, daran teilnimmt. Er kommt aus dem Katholizismus, ist aber ganz Protestant." Quoted in Antje Bultmann Lemke, *Rudolf Bultmanns Werk und Wirkung,* ed. Bernd Jaspert (Darmstadt: Wissenschaftliche Buchgesellschaft, 1984), 202.

4. Martin Heidegger and Elisabeth Blochmann, *Briefwechsel 1918–1969,* ed. Joachim W. Storck (Marbach am Neckar: Dt Schillerges, 1989), 32: "So muß uns der heutige Katholizismus u. all dergleichen, der Protestantismus nicht minder, ein Greuel bleiben."

5. *Martin Heidegger — Karl Jaspers, Briefwechsel 1920–1963,* ed. Walter Biemel and Hans Saner (München: Piper, 1992), 157: "und sonst sind ja auch zwei Pfähle — die Auseinandersetzung mit dem Glauben der Herkunft und das Mißlingen des Rektorats — gerade genug an solchem, was wirklich überwunden sein möchte."

6. Martin Heidegger, "The Word of Nietzsche 'God is Dead,'" in *The Question Concerning Technology and Other Essays,* trans. William Lovitt (New York: Harper & Row, 1977), 90.

7. Martin Heidegger, *The Metaphysical Foundation of Logic,* trans. Michael Heim (Bloomington: Indiana University Press, 1992), 165fn.

8. Martin Heidegger, *Identity and Difference,* trans. Joan Stambaugh (New York: Harper & Row, 1969), 72.

9. Hugo Ott, *Martin Heidegger: Unterwegs zu seiner Biographie* (Frankfurt a.m.: Campus, 1988), 42.

10. Martin Heidegger, *On the Way to Language,* trans. Peter D. Hertz (New York: Harper & Row, 1982), 10.

11. The most extensive study can be found in Anne Marie Gethmann-Siefert, *Das Verhältnis von Philosophie und Theologie im Denken Martin Heideggers* (Freiburg: Karl Alber, 1974). This study, however, had to limit itself to Heidegger's writings published before 1974. See also: John D. Caputo, "Heidegger and Theology," in *The Cambridge Companion to Heidegger,* ed. Charles Guignon (Cambridge: Cambridge University Press, 1993), 270–88 and Richard Schaeffler, "Heidegger und die Theologie," in *Heidegger und die praktische Theologie,* ed. Anne Marie Gethmann-Siefert and Otto Pöggeler (Frankfurt a.m.: Suhrkamp Verlag, 1988), 286–309.

12. See Brkic, 11–27.

NOTES TO CHAPTER ONE

1. Alfred Denker, *Omdat Filosoferen leven is, een archeologie van Martin Heideggers Sein und Zeit* (Best: Damon, 1997), 10.

2. Martin Heidegger, *Reden und andere Zeugnisse eines Lebensweges,* vol. 13 of the *Gesamtausgabe* (Frankfurt a.m.: Vittorio Klostermann, 2000), 3–6. (References to the *Gesamtausgabe* indicated hereafter by GA followed by volume number and page number).

3. GA 16: 11–14.

4. Richard Schaeffler, *Frömmigkeit des Denkens? Martin Heidegger und die katholische Theologie* (Darmstadt: Wissenschaftliche Buchgesellschaft, 1978), 3ff.

5. Martin Heidegger, *Zur Sache des Denkens* (Tübingen: Max Niemeyer Verlag, 1976), 81.

6. *Itinerarium mentis V,* 3, quoted in Schaeffler, *Frömmigkeit des Denkens,* 7: "Wie das Auge, wenn es sich den vielfältigen Unterschieden der Farben zuwendet, das Licht nicht sieht . . ., so bemerkt auch das Auge des Geistes, wenn es sich auf die Seienden im Einzelnen und im Ganzen richtet, das Sein selbst . . . nicht, . . . obgleich nur durch das Sein alles andere ihm begegnet . . . Das Auge unseres Geistes . . . hat den Eindruck, nichts zu sehen . . . ebenso wie der, der das reine Licht sieht, nichts zu sehen meint."

7. Schaeffler, *Frömmigkeit des Denkens,* 3.

8. GA 1:2–3: "so wird begreiflich, daß in seiner Erkenntnistheorie das Realitätsproblem keinen Platz finden konnte."

9. Matthias Jung, *Das Denken des Seins und der Glaube an Gott* (Würzburg: Königshausen & Neumann, 1990), 21.

10. GA 1:15.

11. Ibid., 22.

12. Ibid., 106: "Wird aber trotz dieser wesentlichen Um- und Fortbildung der Urteilslehre das Wesen des Urteils in dem vom Gegenstand geforderten Verhalten des psychischen Subjekts gesehen, dann ist der Psychologismus nicht überwunden."

13. Ibid., 179: "Die Frage nach dem elementaren logische Urteil kann nur so gestellt werden: welches sind die notwendigen und hinreichenden Elemente, die ein Urteil überhaupt allererst möglich machen?"

14. Ibid., 417: "Der Zeitbegriff in der Geschichtswissenschaft": "Welche Struktur muß der Zeitbegriff der Geschichtswissenschaft haben, um als Zeitbegriff dem Ziel dieser Wissenschaft entsprechend in Funktion treten zu können?"

15. Ibid., 179: "Wir wissen, das Urteil der Logik ist Sinn, ein statisches Phänomen, das jenseits jeder Entwicklung und Veränderung steht, das also nicht wird, entsteht, sondern gilt; etwas das allenfalls vom urteilenden Subjekt 'erfaßt' werden kann. Durch dieses Erfassen aber nie alteriert wird."

16. Ibid., 186: "Die wahre Vorarbeit für die Logik und die allein fruchtbringend verwendbare wird nicht von psychologischen Untersuchungen über Entstehung und Zusammensetzung der Vorstellungen geleistet, sondern eindeutige Bestimmungen und Klärungen der Wortbedeutungen."

17. Ibid., 165: "Grundsätzlich ist aber zu bemerken, daß das Wirkliche (worunter hier alles zu verstehen ist, was Gegenstand wird und un der Möglichkeit zur Gegenständlichkeit steht, also auch das 'Unwirkliche') als solches nicht bewiesen, sondern allenfalls nur aufgewiesen werden kann."

18. About the fact that this book, the *Grammaticus Speculativa,* on which Heidegger's research is based, cannot be attributed to Duns Scotus see: Pero Brkic, *Martin Heidegger und die Theologie* (Mainz: Matthias Grünewald Verlag, 1994), 48.

19. GA 1:406.

20. Ibid., 193.

21. Ibid., 198: "Dieses mutige sich ausliefern an den Stoff hält gleichsam das Subjekt in einer Richtung festgebannt, benimmt ihm die innere Möglichkeit und überhaupt den Wunsch zur freien Beweglichkeit. Der Sach-(Objekt)wert dominiert vor dem Ich-(Subjekt)wert."

22. Ibid., 252–53.

23. Ibid., 407–08: *"Der lebendige Geist ist als solcher wesensmäßig historische Geist im weitesten Sinne des Wortes.* Die Wahre Weltanschauung ist weit entfernt von bloßer punktueller Existenz einer vom Leben abgelösten Theorie. Der Geist ist nur begreifen, wenn die ganze Fülle seiner Leistung, d.h. *seine Geschichte,* in sich aufgehoben wird, mit welcher stets wachsenden Fülle in ihrer philosophischen Begriffenheit ein sich fortwährend steigerndes Mittel der lebendigen Begreifung des absoluten Geistes Gottes gegeben wird."

24. This is the way it is summarized in Roderick Stewart, "Signification and Radical Subjectivity in Heidegger's *Habilitationsschrift,*" in *A Companion to Martin Heidegger's Being and Time,* ed. Joseph Kockelmans (Washington, DC: University Press of America, 1986), 14.

25. Manfred Riedel, "Frömmigkeit im Denken," in *Herkunft aber bleibt stets Zukunft, Martin Heidegger und die Gottesfrage,* ed. Paola-Ludovica Coriando (Frankfurt a.M.: Klostermann, 1998), 29.

26. GA 1: 410–11: "Die Philosophie des lebendigen Geistes, der tatvollen Liebe, der verehrenden Gottinnigkeit, deren allgemeinste Richtpunkte nur angedeutet werden konnten, insonderheit eine von ihren Grundtendenzen geleitete Kategorienlehre steht vor der großen Aufgabe einer prinzipiellen Auseinandersetzung mit dem an Fülle wie Tiefe, Erlebnisreichtum und Begriffsbildung gewaltigsten System einer historischen Weltanschauung, als welches es alle vorausgegangenen fundamentalen philosophischen Problemmotive in sich aufgehoben hat, mit Hegel."

27. GA 60:336.

28. Riedel, "Frömmigkeit im Denken," 31.

29. It is not important here to discuss different periods; we are concerned with the gradual change in Heidegger's thinking on religion. Van Buren speaks about three different periods in John van Buren, "Martin Heidegger, Martin Luther," in *Reading Heidegger from the Start, Essays in His Earliest Thought,* ed. Theodore Kisiel and John van Buren (Albany: State University of New York Press, 1994), 159–74.

30. GA 13:113–16.

31. Riedel, "Frömmigkeit im Denken," 24.

32. Ibid., 26.

33. See Thomas Sheehan, "Heidegger's *Introduction to the Phenomenology of Religion, 1920–21*" in *A Companion to Martin Heidegger's Being and Time,* 41 ff.

34. Ibid., 43.

35. C. Ochwadt and E. Tecklenborg, eds., *Das Maß des Verborgenen. Heinrich Ochsner (1891–1970) zum Gedächtnis* (Hannover: Charis-Verlag, 1981), 92.

36. Remainders of this study are published in M. Heidegger, *The Phenomenology of Religious Life*. Translated by Matthias Fritsch and Jennifer Anna Gosetti-Ferencei. (Bloomington: Indiana University Press, 2004), 231–54.

37. Cf. Hugo Ott, *Martin Heidegger: Unterwegs zu seiner Biographie* (Frankfurt a.M.: Campus Verlag, 1988), 106: "Erkenntnistheoretische Einsichten, übergreifend auf die Theorie des geschichtlichen Erkennens haben mir das System des Katholizismus problematisch u. unannehmbar gemacht; nicht aber das Christentum und die Metaphysik, diese allerdings in einem neuen Sinne." See also Thomas Sheehan, "Reading a Life," in *The Cambridge Companion to Heidegger,* ed. Charles Guignon (Cambridge: Cambridge University Press, 1993), 72.

38. Ott, *Martin Heidegger,* 107: "Es ist schwer zu leben als Philosoph — die innere Wahrhaftigkeit sich selbst gegenüber u. mit Bezug auf die, für die man Lehrer sein soll, verlangt Opfer u. Verzichte u. Kämpfe, die dem wissenschaftlichen Handwerker immer fremd bleiben. Ich Glaube, den inneren Beruf zur Philosophie zu haben u. durch seine Erfüllung in Forschung und Lehre für ewige Bestimmungen des inneren Menschen u. nur dafür das in meinen Kräften Stehende zu leisten u. so mein Dasein u. Wirken selbst für Gott zu rechtfertigen."

39. Otto Pöggeler, *Neue Wege mit Heidegger* (Freiburg: Karl Alber, 1992), 22.

40. F.D.E. Schleiermacher, *On Religion: Speeches to its Cultured Despisers,* ed. Richard Crouter (New York: Cambridge University Press, 1996), 51.

41. Ibid., 52.

42. M. Heidegger, *The Phenomenology of Religious Life,* trans. Matthias Fritsch and Jennifer Anna Gosetti-Ferencei (Bloomington: Indiana University Press, 2004), 242.

43. Ibid., 243.

44. Ibid.

45. Ibid.

46. Ibid.

47. Ibid.

48. Ibid., 236–37.

49. Ibid., 236

50. Ibid., 240.

51. Ibid., 241.

52. Ibid., 242–43.

53. Ibid., 244.

54. Ibid., 244.

55. Ibid., 245.

56. Ibid.

57. Ibid., 246.

58. Ibid., 248.

59. Ibid., 252.

60. Ibid., 244.

61. Martin Heidegger, *Phenomenological Interpretations of Aristotle, Initiation into Phenomenological Research,* trans. Richard Rojcewicz (Bloomington: Indiana University Press, 2001), 148.

62. Ibid.

63. Martin Heidegger, *The Fundamental Concepts of Metaphysics, World, Finitude, Solitude,* trans. William McNeill and Nicholas Walker (Bloomington, Indiana University Press, 1995), 2.

64. GA 58:208: "Religiöse Lebenserfahrung erfaßt mich in meinem innersten Selbst, die Erfahrung tritt in die unmittelbare Nähe meines Selbst, ich *bin* sozusagen diese Erfahrung."

65. GA 56/57:207.

66. Martin Luther, *Disputatio Heidelbergae Habita* 1518, vol. 1, *D. Martin Luthers Werke, kritische Gesamausgabe* (Weimar: Böhlau, 1883), 354. Quoted in *The Phenomenology of Religious Life,* 213.

67. Bernd Jaspert, *Sachgemäße Exegese, Die Protokolle aus Rudolf Bultmann Neutestamentlichen Seminaren 1921–1951* (Marburg: Elwert Verlag, 1996), 12, 28–33.

68. Martin Heidegger, *Being and Time,* trans. John Macquarrie and Edward Robinson (San Francisco: Harper & Row, 1962), 30.

69. Martin Heidegger, *"Phänomenologische Interpretationen zu Aristoteles* (1922)," *Dilthey-Jahrbuch* 6 (1989): 250. In English as "Phenomenological Interpretations with Respect to Aristotle," trans. Michael Baur, *Man and World,* 25 (1992): 372. (Now called *Continental Philosophy Review*).

70. *Being and Time,* 499 n. xiii.

71. Riedel, "Frömmigkeit im Denken," 40.

72. Dietrich Papenfuß and Otto Pöggeler, eds., *Zur philosophische Aktualität Heideggers,* vol. 2. (Frankfurt a.M.: Vittorio Klostermann: 1990), 29: "Zu dieser meiner Faktizität gehört — was ich kurz nenne —, daß ich 'christlicher theo*loge*' bin. Darin liegt bestimmte radikale Selbstbekümmerung, bestimmte radikale Wissenschaftlichkeit — *in* der *Faktizität* strenge Gegenständlichkeit; darin liegt das 'geistesgeschichtliche' Bewußtsein, — und ich bin das im Lebenszusammenhang der *Universität.*"

73. "Phenomenological Interpretations with Respect to Aristotle," 367.

74. Ibid., 393n.

75. Martin Heidegger, *Introduction to Metaphysics,* trans. Gregory Fried and Richard Polt (New Haven: Yale University Press, 2000), 8.

76. Martin Heidegger, "The Question Concerning Technology," in *The Question Concerning Technology and Other Essays,* trans. William Lovitt (New York: Harper & Row, 1977), 35.

Notes to Chapter Two

1. Cf. Thomas Sheehan, "Heidegger's *Introduction to the Phenomenology of Religion,* 1920–21" in *A Companion to Martin Heidegger's Being and Time,* ed. Joseph Kockelmans (Washington, DC: University Press of America, 1986), 45 ff.

2. Karl Lehmann, "Christliche Geschichtserfahrung und ontologische Frage beim jungen Heidegger," *Philosophisches Jahrbuch* 74 (1966): 128 ff.

3. Quoted in Sheehan, "Phenomenology of Religion," 59.

4. Otto Pöggeler, *Der Denkweg Martin Heideggers* (Pfullingen: Neske), 36.

5. Lehman, "Christliche," 135. Here it is about structures of historicity, which are placeless with respect to content. (This has made possible Bultmann's interpretation of demythologizing). Whereas Heidegger wants to understand human historicity as facticity, the problem is solved for Bultmann: "die Geschichte ist die Geschichte des Menschen;" their acts arise from the "Intentionen der menschlichen Individuen," and "das Subjekt der Geschichte ist der Mensch." For Heidegger the essence of humankind has still to be explicated in his research. Bultmann's approach abandons Heidegger's real problem from the beginning. See Rulolf Bultmann, *Geschichte und Eschatologie* (Tübingen: Mohr, 1958), 171.

6. Martin Heidegger, *The Phenomenology of Religious Life.* trans. by Matthias Fritsch and Jennifer Anna Gosetti-Ferencei. (Bloomington: Indiana University Press, 2004), 4. This text is a lecture course by Heidegger presented in Freiburg during winter semester 1920/21 and summer semester 1921.

7. Ibid., 11.

8. Ibid., 11.

9. Werner Schüßler, ed., *Religionsphilosophie* (Freiburg: Karl Alber, 2000), 17–18.

10. Heidegger, *The Phenomenology of Religious Life,* 20.

11. Ibid., 22.

12. Ibid., 33.

13. Ibid., 35.

14. Ibid., 38.
15. Ibid., 7.
16. Cf. Theodore Kisiel, "Die formale Anzeige, Die methodische Geheimwaffe des frühen Heidegger," in *Heidegger — neu gelesen,* ed. M. Happel (Würzburg: Königshausen & Neumann, 1997), 30.
17. Heidegger, *The Phenomenology of Religious Life,* 11.
18. Ibid., 43.
19. Heidegger sees a cause of this hidden enactment-sense in religion. GA 58:261: "Der Vollzugssinn ist verdrängt, die Situation verläuft im Bezugssinn. Das findet sich in ästhetischen und religiösen Welten."
20. Sheehan sees in these three concepts of content-sense, relation-sense and enactment-sense a primitive articulation of the later distinction between *das Seiende* (the thematic entity), *Seiendheit* (the beingness of that entity = the Greek *ousia*) and *das Sein selbst* (the event of being itself). See "Heidegger's *Introduction,*" 51.
21. Heidegger, *The Phenomenology of Religious Life,* 43.
22. D.O. Dahlstrom, "Heidegger's Method: Philosophical Concepts as Formal Indications," *The Review of Metaphysics* 47 (1993/94): 782–83.
23. During the winter semester of 1921/22 Heidegger again queries the facticity of human existence. Martin Heidegger, *Phenomenological Interpretations of Aristotle, Initiation into Phenomenological Research,* trans. Richard Rojcewicz (Bloomington: Indiana University Press, 2001).
24. Ibid., 105.
25. Ibid., 25–26.
26. Dahlstrom, "Heidegger's Method," 784.
27. Heidegger, *The Phenomenology of Religious Life,* 184.
28. Ibid., 47.
29. Rudolf Otto, *The Idea of the Holy,* trans. John W. Harvey (London: Oxford University Press, 1958), 6.
30. Ibid., 112 ff.
31. Ibid., 175.
32. Carl-Friedrich Gethmann, "Philosophie als Vollzug und als Begriff. Heideggers Identitätsphilosophie des Lebens in der Vorlesung vom Wintersemester 1921/22 und ihr Verhältnis zu 'Sein und Zeit,'" *Dilthey-Jahrbuch* (1986/87): 44.
33. Matthias Jung, *Das Denken des Seins und der Glaube an Gott* (Würzburg: Könighausen & Neumann), 53.
34. Heidegger later repeats this point in his analysis of Aristotle's *phronesis.* See the "Phenomenological Interpretations with Respect to Aristotle," trans. Michaul Baur, *Man and World* 25 (1992). (Now called *Continental Philosophy Review*). When Heidegger was asked to apply for a job in Marburg or in Göttingen in 1922, the problem was that he had not pub-

lished much. The only publications were his dissertation and his *Habilitationschrift*. To solve this problem, he was asked to write some of his ideas and his plans for the future. This resulted in the "Phänomenologische Interpretationen zu Aristoteles." Those who had to judge this paper reacted in a different way. In Göttingen they were rather critical and skeptical, saying that Heidegger presented only his own ideas and that it was not really research on Aristotle, so he became second on the list. In Marburg the reaction was different: there they were enthusiastic, and they praised Heidegger's new approaches to philosophy. It was Natorp, a professor in Marburg and Neo-Kantian, who gave the paper to Gadamer, who was Heidegger's assistant in Marburg. Unfortunately, this copy was destroyed by an air raid in the Second World War. However, the copy Heidegger sent to Göttingen has been saved in the archives of a student of Nicolai Hartmann. In his estate was the copy that is now published in the *Dilthey Jahrbuch* with an introduction by H.G. Gadamer, and an afterword by Hans Ulrich Lessing. "Phänomenologische Interpretationen zu Aristoteles (Anzeige der hermeneutischen Situation)," *Dilthey Jahrbuch* 6 (1989).

35. Sheehan, "Heidegger's *Introduction*," 314.

36. Heidegger, *The Phenomenology of Religious Life*, 55.

37. Ibid., 89.

38. The first letter is important for an analysis of the early Christian experience of life, because it is the oldest New Testament writing, probably written in Corinth between 50 and 52 AD. The authenticity is not questioned, in contrast to the second letter to the Thessalonians, according to historical critical exegesis.

39. Heidegger, *The Phenomenology of Religious Life*, 43.

40. Ibid., 57.

41. 1 Thess. 5:2.

42. Heidegger, *The Phenomenology of Religious Life*, 85.

43. 1 Cor. 7:29–31.

44. Heidegger, *The Phenomenology of Religious Life*, 86.

45. Ibid., 87.

46. Ibid., 10.

47. Walter Strolz, "*Martin Heidegger und der christliche Glaube*," ed. Hans-Jürg Braun (Zürich: Theologischer Verlag, 1990), 28.

48. Heidegger, *The Phenomenology of Religious Life*, 115–227.

49. I am following Heidegger here; the references are not to Augustine's work.

50. Heidegger, *The Phenomenology of Religious Life*, 142–43.

51. Ibid., 153.

52. Ibid., 212.

53. Ibid., 193.
54. Ibid., 219.
55. Ibid., 222.
56. Heidegger developed this notion further in *Being and Time,* §36.
57. Ibid., 9.

Notes to Chapter Three

1. Matthias Jung, *Das Denken des Seins und der Glaube an Gott* (Würzburg: Königshausen & Neumann, 1990), 113.
2. Martin Heidegger, "Phenomenology and Theology," trans. James G. Hart and John C. Maraldo, in *Pathmarks,* ed. William McNeill (New York: Cambridge University Press, 1998).
3. It is likely that Hans Jonas was invited for this meeting. See Hans Jonas, *Heidegger und die Theologie,* ed. Gerhard Noller (München: Kaiser Verlag, 1967), 316.
4. Heidegger, "Phenomenology and Theology," 39: "In the Introduction to *Being and Time* (1927) §7, pp. 27ff., one finds a discussion of the notion of phenomenology (as well as its relation to the positive sciences) that guides the presentation here."
5. From the Latin *positum* (positioned).
6. Heidegger, "Phenomenology and Theology," 41.
7. Ibid., 42: "The most central question is whether, indeed, theology in general is a science."
8. Heidegger, *Being and Time,* trans. John Macquarrie and Edward Robinson (Oxford: Basil Blackwell, 1962), §66b.
9. Jung, *Das Denken des Seins,* 118.
10. Heidegger, "Phenomenology and Theology," 43.
11. As appears in a letter from December 28, 1945; GA 16:416.
12. Heidegger, "Phenomenology and Theology," 43–44.
13. Ibid., 44.
14. Ibid.
15. Jung emphasizes this constantly: cf. Jung, *Das Denken des Seins,* 120.
16. For this analysis see Jung, *Das Denken des Seins,* 122 ff.
17. Heidegger, "Phenomenology and Theology," 44.
18. Ibid., 45.
19. Jung, 125.
20. Ibid., 44.
21. Martin Heidegger, *Being and Time,* 413–14.
22. Heidegger, "Phenomenology and Theology," 53.
23. Martin Heidegger, *What is Called Thinking?* trans. J. Glenn Gray (New York: Harper & Row, 1968), 177.

24. Martin Heidegger, *Introduction to Metaphysics,* trans. Gregory Fried and Richard Polt (New Haven: Yale University Press, 2000), 7.

25. Karl Jaspers, *Der philosophische Glaube angesichts der Offenbarung* (München: Piper, 1962).

26. Jung, *Das Denken des Seins,* 128.

27. Martin Heidegger, "Letter on 'Humanism,'" trans. Frank A. Capuzzi, in *Pathmarks*, ed. William McNeill (New York: Cambridge University Press, 1998), 253.

28. Heidegger, "Phenomenology and Theology," 46.

29. Martin Heidegger, *Ontology — The Hermenutics of Facticity,* trans. John van Buren (Bloomington: Indiana University Press, 1999), 11. Cf. Ben Vedder, *Was ist Hermeneutik?* (Stuttgart: Kohlhammer, 2000), 93–113.

30. Heidegger, "Phenomenology and Theology," 46.

31. Ibid., 49.

32. Eduard Landolt, *Der einzige Heidegger. Eine Deutung nach dem systematischen Index* (Heidelberg: C. Winter, 1992), 30: "Das 'Heideggerische Sein' ist nicht das 'biblische Sein,' wenn Heidegger sagt, daß er sonst 'seine Werkstatt hätte schließen können,' da er (d.h.) der Mensch ganz vom Glauben beschlagnahmt wäre und die Philosophen, bzw. die Philosophie keinen Platz mehr im Dasein des Menschen hätte."

33. Jung, *Das Denken des Seins,* 132.

34. Heidegger, "Phenomenology and Theology," 47.

35. Ibid.

36. Ibid., 48.

37. Ibid.

38. Ibid, 49.

39. Jung, *Das Denken des Seins,* 135.

40. Heidegger, "Phenomenology and Theology," 50.

41. Ibid., 51.

42. G. W. F. Hegel, *Lectures on the philosophy of Religion,* Translated by R. F. Hodgson and J. M. Stewart (Berkeley: University of California Press, 1984–1987).

43. Heidegger, "Phenomenology and Theology," 51.

44. Heidegger, *Being and Time,* 365 n. 2.

45. Heidegger, "Phenomenology and Theology," 52.

46. Heidegger, *Being and Time,* 224; Jung, *Das Denken des Seins,* 141.

47. Heidegger, *Being and Time,* 496 n. ii.

48. Heidegger, "Phenomenology and Theology," 52.

49. Jung, *Das Denkend des Seins,* 143.

50. One can see this in his lecture course from winter semester 1921/

1922. Martin Heidegger, *Phenomenological Interpretations of Aristotle, Initiation into Phenomelogical Research,* trans. Richard Rojcewicz (Bloomington: Indiana University Press, 2001), 138–39.

51. Heidegger, *Being and Time,* 387.

52. Heidegger, "Phenomenology and Theology," 52.

53. Ibid., 53.

54. Ibid., 52–3.

55. Ibid., 53.

56. "Phenomenological Interpretations with Respect to Aristotle," trans. Michael Baur, *Man and World* 25 (1992): 393.

57. Jung summarizes this concisely: "*Wenn* sich aber aus dem Glauben heraus einen Wissenschaft der Theologie konstituiert hat, *dann* kann die Philosophie vorab eine Bedeutung für diese Wissenschaft beanspruchen, insofern in ihren Begriffen ein nichttheologischer, vorgläubiger Gehalt aufgehoben ist." Jung, *Das Denken des Seins,* 146. On page 147 n.73, Jung describes how superficially this text by Heidegger is for the most part read.

58. Ibid., 147.

59. Heidegger, "Phenomenology and Theology," 53.

60. Ibid. Heidegger has always taken the position of a philosopher in his conversation with theology. As a philosopher he keeps faith at a distance, according to his contention: "Wenn ich vom Glauben so angesprochen wäre, würde ich die Werkstatt schliessen." In: Gollwitzer and Weischedel eds., *Denken und Glauben,* 2nd ed. (Stuttgart: Kohlhammer, 1965). Quoted by François Fédier, *"Heidegger et Dieu,"* in *Heidegger et la Question de Dieu,* ed. R. Kearny and J. O'Leary (Paris: Bernard Grasset, 1980), 37.

61. Martin Heidegger, *The Concept of Time,* trans. William McNeill (Oxford: Blackwell, 1992), 1–2.

62. Heidegger, *Introduction to Metaphysics,* 8.

Notes to Chapter Four

1. Plato *Sophist* 244a.

2. Heidegger, *Being and Time,* trans. John Macquarrie and Edward Robinson (Oxford: Basil Blackwell, 1962), 19.

3. Martin Heidegger, "Onto-theo-logical Constitution of Metaphysics," *Identity and Difference,* trans. Joan Stambaugh (New York: Harper & Row, 1969).

4. Martin Heidegger, "Phenomenological Interpretations with Respect to Aristotle," trans. Michale Baur, *Man and World* 25 (1992) 358–393.

5. Ibid., 386.

6. Ibid.

7. Martin Heidegger, *Plato's Sophist,* trans. Richard Rojcewicz and André Schuwer (Bloomington: Indiana University Press, 1997), 153.

8. Ibid.

9. Ibid., 437–38.

10. Ibid., 154.

11. Ibid.

12. Ibid.

13. For the following analysis I owe a large debt of gratitude to my former assistant Koos Verhoof.

14. GA 22:1: "Absicht: Eindringen in das Verständnis der *wissenschaftlichen Grundbegriffe,* die nicht nur alle nachkommende Philosophie bestimmt haben und entscheidend bestimmten, sondern die abendländische Wissenschaft überhaupt möglich machten und heute noch tragen."

15. Ibid., 13: "Notwendigkeit einer radikaleren Fragestellung gegenüber der griechischen. Das nur, wenn wir zuvor die griechische Philosophie *ganz aus ihr selbst verstanden* haben, nicht moderne Probleme hineindeuten."

16. Ibid., 6: "Und wenn Philosophie auch ihr Thema vorfindet und nicht erfindet, dann muß etwas zum Thema gemacht werden können, was *nicht vorliegt,* d.h. *kein Seiendes* ist."

17. Ibid., 22: "Er vereinigt positiv die Grundmotive der vorangehenden Philosophie, nach ihm Abfall."

18. Ibid., 149: "das der Idee von Sein am angemessensten genügt."

19. Ibid., 249: "das Sein des Seienden überhaupt . . . zu bestimmen."

20. Ibid.: "Der *Doppelbegriff* der Fundamentalwissenschaft: 1. Wissenschaft vom *Sein*; 2. Wissenschaft vom *höchsten und eigentlichen Seienden.*"

21. Ibid., 149: "ein merkwürdiges Stadium des Schwankens."

22. Ibid., 150: "von woher Sein als solches zu bestimmen ist."

23. Ibid., 31: "Warum soviel und warum diese?"

24. Ibid., 223: "Warum gibt es ein Warum, einen Grund? . . . Die Griechen haben diese Frage nicht gestellt."

25. Ibid., 328: "von dem sie ewig und ständig gleichmäßig entfernt ist."

26. Ibid.: "reine *energeia,* reine, pure Anwesenheit."

27. Ibid., 178: "eigenständige ständige Anwesenheit von ihm selbst her."

28. Ibid., 30: "Es bleibt dabei: sophia ist das höchste Verstehen und eigentliche Wissenschaft. Sie ist die göttlichste."

29. Ibid., 325.

30. Ibid., 179.

31. Ibid., 329–30: "wie das Problem des Seins notwendig auf ein eigentlich Seiendes gedrängt wird; ob es überhaupt eine Ontologie gibt, die rein gewissermaßen sich aufbaut ohne Orientierung an einem ausgezeichneten Seienden."

32. Aristotle *Metaphysics* IX. 8; 1050 b3 ff.

33. GA 22:180: "Doppelbegriff der Fundamentalwissenschaft ist nicht eine Verlegenheit oder das Zusammenbestehen zweier verschiedener Ansätze, die nichts zu tun haben miteinander, sondern immer sachliche Notwendigkeit des Problems, das Aristoteles nicht bewältigte, als solches auch nicht formulierte, weshalb es künftig auch völlig in Vergessenheit geriet."

34. Ibid., 22: "an die Grenzen vorgestoßen, die mit dem Problemansatz der griechischen Philosophie überhaupt gegeben sind."

35. Ibid., 150: "Hier liegt der Knoten des Problems, der Doppelbegriff von einer Wissenschaft vom Sein als ontische Erklärung und ontologische Auslegung. Ursachen für Seiendes: Thema ist das Sein des Seienden. Ursachen für das Sein: Seiendes ist Ursache für das Sein."

36. Martin Heidegger, *The Metaphysical Foundations of Logic,* trans. Michael Heim (Bloomington: Indiana University Press, 1984).

37. Ibid., 9.

38. Aristotle, *Metaphysics* IV. 1; 1003a 21 ff.

39. Heidegger, *Metaphysical Foundations,* 10.

40. Ibid., 11.

41. Ibid.

42. Ibid.

43. Ibid., 14.

44. Ibid.

45. Martin Heidegger, *Kant and the Problem of Metaphysics,* 5th ed., enlarged, trans. Richard Taft (Bloomington: Indiana University Press, 1997), 5. This book (from 1929) contains the lecture course from winter semester 1927/28 on Kant's *Critique of Pure Reason.*

46. Ibid.

47. Martin Heidegger, "What Is Metaphysics?" trans. David Farell Krell, in *Pathmarks,* ed. William McNeill (New York: Cambridge University Press, 1998), 93.

48. Martin Heidegger, *The Fundamental Concepts of Metaphysics, World, Finitude, Solitude,* trans. William McNeill and Nicholas Walker (Bloomington: Indiana University Press, 1995), 34.

49. Ibid., 42–43.

50. Ibid., 33.

51. Ibid., 34.

52. Martin Heidegger, *The Essence of Human Freedom, an Introduction to Philosophy,* trans. Ted Sadler (New York: Continuum, 2002), 1n.

53. Ibid., 61–62.

54. Ibid., 75.

55. Martin Heidegger, *Hegel's Phenomenology of Spirit,* trans. Parvis Emad and Kenneth Maly (Bloomington: Indiana University Press, 1988), 98.

56. W.F. Hegel, *Aesthetics,* trans. T. Knox (London: Oxford University Press, 1975), 1:101.

57. Martin Heidegger, *Schelling's Treatise on the Essence of Human Freedom,* trans. Joan Stambaugh (Athens,Ohio: Ohio University Press, 1985), 51.

58. Ibid., 64.

59. Ibid., 65.

60. Ibid.

61. Ibid., 66.

62. Ibid.

63. Martin Heidegger, *Nietzsche,* vol. 3/4, ed. David Krell (San Francisco: Harper & Row, 1991), 209.

64. Martin Heidegger, "Introduction to 'What Is Metaphysics?'" trans. Walter Kaufmann, in *Pathmarks,* ed. William McNeil (New York: Cambridge University Press, 1998), 287.

65. Ibid., 287–88. Here also Heidegger emphasizes that this concept of theology has nothing to do with Christian theology. It is because of the theological structure of ontology that Christian believers can use it; but "will Christian theology one day resolve to take seriously the word of the apostle and thus also the conception of philosophy as foolishness?"

66. Heidegger, *Identity and Difference,* 54.

67. We see this in 1961 in Heidegger, "Kant's Thesis about Being," trans. Ted E. Klein Jr. and William E. Pohl, in *Pathmarks,* ed. William McNeill (New York: Cambridge University Press, 1998), 340.

68. Heidegger, "Introduction to 'What Is Metaphysics?'" 288.

69. Martin Heidegger, *The Principle of Reason,* trans. Reginald Lilly (Bloomington: Indiana University Press, 1991), 35 ff.

NOTES TO CHAPTER FIVE

1. Hans Köchler, *Politik und Theologie bei Heidegger* (Innsbruck: Arbeitsgemeinschaft für Wissenschaft und Politik, 1991), 32 ff.

2. In this way Thomas Aquinas understands also the biblical "Sum quod Sum." *Summa contra Gentiles I,* c. 22; S. Theol I, qu. 13, art. 11: "Utrum hoc nomen qui est sit maxime nomen Dei proprium."

3. Thomas Aquinas, *Quaestiones disputatae: De potentia,* qu. 1, art. 1. "Deo autem convenit esse actum purum et primum."

4. Köchler, *Politik und Theologie,* 33.

5. Thomas Aquinas, *Quaest. disputatae: De veritate,* qu. 22, art. 2, ad 2: "ipsum esse est similitudo divinae bonitatis; unde inquantum aliqua desiderant esse, desiderant Dei similitudinem et Deum implicite."

6. Martin Heidegger, *The Principle of Reason,* trans. Reginald Lilly (Bloomington: Indiana University Press, 1991), 79.

7. Thomas Aquinas, *Summa Theologica I,* qu. 45, art. 1: "emanatio totius entis a causa universali, quae est deus; et hanc quidem emanationem designamus nomine creationis."

8. Martin Heidegger, *The Question Concerning Technology and Other Essays,* trans. William Lovitt (New York: Harper & Row, 1977), 161.

9. Martin Heidegger, *The End of Philosophy,* trans. Joan Stambauch (London: Souvenier Press, 1975), 15.

10. Ibid., 65.

11. Martin Heidegger, *Introduction to Metaphysics,* trans. Gregory Fried and Richard Polt (New Haven: Yale University Press, 2000), 207.

12. Pico della Mirandola, *On the Dignity of Man, On Being and the One, Heptaplus,* trans. Charles Glenn Wallis, Paul J.W. Miller, Douglas Charmichael (Indianapolis: Bobbs-Merrill, 1965), 4–5.

13. Ludwig Feuerbach, *The Essence of Christianity,* trans. George Eliot (New York: Harper & Row, 1957), xxxvii.

14. Ibid., 12.

15. Martin Heidegger and Erhart Kästner, *Briefwechsel, 1953–1974,* ed. Heinrich W. Petzet (Frankfurt: Insel Verlag, 1986), 23: "aber die heutigen Theologen meinen, sie müßten ihre Geschäfte mit der Psychoanalyse und der Soziologie machen."

16. Martin Heidegger, *Hegel's Phenomenology of Spirit,* trans. Parvis Emad and Kenneth Maly (Bloomington: Indiana University Press, 1988), 126.

17. Heidegger, *The Principle of Reason,* 3 ff.

18. Martin Heidegger, "On the Essence of Ground," in *Pathmarks,* ed. and trans. William McNeill (New York: Cambridge University Press, 1998), 98–99.

19. Heidegger, *The Principle of Reason,* passim.

20. Baruch Spinoza, *The Ethics,* Chapter I. def. 1.

21. Wolfgang Stegmüller, *"Das Problem der Kausalität,"* in *Probleme der Wissenschaftstheorie, Festschrift für V. Kraft,* ed. Ernst Topitsch (Wien: Springer, 1960), 189.

22. Heidegger, *The Principle of Reason,* 71–72.

23. Immanuel Kant, *Critique of Pure Reason,* trans. Werner S. Pluhar (Indianapolis: Hackett, 1966), 134, 139.

24. Edmund Husserl, *Formal and Transcendental Logic,* trans. Dorion Cairns (The Hague: Nijhoff, 1969).

25. Jean Paul Sartre, *Existantialism and Humanism,* trans. Philip Mairet (London: Eyre Methuen, 1989).

26. Heidegger, *The Principle of Reason,* 23.

27. Ibid., 24.

28. Martin Heidegger, *Discourse on Thinking,* trans. John M. Anderson and E. Hans Freund (New York: Harper & Row, 1966), 49.

29. Martin Heidegger, *Nietzsche,* ed. and trans. David Krell (San Francisco: Harper & Row, 1991), 3: 174.

30. Martin Heidegger, *Kant and the Problem of Metaphysics,* 5th ed., trans. Richard Taft. (Bloomington: Indiana University Press, 1997), 147.

31. Ben Vedder, *Was ist Hermeneutik?* (Stuttgart: Kohlhammer, 2000), 69–91.

32. Martin Heidegger, *Four Seminars,* trans. Andrew Mitchell and Francois Raffoul. (Bloomington: Indiana University Press, 2003), 73: "Marxism as a whole rests upon this thesis, Heidegger explains. Indeed Marxism thinks on the basis of production: social production of society (society produces itself) and the self-production of the human being as a social being."

33. Karl Marx and Frederick Engels, "Contribution to the Critique of Hegel's Philosophy of Law," in *Collected Works* (London: Lawrence & Wishart, 1975), 3:182.

34. Heidegger, *Four Seminars,* 76–77.

35. Baruch Spinoza, *The Ethics and Selected Letters,* trans. Samuel Shirley (Indianapolis: Hackett, 1982), 109.

36. Ibid., 156.

37. Robert Spaemann and Reinhard Löw, *Die Frage Wozu? Geschichte und Wiederentdeckung des teleologischen Denkens* (München: Piper, 1981), 290.

38. Karl Marx and Frederick Engels, "Critique of the Gotha Programme," in *Collected Works* (London: Lawrence & Wishart, 1989), 24:75–99.

39. GA 66:16–25.

40. Heidegger, *Nietzsche,* 3:174–75.

41. Martin Heidegger *Parmenides*, trans. André Schuwer and Richard Rojcewicz (Bloomington: Indiana University Press, 1998), 56.

42. Heidegger, *Nietzsche,* 3:177–78.

43. Ibid., 178.

44. P. Hadot, "Causa sui," in *Historisches Wörterbuch der Philosophie* (Darmstadt: Wissenschaftliche Buchgesellschaft, 1971), 1:976.

45. Thomas Aquinas, *Summa contra Gentiles* II.48: "Liberum est quod sui causa est."; cf. Aristotle *Metaphysics,* I. 2. 982 b 26.

46. Martin Heidegger, "Overcoming Metaphysics," in *The End of Philosophy,* trans. Joan Stambauch (London: Souvenier Press, 1975), 106.

47. GA 48:131.

48. Heidegger, *The Principle of Reason,* 122.

49. Martin Heidegger, *Being and Time,* trans. John Macquarrie and Edward Robinson (Oxford: Basil Blackwell, 1962), 330.

50. Heidegger, *Nietzsche,* 3:174.

51. Heidegger, *The Principle of Reason,* 127.

52. Heidegger, *The Question Concerning Technology,* 180–82.

53. Heidegger, *Being and Time,* §74.

54. Heidegger, *The Principle of Reason,* 128.

NOTES TO CHAPTER SIX

1. Martin Heidegger, "Phenomenology and Theology," trans. James G. Hart and John C. Maraldo, in *Pathmarks,* ed. William McNeill (New York: Cambridge University Press, 1998), 40. The article "The Word of Nietzsche: 'God is dead'" is published in Martin Heidegger, *The Question Concerning Technology and Other Essays,* trans. William Lovitt (New York: Harper & Row, 1977), 53–112; The texts "European Nihilism" and "The Determination of Nihilism in the History of Being," are published in Martin Heidegger, *Nietzsche* vol. 4, ed. and trans. David Farrell Krell (San Francisco: Harper & Row, 1982).

2. Martin Heidegger, "The Self-Assertion of the German University," trans. Karsten Harries, *Review of Metaphysics* 38 (1985): 474.

3. The quotations from Nietzsche are taken from this article.

4. These lecture courses are published in GA 43, 44, 47, 48 and 50.

5. Martin Heidegger, *Identity and Difference,* trans. Joan Stambaugh (New York: Harper & Row, 1969), 57.

6. Rainer Thurnher, "Gott und Ereignis — Heideggers Gegenparadigma zur Onto-Theologie," *Heidegger Studies* 8 (1992): 90.

7. Heidegger, *Identity and Difference,* 59.

8. Ibid., 58.

9. Martin Heidegger, "Plato's Doctrine of Truth," trans. Thomas Sheehan, in *Pathmarks,* 180–81.

10. Heidegger, *Identity and Difference,* 69. Thurner, "Gott und Ereignis" 92.

11. Martin Heidegger, *Introduction to Metaphysics,* trans. Gregory Fried and Richard Polt (New Haven: Yale University Press, 2000), 206 ff.

12. Cf. Aristotle, *Metaphysics* 6.1.1028a31 ff.; 7.3.1029b3 ff.; *Physics* 1.1.184a 17 ff.

13. Heidegger, *Identity and Difference,* 72.

14. Martin Heidegger, "Science and Reflection" in *The Question Concerning Technolog and Other Essays,* 161.

15. Martin Heidegger, *The End of Philosophy,* trans. Joan Stambaugh (London: Souvenir Press, 1975), 12–14.

16. GA 41:110–11.

17. Heidegger, *Identity and Difference,* 66.

18. Martin Heidegger, *Nietzsche,* ed. and trans. David Farrell Krell (San Francisco: Harper & Row, 1991), 1:203–05.

19. Heidegger, *Nietzsche,* 3:60; *Introduction to Metaphysics,* 111.

20. Heidegger, *Nietzsche,* 3:202.

21. Ibid., 226.

22. Heidegger, "Plato's Doctrine of Truth," 155.

23. Ibid., 170.

24. Heidegger, *Introduction to Metaphysics,* 197; "Plato's Doctrine of Truth," 176/177.

25. Martin Heidegger, *Being and Time,* trans. John Macquarrie and Edward Robinson (San Francisco: Harper & Row, 1962), 257.

26. Heidegger, "On the Essence of Truth," trans. John Sallis, in *Pathmarks,* 138.

27. Ibid., 139.

28. Martin Heidegger, "The Origin of the Work of Art," in *Poetry, Language, Thought,* trans. Albert Hofstadter (New York: Harper & Row, 1971), 51.

29. Martin Heidegger, *What is Called Thinking,* trans. J. Glenn Gray (New York: Harper & Row, 1968), 91.

30. Heidegger, *Nietzsche,* 4:210.

31. GA 48:76–80.

32. GA 43, 190–93.

33. Heidegger, "The Word of Nietzsche," 58.

34. Ibid., 58–59.

35. GA 43:191: "Der Satz 'Gott ist todt' ist keine Verneinung, sondern das innerste Ja zum Kommenden."

36. Friedrich Nietzsche, *The Gay Science,* trans. Walter Kaufmann (New York: Vintage, 1974), 279.

37. GA 44:67–71.

38. Friedrich Nietzsche, *The Portable Nietzsche,* ed. and trans. Walter Kaufmann (New York: Viking 1980), 95.

39. Heidegger, "The Word of Nietzsche," 66.

40. GA 48:101.

41. Heidegger, "The Word of Nietzsche," 71.

42. GA 48:108–13.

43. Heidegger, "The Word of Nietzsche," 74.

44. GA 48:107.

45. Heidegger, "The Word of Nietzsche," 77.

46. Ibid., 80.

47. Ibid., 93.

48. Ibid., 60.

49. Ibid., 99.

50. GA 50:50.

51. Heidegger, "The Word of Nietzsche," 105–06.

52. Cf. Guörgy Tatár, "Gott ist tot," in *Wege und Irrwege des neueren Umganges mit Heideggers Werk, Ein deutsch-ungarisches Symposium,* ed. István M. Fehér (Berlin: Duncker & Humblot, 1991), 193–203.

53. Friedrich Nietzsche, *Sämtliche Werke. Kritische Studienausgabe,* vol. 9, ed. G. Colli und M. Montinari (München: Dt Taschenbuch-Verlag, 1980), 577: "Wenn wir nicht aus dem Tode Gottes eine großartige Entsagung und einen fortwährenden Sieg über uns machen, so haben wir den Verlust zu tragen." (abbreviated as KSA)

54. KSA 9:590: "Gott ist todt — wer hat ihn dan getödtet? Auch dies Gefühl, den Heiligsten Mächtigsten getödtet zu haben, muß noch über einzelne Menschen kommen."

55. KSA 9:624: "noch einen eigenen Schöpfer, oder zerquälten uns mit dem Problem des Woher".

56. KSA 9:590: "Muß er nicht der allmächtigste und heiligste Dichter selber werden?"

57. KSA 14:256. The original manuscript of the *The Gay Science* reads: "Einmal zündete Zarathustra am hellen Vormittage eine Laterne an, lief auf den Markt und schrie: Ich suche Gott! Ich suche Gott! . . ."

58. Heidegger, "The Word of Nietzsche," 60.

59. Heidegger, "The Word of Nietzsche," 109.

60. GA 50:105–15.

61. Heidegger, "The Word of Nietzsche," 112.

62. Heidegger, *Nietzsche,* 1:156.

63. Heidegger, "The Word of Nietzsche," 61.

64. Heidegger, *Nietzsche,* 2:77.

65. Heidegger, "The Word of Nietzsche," 69.

66. Heidegger, *Nietzsche,* 3:203.

67. Heidegger, *Nietzsche,* 4:211.

68. Ibid., 210.

69. Heidegger, "On the Question of Being," trans. William McNeill, in *Pathmarks,* 306.

70. Martin Heidegger, *Elucidations of Hölderlin's Poetry,* trans. Keith Hoeller (Amherst, New York: Humanity Books, 2000), 46.

71. Ibid.

72. Heidegger, "What are Poets for?" in *Poetry, Language, Thought,* 91.

73. Heidegger, "Poetically Man Dwells," in *Poetry, Language, Thought,* 214.

74. GA 43:191: "Die gewöhnliche Auslegung des Wortes 'Got ist todt' lautet: Nietzsche sagt hier ganz unzweideutig: Der einzig mögliche Standpunkt ist heute nur noch der Atheismus. Aber genau das Gegenteil und noch einiges mehr ist die wahre Meinung Nietzsches. Die Grundstellung, aus der heraus er zum Seienden stand, war das Wissen, daß ein geschtliches Dasein ohne den Gott und ohne die Götter nicht möglich ist. Aber der Gott ist nur der Gott, wenn er kommt und kommen muß, und das ist nur möglich, wenn ihm die schaffende Bereitschaft und das Wagnis aus dem Letzten entgegengehalten wird, aber nicht ein übernommener und nur noch überkommener Gott, zu dem wir nicht gedrungen und von dem wir nicht gezwungen sind. Der Satz 'Gott ist todt' ist keine Verneinung, sondern das innerste Ja zum kommenden."

75. One does not see the radicality of Heidegger's position if one places above this history a God that is the Master of history, like Tatár does. See Tatár, "Gott ist tot" 200.

NOTES TO CHAPTER SEVEN

1. GA 65, *Beiträge zur Philosophie (Vom Ereignis),* in English as *Contributions to Philosophy (From Enowning),* trans. Parvis Emad and Kenneth Maly (Bloomington: Indiana University Press, 1999). Mainly, I follow the translation of Emad and Maly, because it is the most available one. Other individual translations of parts of the Beiträge have also been made. Therefore I translate the German *"Ereignis"* as enowning and not as appropriation. See for instance Joan Stambaugh, trans. *The Finitude of Being* (Albany: State University of New York Press, 1992), 111–51.

2. Cf. David R. Law, "Negative theology in Heidegger's *Beiträge zur Philosophie,"* in *International Journal for Philosophy of Religion* 48 (2000): 139.

3. Heidegger, *Contributions,* 307.

4. Ibid., 332.

5. Martin Heidegger and Karl Jaspers, *Briefwechsel, 1920–1963,* ed.

Walter Biemel (München: Piper, 1992), 171–72. "Die Wächter des Denkens sind in der steigenden Weltnot nur noch wenige; dennoch müssen sie gegen den Dogmatismus jeder Art ausharren, ohne auf Wirkung zu rechnen. Die Weltöffentlichkeit und ihre Organisation ist nicht der Ort, an dem das Geschick des Menschenwesens sich entscheidet. — Man soll nich über Einsamkeit reden. Aber sie bleibt die einzige Ortschaft, an der Denkende und Dichtende nach menschlichem Vermögen dem Sein bei stehen."

6. Cf. David Law with regard to the translation of these German words and their original meaning. Law, "Negative Theology" 154.

7. Heidegger, *Contributions*, 6.

8. See for the previous summary Law, "Negative Theology" 140–41. See also Heidegger, *The Finitude of Being*, 111–51.

9. Heidegger, *Contributions*, 63.

10. Ibid., 88.

11. Ibid., 77.

12. Ibid., 88.

13. Ibid., 79.

14. Ibid., 107.

15. This clearly appears in the correspondence with Elisabeth Blochmann from June 22, 1932. Martin Heidegger and Elisabeth Blochmann, *Briefwechsel 1918–1969*, ed. Joachim W. Storck (Marbach am Neckar: Dt Schillerges, 1989), 52.

16. Heidegger, *Contributions*, 283.

17. Ibid., 98.

18. Ibid., 97.

19. Ibid., 147.

20. Ibid.

21. Ibid., 153.

22. Ibid., 156–7.

23. Ibid., 245.

24. Ibid., 308.

25. Ibid., 309.

26. Ibid.

27. Ibid., 172.

28. See also: Ben Vedder, "Heidegger on Desire," in *Continental Philosophy Review* 31 (1998): 353–68 and Kearney, "Heidegger and the Possible," in *Philosophical Studies* 27 (1980): 176–95.

29. Heidegger, *Contributions*, 309.

30. Ibid., 166.

31. Ibid., 172.

32. Ibid., 309.

33. Ibid., 69.

34. Ibid.

35. "Only a God Can Save Us: *Der Spiegel*'s Interview with Martin Heidegger," in *Philosophy Today* 20 (1976): 267–84.

36. Heidegger, *Contributions,* 337.

37. Ibid., 207.

38. Ibid., 178.

39. Ibid., 195.

40. See Jean Grondin, *Sources of Hermeneutics* (Albany: State University of New York Press, 1995), 4.

41. See Christian Müller, *Der Tod als Wandlungsmitte, Zur Frage nach Entscheidung, Tod und letztem Gott in Heideggers "Beiträgen zur Philosophie,"* (Berlin: Duncker & Humblot, 1999).

42. Jean-François Courtine, "Les traces et le passage du Dieu dans les 'Beiträge zur Philosophie'," in *Filosofia della rivelazione,* ed. Marco-M. Olivetti (Padova: CEDAM, 1994), 523–24.

43. Otto Pöggeler, *Heideggers Begegnung mit Hölderlin,* Man and World 1 (1978): 15.

44. Courtine, "Les traces" 519.

45. GA 39: 54, 111.

46. Heidegger, *Contributions,* 332.

47. GA 43:1.

48. Manfred Frank, *Der kommende Gott, Vorlesungen über die neue Mythologie* (Frankfurt am Main: Suhrkamp), 1982.

49. Heidegger, *Contributions,* 293.

50. Ibid., 289.

51. GA 39:111: "sondern gerade das Vorbeigehen ist die Art der Anwesenheit der Götter, die Flüchtigkeit eines kaum faßbaren Winkes, der im Nu des Vorüberganges alle Seligkeit und alle Schrecken zeigen kann. Der Gott hat eigene Maße, einen Augenblick nur währt er, kaum berührend die Wohnungen der Menschen, und diese wissen eigentlich nicht, was es ist, und sie können es auch nicht wissen, solange sie in der Art des Wissens festhängen, nach der sie die Dinge und Umstände und sich selbst allemal wissen."

52. Heidegger, *Contributions,* 289.

53. Heidegger, *The Finitude of Being,* 139–44.

54. Günter Figal, "Forgetfulness of God: Concerning the Center of Heidegger's Contributions to Philosophy," in *A Companion to Heidegger's 'Contributions to philosophy,'* ed. Charles Scott et al. (Bloomington: Indiana University Press, 2001), 206.

55. Martin Heidegger, *Being and Time*, trans. John Macquarrie and Edward Robinson (Oxford: Basil Blackwell, 1962), 193.

56. Martin Heidegger, *The Essence of Truth, On Plato's Cave Allegory and Theaetetus*, trans. Ted Sadler (New York: Continuum, 2002), 12–13.

57. Otto Pöggeler, "*Destruktion und Augenblick*," in *Destruktion und Übersetzung, Zu den Aufgaben von Philosophiegeschichte nach Martin Heidegger*, ed. Thomas Buchheim (Weinheim: VCH, Acta Humaniora, 1989), 26–27.

58. Heidegger, *Contributions*, 17.

59. Ibid., 285.

60. Ibid.

61. Heidegger, *Being and Time*, §53.

62. Heidegger, *Contributions*, 287.

63. Ibid., 289.

64. Ibid., 290.

65. Ibid., 292.

66. Ibid.

67. Ibid., 334.

68. Ibid., 335.

69. Ibid.

70. Ibid., 293.

71. Ibid.

72. Ibid., 287.

73. Ibid., 332.

74. Ibid., 181.

75. Ibid., 277.

76. Ibid., 10.

77. Ibid. It is obvious that Heidegger saw himself as one of the few. See for instance the aforementioned letter to K. Jaspers: "Die Wächter des Denkens sind in der steigenden Weltnot nur noch wenige; dennoch müssen sie gegen den Dogmatismus jeder Art ausharren, ohne auf Wirkung zu rechnen. Die Weltöffentlichkeit und ihre Organisation ist nicht der Ort, an dem das Geschick des Menschenwesens sich entscheidet. — Man soll nich über Einsamkeit reden. Aber sie bleibt die einzige Ortschaft, an der Denkende und Dichtende nach menschlichem Vermögen dem Sein bei stehen."

78. Heidegger mentions this other basic mood of the other beginning as opposite to wonder as the basic mood of the first beginning. See Martin Heidegger, *Basic Questions of Philosophy, Selected "Problems" of "Logic,"* trans. Richard Rojcewicz and André Schuwer (Bloomington: Indiana University Press, 1994), 4; 131–55.

79. Heidegger, *Contributions,* 13.

80. Ibid., 25.

81. Ibid., 285.

82. Heidegger, *Basic Questions of Philosophy,* 135. Heidegger describes the phenomenon of wonder, in which he refers to Plato (*Theaetetus* 155d2 ff) and Aristotle (*Metaphysics* 982b11ff) where wonder expressly is mentioned as the beginning of philosophy.

83. See Ben Vedder, "*Die Faktizität der Hermeneutik: Ein Vorschlag,*" in *Heidegger Studies* 12 (1996): 95–107.

84. Martin Heidegger, *On Time and Being,* trans. Joan Stambaugh (Chicago: University of Chicago Press, 2002), 35. "A further characteristic of the thinking which is also decisive for the realization of the question of Being is closely bound up with the fact that thinking receives its decisive determination only when it enters Appropriation. Echoes of this can already be found in the discussion of the step back. This characteristic is its provisionalness. Above and beyond the most obvious meaning that this thinking is always merely preparatory, provisionalness has the deeper meaning that this thinking always anticipated — and this in the mode of the step back. Thus the emphasis on the provisional character of these considerations does not stem from any kind of pretended modesty, but rather has a strict, objective meaning which is bound up with the finitude of thinking and of what is to be thought. The more stringently the step back is taken, the more adequate anticipatory Saying becomes."

85. Martin Heidegger, "Letter on 'Humanism,'" trans. Frank A. Capuzzi, in *Pathmarks,* ed. William McNeill (New York: Cambridge University Press, 1998), 276.

86. Heidegger, *Contributions,* 280.

87. Ibid., 281.

88. Ibid., 288.

89. Ibid., 289.

90. Ibid., 292.

91. Ibid., 285.

92. Otto Pöggeler, *Martin Heidegger's Path of Thinking,* trans. Daniel Magurshak and Sigmund Barber (Atlantic Highlands: Humanities Press International, 1995). I doubt therefore whether Otto Pöggeler is right when he writes on page 214 that, "the 'last god' is also not simply another god compared with the gods that have been; rather, he gathers these others into the final and highest essence of the divine." It seems to me that Heidegger does not mean such a gathering god.

93. Heidegger, *Being and Time,* 307. See also footnote 1: "dessen Seinsart das Vorlaufen selbst ist." The earlier editions have 'hat' instead of 'ist.'

94. Heidegger, *Contributions,* 291.

95. Ibid., 57.

96. GA 39: 111: "sondern gerade das Vorbeigehen ist die Art der Anwesenheit der Götter, die Flüchtigkeit eines kaum faßbaren Winkes, der im Nu des Vorüberganges alle Seligkeit und alle Schrecken zeigen kann. Der Gott hat eigene Maße, einen Augenblick nur währt er, kaum berührend die Wohnungen der Menschen, und diese wissen eigentlich nicht, was es ist, und sie können es auch nicht wissen, solange sie in der Art des wissens festhängen, nach der sie die Dinge und Umstände und sich selbst allemal wissen."

97. Heidegger, *Contributions,* 288. With regard to Heidegger's interpretation of the gods Karl Jaspers had his doubts; in January 1950 he wrote after reading *Holzwege:* "Was . . . ihr eigentliches Absehen ist, das könnte ich nicht sagen . . . Ich bleib in der fragenden Spannung: ob es eine phantastische-täuschende Möglichkeit von Denken-Dichten werde, oder ob hier ein behutsames Öffnen der Pforte beginne, — ob gnostische Gottlosigkeit hier Wort finde oder das Spüren zur Gottheit hin."

98. Martin Heidegger, "Das Sein (Ereignis)," *Heidegger Studies* 15 (1999): 9. "Nicht *nach* dem Tod, sondern *durch* den Tod erscheinen die Götter. Durch den Tod — will sagen: nicht durch den Vorgang des Ablebens, sondern dadurch, daß der Tod in das Dasein hereinsteht."

99. Heidegger, *Contributions,* 163.

100. Costantino Esposito, "Die Geschichte des letzten Gottes in Heideggers 'Beiträge zur Philosophie'," *Heidegger Studies* 11 (1995): 52.

101. Otto Pöggeler, *Neue Wege mit Heidegger* (Freiburg: Karl Alber, 1992), 475.

102. Ibid., 476.

103. Heidegger, *Contributions,* 293.

104. Ibid.

105. Pöggeler, *Neue Wege,* 478.

106. For instance Hans Jonas considers Heidegger's gods as pagan gods. See *Heidegger und die Theologie,* ed. Gerhard Noller (München: Kaiser Verlag, 1967), 327.

107. GA 52:132.

108. Friedrich-Wilhelm von Hermann, *Wege ins Ereignis Zu Heideggers 'Beiträge zur Philosophie'* (Frankfurt a.M.: Klostermann, 1994), 366.

109. As is the case in David J. Krieger, "Das Andere des Denkens und das andere Denken — Heideggers Dekonstruktion und die Theologie," in *Martin Heidegger und der christliche Glaube,* ed. Hans-Jürg Braun (Zürich: Theologischer Verlag, 1990), 89–114.

110. Esposito, "Die Geschichte des letzten Gottes," 49 ff.

NOTES TO CHAPTER EIGHT

1. Martin Heidegger, "Letter on 'Humanism,'" trans. Frank A. Capuzzi, in *Pathmarks,* ed. William McNeill (New York: Cambridge University Press, 1998), 239.

2. Ibid., 266.

3. Ibid., 267.

4. Martin Heidegger, "The Word of Nietzsche: 'God is dead,'" *The Question Concerning Technology and Other Essays,* trans. William Lovitt (New York: Harper & Row, 1977), 112.

5. Heidegger, "Letter on 'Humanism,'" 267.

6. See Friedrich-Wilhelm von Hermann, *Wege ins Ereignis, zu Heideggers 'Beiträge zur Philosophie,'* (Frankfurt a.M.: Vittorio Klostermann, 1994), 39, 61, 97, 350, 366, 385. See also Paola-Ludovica Coriando, *Der letzte Gott als Anfang. Zur ab-gründigen Zeit-Räumlichkeit des Übergangs in Heideggers 'Beiträge zur Philosophie'* (München: Wilhelm Fink Verlag, 1998), 117.

7. Holger Helting, *Heidegger und Meister Eckehart. Vorbereitende Überlegungen zu ihrem Gottesdenken* (Berlin: Duncker & Humblot, 1997), 37.

8. Martin Heidegger, *On the Way to Language,* trans. Peter D. Hertz (San Francisco: Harper & Row, 1982), 164–65.

9. Helting, *Heidegger und Meister Eckehart,* 44.

10. GA 13:154: "Dies sagt für das sinnende Denken: Der Gott als Wert gedacht, und sei er der höchste, ist kein Gott. Also ist Gott nicht tot. Denn seine Gottheit lebt. Sie ist sogar dem Denken näher als dem Glauben, wenn anders die Gottheit als Wesendes seine Herkunft aus der Wahrheit des Seins empfängt und das Sein als ereignender Anfang Anderes 'ist' denn Grund und Ursache des Seienden."

11. Martin Heidegger, *Contributions to Philosophy (From Enowning),* trans. Parvis Emad and Kenneth Maly (Bloomington: Indiana University Press, 1999), 291.

12. Martin Heidegger, *What is Called Thinking?* trans. J. Glenn Gray (New York: Harper & Row, 1968), 115.

13. Ibid., 187.

14. Martin Heidegger, *Early Greek Thinking,* trans. David Farrell Krell and Frank A. Capuzzi (San Francisco: Harper & Row, 1975), 51–52.

15. Heidegger, *Contributions,* 293.

16. Heidegger, "Letter on 'Humanism,'" 267.

17. Heidegger, *Nietzsche,* ed. and trans. David Farrell Krell (San Francisco: Harper & Row, 1991), 2:106.

18. Martin Heidegger, *Identity and Difference,* trans. Joan Stambaugh (New York: Harper & Row, 1969), 72.

19. Ibid.

20. Martin Heidegger, "What are Poets For?" in *Poetry, Language, Thought,* trans. Albert Hofstadter (New York: Harper & Row, 1971), 91.

21. Martin Heidegger, "The Age of the World Picture," in *The Question Concerning Technology and Other Essays,* trans. William Lovitt (New York: Harper & Row, 1977), 116–17.

22. Gerhard Noller, "Ontologische und theologische Versuche zur Überwindung des Anthropologischen Denkens," in *Heidegger und die Theologie,* ed. Gerhard Noller (München: Kaiser Verlag, 1967), 292.

23. Ibid.; With regard to Bultman's reception of Heidegger see: Annemarie Gethmann-Siefert, *Das Verhältnis von Philosophie und Theologie im Denken Martin Heideggers* (Freiburg: Karl Alber, 1974), 140 ff.

24. Noller, "Ontologische" 26.

25. Bernd Trocholepczy, *Rechtfertigung und Seinsfrage, Anknüpfungen und Widerspruch in der Heidegger-Rezeption Bultmanns* (Herder: Freiburger theologischer Studien, 1991) 6, 114, 102–130. See also John Macquarrie, *An Existentialist Theology, a Comparison of Heidegger and Bultmann* (Harmondworth: Pinguin Books, 1973).

26. Heidegger, "The Age of the World Picture," 148.

27. Noller, "Ontologische" 295.

28. Noller, "Ontologische" 299.

29. Heidegger, "The Age of the World Picture," 117.

30. Heidegger, "Letter on 'Humanism,'" 265.

31. Heidegger, "The Word of Nietzsche," in *The Question Concerning Technology,* 63–64.

32. See Ludwig Heyde, *The Weight of Finitude, On the Philosophical Question of God,* trans. Alexander Harmsen and William Desmond (Albany: State University of New York Press, 1999), 120 ff.

33. Martin Heidegger, *The End of Philosophy,* trans. Joan Stambaugh (London: Souvenir Press, 1975), 67.

34. Heidegger, "The Word of Nietzsche," 94.

35. See Ben Vedder, "Religion and Hermeneutic Philosophy," *International Journal for the Philosophy of Religion* 51 (2002): 39–54.

36. Heidegger, "The Age of the World Picture," 117.

37. Heidegger, "The Turning," in *The Question Concerning Technology,* 49.

38. Heidegger, "Letter on 'Humanism,'" 258.

39. Ibid., 252, 253, 261.

40. Heidegger, *What is Called Thinking?* 68, 61, 93.

41. Martin Heidegger, *Parmenides,* trans. André Schuwer and Richard Rojcewicz (Bloomington: Indiana University Press, 1998), 110.

42. Ibid., 110–11.

43. Heidegger, "Letter on 'Humanism,'" 258.

44. Martin Heidegger, *Elucidations of Hölderlin's Poetry,* trans. Keith Hoeller (Amherst, New York: Humanity Books, 2000), 133.

45. Heidegger, "The Thing," in *Poetry, Language, Thought,* 184.

46. Heidegger, "What Are Poets For?" 91.

47. Ibid., 92.

48. Ibid.

49. Heidegger, *Elucidations,* 46.

50. Heidegger, "What are Poets For?" 97.

51. Heidegger, *Parmenides,* 112.

52. Heidegger, "What Are Poets For?" 117.

53. Heidegger, *Elucidations,* 141.

54. Ibid., 126.

55. Emil Kettering, "Nähe als Raum der Erfahrung des Heiligen. Eine topologische Besinnung," in *Auf der Spur des Heiligen: Heideggers Beitrag zur Gottesfrage,* ed. Günther Pöltner (Wien: Böhlau Verlag, 1991), 18.

56. Heidegger, "The Thing," in *Poetry, Language, Thought,* 178.

57. Heidegger, "Building, Dwelling, Thinking," in *Poetry Language Thought,* 150.

58. Martin Heidegger, *The Principle of Reason,* trans. Reginald Lilly (Bloomington: Indiana University Press, 1991), 128.

59. Heidegger, "The Thing," 180.

60. Heidegger, "What Are Poets For?" 96.

61. Walter Strolz, *"Martin Heidegger und der christliche Glaube,"* ed. Hans-Jürg Braun (Zürich: Theologischer Verlag, 1990), 48.

62. Heidegger writes to Strolz: "Ist im Prinzip der Unterschlupf ins seinsgeschichtliche Denken etwas anderes als der in die aristotelisch-scholastische-hegelsche Metaphysik? Ist dies alles nicht ein Beweis des Unglaubens an den Glauben, ein Versuch, diesem eine Stütze und eine Krücke von welcher Art auch immer, zu verschaffen? Ist der Glaube nicht nach dessen eigenem Sinn die Tat Gottes? Wozu 'Seinsverständnis' und 'Seinsgeschichte'? 'ontologische Differenz'? Es gibt in der biblischen Botschaft keine Lehre vom 'Sein.' Wer aber — ich meine in diesem Fall nicht Sie — aus dem alltestam. Wort 'Ich bin, der Ich bin' eine Ontologie herauszaubert, weiß nicht was er tut. Ist solches Hantieren mit der Philosophie und das Schielen nach ihr nicht einen einzige Kleingläubigkeit? Mir scheint, die moderne Theologie beider Konfessionen sucht nur immer die

Zeitgemässheit des Christentums, aber nicht die von Kierkegaard in der Verzweiflung gedachte Gleichzeitigkeit mit dem Christlichen." Quoted from Strolz, 51, from a letter by Heidegger addressed to him, dated June 14, 1965.

63. Heidegger, *Identity and Difference,* 54–55.

64. See the work of John Caputo. See also: Holger Helting, *Heidegger und Meister Eckehart, Vorbereitende Überlegungen zu ihrem Gottesdenken* (Berlin: Duncker & Humblot, 1997). In 1986 Derrida presented an interpretation of the dimension of the "Verneinung" in Heidegger's thinking. He related this with Dionysius Areopagita and Meister Eckehart. The text is published in Jacques Derrida, *Psyché. Inventions de l'autre* (Paris: Galilée, 1987).

NOTES TO CHAPTER NINE

1. Martin Heidegger, "Postscript to 'What Is Metaphysics?' " in *Pathmarks,* trans. and ed. William McNeill (New York: Cambridge University Press, 1998), 237. About the difference between the poetic and the thinking experience, see Martin Heidegger, "The Nature of Language," in *On the Way to Language,* trans. Peter D. Hertz (San Francisco: Harper & Row, 1971), 69–70.

2. Emilio Brito, *Heidegger et l'Hymne du Sacré* (Leuven: Leuven University Press, 1999), 29. For references on the issue of the holy in Heidegger see also: Jean Greisch, "Hölderlin et le chemin vers le Sacré," in *Cahier de l' herne, Martin Heidegger,* Ed. Michel Haar (Paris: Editions de L'Herne, 1983), 543–67; Emilio Brito, "Le Sacré dans les 'Éclaircissemnets pour la poésie de Hölderlin' de M. Heidegger," in *Ephemerides Theologicae Lovanienses* 71 (1995): 337–69; Holger Helting, *Heideggers Auslegung von Hölderlins Dichtung des Heiligen, Ein Beitrag zur Grundlagenforschung der Daseinsanalyse* (Berlin: Duncker & Humblot, 1999).

3. However, Heidegger had already mentioned the notion of the holy earlier, namely with respect to the work of Rudolf Otto. See chapter 1 on the pre-historical Heidegger.

4. GA 4: 33–48. The English translation of this volume appears as Martin Heidegger, *Elucidations of Hölderlin's Poetry,* trans. Keith Hoeller (Amherst, New York: Humanity Books, 2000). These elucidations are a result of Heidegger's lecture courses from 1934–35. The oldest text of this volume, "Holderlin and the Essence of Poetry" resurrects the important parts of sections 4–7 of the lecture course from 1934 published in GA 39, *Hölderlins Hymnen "Germanien" und "Der Rhein";* See also GA 52,

Hölderlins Hymne "Andenken," and GA 53, *Hölderlins Hymne "der Ister."*

5. Heidegger, *Elucidations, 52.*

6. Ibid., 60.

7. Ibid., 64.

8. Heidegger, *Elucidations,* 80.

9. Ibid., 80–81.

10. See *Besinnung,* GA 66: 253: "Ewige Götter *sind* keine Götter, wenn 'ewig' gedacht wird in der Bedeutung des aei und der aeternitas und vollends gar der sempiternitas, des neuzeitlichen fortschreitend öderen Und-so-weiter."

11. Heidegger, *Elucidations,* 82.

12. Helmut Danner, *Das Göttliche und der Gott bei Heidegger* (Meisenheim am Glan: Verlag Anton Hain, 1971), 66.

13. Heidegger, *Elucidations,* 85.

14. Ibid., 85–86.

15. Ibid., 87.

16. Ibid., 94.

17. Ibid., 90.

18. Ibid., 91.

19. Ibid.

20. Ibid., 97.

21. Ibid.

22. Ibid., 98.

23. Rainer Thurnher, "Gott und Ereignis — Heideggers Gegenparadigma zur Onto-theologie," in *Heidegger Studies* 8 (1992): 81–102.

24. Martin Heidegger, "The Nature of Language," in *On the Way to Language,* trans. Peter D. Hertz (San Francisco: Harper & Row, 1982), 106–08; D. Thomä, *Die Zeit des Selbst und die Zeit danach. Zur Kritik der Textgeschichte Martin Heideggers 1910–1976* (Frankfurt a. M.: Suhrkamp Verlag, 1990), 829 ff.

25. Martin Heidegger, "The Thing," in *Poetry, Language Thought,* trans. Albert Hofstader (New York: Harper & Row, 1971), 178.

26. Heidegger, "Poetically Man Dwells," in *Poetry, Language, Thought,* 223.

27. Heidegger, *Elucidations,* 191.

28. Heidegger, "Building Dwelling Thinking," in *Poetry Language Thought,* 150.

29. Heidegger, "The Thing," in *Poetry, Language, Thought,* 179.

30. Ibid., 178.

31. Ibid., 179.

32. Heidegger, *Elucidations, 188.*

33. Ibid., 194–95.

34. Ibid., 194.

35. Ibid., 200.

36. Ibid.

37. Ibid., 202.

38. Martin Heidegger, *Hölderlin's Hymn "The Ister,"* trans. William McNeill and Julia Davis (Bloomington: Indiana University Press, 1996), 55.

39. Heidegger, "Building Dwelling Thinking," in *Poetry, Language, Thought,* 150.

40. Heidegger, *Elucidations,* 94ff.

41. Ibid., 98.

42. Ibid., 82.

43. Ibid., 90.

44. Heidegger, "The Thing," 173.

45. Heidegger, "Building Dwelling Thinking," 150.

46. Ibid., 151.

47. Ibid., 150.

48. GA 52: 132.

49. See Heidegger, "The Nature of Language," 98–101.

50. Cf. Emil Kettering, "Nähe als Raum der Erfahrung des Heiligen. Eine topologische Besinnung," in *Auf der Spur des Heiligen, Heideggers Beitrag zur Gottesfrage,* ed. Günther Pöltner (Wien: BöhlauVerlag, 1991), 9.

51. Heidegger, "Poetically Man Dwells," 213–29.

52. Ibid., 216.

53. Heidegger, "The Nature of Language," 72.

54. Heidegger, "Poetically Man Dwells," 216.

55. Ibid., 218.

56. Ibid., 220.

57. Ibid., 222.

58. Ibid., 221.

59. Ibid., 224.

60. Heidegger, *Elucidations,* 169–70.

61. Jörg Splett, *Die Rede vom Heiligen, über ein religionsphilosophisches Grundwort* (Freiburg: Verlag Karl Alber, 1971), 144.

62. Martin Heidegger, "The Anaximander Fragment," in *Early Greek Thinking,* trans. David Farrell Krell and Frank A. Capuzzi (San Francisco: Harper & Row, 1984), 56.

63. According to Löwith, Heidegger's philosophy has a religious

motive which is separated from Christian faith, which in its undogmatic dissoluteness appeals to those who want to be religious without being a Christian. That is the reason for his broad effect. Karl Löwith, *Heidegger — Denker in dürftiger Zeit* (Göttingen: Vandenhoeck & Ruprecht, 1965), 111.

64. For the following see: Schaeffler Richard, "Der Gruß des 'Heiligen' und die 'Frömmigkeit des Denkens' Heideggers Beitrag zu einer Phänomenologie der Religion," in *Auf der Spur des Heiligen Heideggers Beitrag zur Gottesfrage,* ed. Günther Pöltner (Wien: Böhlau Verlag, 1991), 62 ff.

65. Heidegger, *Identity and Difference,* 72.

66. Heidegger, *What is Called Thinking?* trans. J. Glenn Gray. (New York: Harper & Row, 1968), 146.

67. Heidegger, *Elucidations,* 98.

68. Heidegger, "The Question Concerning Technology," 35.

69. Martin Heidegger, *Being and Time,* trans. John Macquarrie and Edward Robinson (San Francisco: Harper & Row, 1962), 59.

70. Heidegger, "On the Essence of Truth," in *Pathmarks,* 148.

71. As Richard Schaeffler does: Schaeffler, "Der Gruß des Heiligen," 72.

72. Heidegger, *On the Way to Language,* 29.

73. Heidegger, "Letter on 'Humanism,'" in *Pathmarks,* 267.

74. Heidegger, "Postscript to 'What Is Metaphysics?'" 236.

75. Heidegger, "Letter on Humanism," 274.

76. Heidegger, *Elucidations,* 98.

77. Ibid., 128–30.

78. Ibid., 64.

Notes to Chapter Ten

1. Martin Heidegger, "Building Dwelling Thinking," in *Poetry, Language, Thought,* trans. Albert Hofstadter (New York: Harper & Row, 1971), 150.

2. For a more detailed interpretation of the notion of desire in Heidegger, see Ben Vedder, "Heidegger on Desire," *Continental Philosophy Review* 31(1998): 353–68.

3. Martin Heidegger, *Plato's Sophist,* trans. Richard Rojcewicz and André Schuwer (Bloomington: Indiana University Press, 1997), 446.

4. Martin Heidegger, *The Metaphysical Foundations of Logic,* trans. Michael Heim (Bloomington: Indiana University Press, 1984), 143; Plato, *Theaetetus,* 186 a. See also GA 34:200–33. There Heidegger presents an extensive interpretation of the notion of *eros* in Plato.

5. Martin Heidegger, *The Basic Problems of Phenomenology*, trans. Albert Hofstadter (Bloomington: Indiana University Press, 1988), 136.

6. Immanuel Kant, *Grundlegung zur Metaphysik der Sitten, Werke in zehn Bänden*, ed. W. Weischedel (Darmstadt: Wissenschaftliche Buchgesellschaft, 1975), 6:28.

7. Aristotle, *Ethica Nicomachea*, VI. 1139 a 20.

8. Martin Heidegger, *Kant and the Problem of Metaphysics*, 5th ed., trans. Richard Taft (Bloomington: Indiana University Press, 1990), 112.

9. Heidegger, *The Metaphysical Foundations of Logic*, 210–11.

10. Ibid., 192.

11. Martin Heidegger, "On the Essence of Ground," in *Pathmarks*, trans. and ed. William McNeill (New York: Cambridge University Press, 1998), 123.

12. Ibid., 126.

13. GA 21:234–35.

14. Heidegger, "On the Essence of Ground," 128.

15. Martin Heidegger, *Being and Time*, trans. John Macquarrie and Edward Robinson (San Francisco: Harper & Row, 1962), 63; *The Basic Problems of Phenomenology*, 308; *The Metaphysical Foundations of Logic*, 216.

16. Heidegger, *Being and Time*, 185.

17. Heidegger, *Being and Time*, 214–17.

18. Ibid., 397.

19. Martin Heidegger, *The History of the Concept of Time*, trans. Theodore Kissiel (Bloomington: Indiana University Press, 1992), 317; *Being and Time*, 305.

20. Heidegger, *Being and Time*, 187.

21. Martin Heidegger, *What is Called Thinking?* trans. J. Glenn Gray (New York: Harper & Row, 1968), 117.

22. Ibid., 20.

23. Ibid., 9.

24. Martin Heidegger, *Elucidations of Hölderlin's Poetry*, trans. Keith Hoeller (Amherst, New York: Humanity Books, 2000), 135–36.

25. Ibid.; See also Martin Heidegger, *Basic Concepts*, trans. Gary E. Aylesworth (Bloomington: Indiana University Press, 1993), 22, and *Hölderlins Hymne 'Andenken,'* GA 52:118–22.

26. Heidegger, *Elucidations*, 136–37.

27. See also Friedrich-Wilhelm von Herrmann, "Dichterische Einbildungskraft und andenkendes Denken," in *Wege ins Ereignis: zu Heideggers 'Beiträge zur Philosophie'* (Frankfurt a.M.: Klostermann, 1994), 264–306.

28. Heidegger, *Being and Time*, 25.

29. Heidegger, "Language" in *Poetry, Language, Thought,* 197.

30. Martin Heidegger, "The Onto-theological-constitution of Metaphysics," in *Identity and Difference,* trans. Joan Stambaugh (New York: Harper & Row, 1969), 54.

31. Heidegger, "Language," 198.

32. Martin Heidegger, *Introduction to Metaphysics,* trans. Gregory Fried and Richard Polt (New Haven: Yale University Press, 2000), 108–09.

33. Heidegger, *Introduction to Metaphysics,* 131.

34. Ibid., 136; Martin Heidegger, "Logos," in *Early Greek Thinking,* trans. David Farrell Krell and Frank A. Capuzzi (San Francisco: Harper & Row, 1984), 66 ff.

35. Heidegger, *Introduction to Metaphysics,* 143.

36. Heidegger, "Anaximander," in *Early Greek Thinking,* 18.

37. Heidegger, "Logos," 62.

38. Martin Heidegger, *Die Frage nach dem Ding* (Tübingen: Max Niemeyer, 1962), 146.

39. Heidegger, "Logos," 61.

40. Martin Heidegger, *The Principle of Reason,* trans. Reginald Lilly. (Bloomington: Indiana University Press, 1991), 107.

41. Heidegger, *Being and Time,* §7b; "Logos," 63.

42. Martin Heidegger, "The Nature of Language," in *On the Way to Language,* trans. Peter D. Hertz (San Francisco: Harper & Row, 1982), 80.

43. Heidegger, "On the Essence and Concept of Phusis," in *Pathmarks,* 213.

44. Heidegger, "Logos," 70.

45. Heidegger, "The Nature of Language," 57–108.

46. Heidegger, *Introduction to Metaphysics,* 15.

47. Heidegger, "Language," 209.

48. Heidegger, *Introduction to Metaphysics,* 184.

49. Heidegger, "Language," 192.

50. Heidegger, "Poetically Man Dwells," in *Poetry, Language, Thought,* 216.

51. Heidegger, "Language," 190.

52. Heidegger, "Logos," 65.

53. Ibid.

54. Heidegger, *The Principle of Reason,* 47.

55. Heidegger, *What is Called Thinking?* 130.

56. W. F. Otto, *Die Musen und der Göttliche Ursprung des Singens und des Sagens* (Düsseldorf: Dietrichs, 1955); W. F. Otto, *Das Wort der Antike* (Stuttgart: Klett, 1962).

57. Lawrence J. Hatab, "Heidegger and Myth: a Loop in the History of Being," *Journal of the British Society for Phenomenology* 22 (1991): 45–64.

58. Otto, *Das Wort der Antike,* 369–71.

59. GA 4:42: "Dichten ist das ursprüngliche Nennen der Götter. Aber dem dichterischen Wort wird erst dann seine Nennkraft zuteil, wenn die Götter selbst und zur Sprache bringen. Wie sprechen die Götter?" Remarkably this passage is not given in the English translation by Keith Hoeller, "Hölderlin and the Essence of Poetry," in Heidegger, *Elucidations,* 63.

60. Friedrich Nietzsche, *Die Fröhliche Wissenschaft,* in *Kritische Studienausgabe,* ed. G. Colli and M. Montinari (München: Dt. Taschenbuch-Verlag, 1980), 3:439–40.

61. Friedrich Nietzsche, *Die Geburt der Tragödie,* in *Kritische Studienausgabe,* ed. G. Colli and M. Montinari (München: Dt. Taschenbuch-Verlag, 1980) 1:153–56.

62. Otto, *Die Musen,* 72.

63. Ibid., 72–79.

64. Ibid., 85.

65. Martin Heidegger, *Was ist das — die Philosophie?* (Pfullingen: Neske, 1966), 29.

66. Heidegger, ". . . Poetically Man Dwells . . .," 216.

67. Heidegger, "The Way to Language," in *On the Way to Language,* 124.

68. Heidegger, "The Origin of the Work of Art," in *Poetry, Language, Thought,* 72.

69. Heidegger, "Logos," 72.

70. Heidegger, "The Nature of Language," 66.

71. Heidegger, *Elucidations,* 55.

72. Ibid., 57.

73. Ibid., 58.

74. Ibid., 60.

75. Heidegger, "Language," 208.

76. Heidegger, *Elucidations,* 136–37.

77. Heidegger, "The Nature of Language," 91. Parts of the German text are omitted in the English translation. The complete text is as follows. "Der Weg ist, hinreichend gedacht, solches, was uns gelangen läßt, und zwar in das, was nach uns langt, indem es uns be-langt. Wir verstehen freilich das Zeitwort, belangen' nur in einem gewöhnlichen Sinne, der meint: sich jemandem vornehmen zur Vernehmung, zum Verhör. Wir können aber auch das Be-langen in einem hohen Sinne denken: be-langen, be-rufen, be-hüten, be-halten. Der Be-lang: das, was, nach unserem

wesen auslangend, es verlangt und so gelangen läßt in das, wohin es gehört. Der Weg ist solches, was uns in das gelangen läßt, was uns belangt." In *Unterwegs zur Sprache,* 197.

78. Heidegger, *Elucidations,* 45.

79. Ibid., 80.

80. Ibid., 219.

81. Heidegger, "The Nature of Language," 78.

Bibliography

Works by Heidegger

Basic Concepts. Translated by Gary E. Aylesworth. Bloomington: Indiana University Press, 1993.

The Basic Problems of Phenomenology. Translated by Albert Hofstadter. Bloomington: Indiana University Press, 1997.

Basic Questions of Philosophy: Selected "Problems" of "Logic." Translated by Richard Rojcewicz and André Schuwer. Bloomington: Indiana University Press, 1994.

Being and Time. Translated by John Macquarrie and Edward Robinson. Oxford: Basil Blackwell, 1962.

Martin Heidegger — Elisabeth Blochmann, Briefwechsel 1918–1968. Edited by Joachim W. Storck. Marbach am Neckar: Dt Schillerges, 1989.

Martin Heidegger — Karl Jaspers, Briefwechsel 1920–1963. Edited by Walter Biemel and Hans Saner. Munich: Piper, 1992.

Martin Heidegger — Erhart Kästner, Briefwechsel 1953–1974. Edited by Heinrich W. Petzet. Frankfurt: Insel Verlag, 1986.

The Concept of Time. Translated by William McNeill. Oxford: Blackwell, 1992.

Contributions to Philosophy (from Enowning). Translated by Parvis Emad and Kenneth Maly. Bloomington: Indiana University Press, 1999.

Discourse on Thinking. Translated by John M. Anderson and E. Hans Freund. New York: Harper & Row, 1966.

Early Greek Thinking. Translated by David Farrell Krell. San Francisco: Harper & Row, 1984.

317

Elucidations of Hölderlin's Poetry. Translated by Keith Hoeller. Amherst: Humanity Books, 2000.

The End of Philosophy. Translated by Joan Stambaugh. London: Souvenir Press, 1975.

The Essence of Human Freedom. Translated by Ted Sadler. London: Continuum, 2002.

The Essence of Truth. Translated by Ted Sadler. London: Continuum, 2002.

The Finitude of Being. Translated by Joan Stambaugh. Albany: State University of New York Press, 1992.

Die Frage nach dem Ding. Tübingen: Max Niemeyer, 1962.

Four Seminars. Translated by Andrew Mitchell and Francois Raffoul. Bloomington: Indiana University Press, 2003.

The Fundamental Concepts of Metaphysics: World, Finitude, Solitude. Translated by William McNeill and Nicholas Walker. Bloomington: Indiana University Press, 1995.

Hegel's Phenomenology of Spirit. Translated by Parvis Emad and Kenneth Maly. Bloomington: Indiana University Press, 1988.

The History of the Concept of Time. Translated by Theodore Kissiel. Bloomington: Indiana University Press, 1992.

Hölderlin's Hymn "Der Ister." Translated by William McNeill and Julia Davis. Bloomington: Indiana University Press, 1996.

Identity and Difference. Translated by Joan Stambaugh. New York: Harper & Row, 1969.

Introduction to Metaphysics. Translated by Gregory Fried and Richard Polt. New Haven: Yale University Press, 2000.

Kant and the Problem of Metaphysics. 5th ed. Translated by Richard Taft. Bloomington: Indiana University Press, 1997.

The Metaphysical Foundations of Logic. Translated by Michael Heim. Bloomington: Indiana University Press, 1992.

Nietzsche. Vols. 1–4. Translated and edited by David Farrell Krell. San Francisco: Harper & Row, 1991.

On the Way to Language. Translated by Peter D. Hertz. San Francisco: Harper & Row, 1982.

"Only a God Can Save Us: Der Spiegel's Interview with Martin Heidegger." *Philosophy Today* 20 (1976): 267–84.

Ontology — The Hermeneutics of Facticity. Translated by John van Buren. Bloomington: Indiana University Press, 1999.

Parmenides. Translated by André Schuwer and Richard Rojcewicz. Bloomington: Indiana University Press, 1992.

Pathmarks. Edited by William McNeill. New York: Cambridge University Press, 1998.

Phänomenologie und Theologie. Frankfurt am Main: Vittorio Klostermann, 1970.

"Phänomenologische Interpretationen zu Aristoteles." *Dilthey-Jahrbuch* 6 (1989): 237–74.

Phenomenological Interpretations of Aristotle, Initiation into Phenomenological Research. Translated by Richard Rojcewicz. Bloomington: Indiana University Press, 2001.

The Phenomenology of Religious Life. Translated by Matthias Fritsch and Jennifer Anna Gosetti-Ferencei. Bloomington: Indiana University Press, 2004.

"Phenomenological Interpretations with Respect to Aristotle." Translated by Michael Baur. *Man and World* 25 (1992): 358–93.

Plato's Sophist. Translated by Richard Rojcewicz and André Schuwer. Bloomington: Indiana University Press, 1997.

Poetry, Language, Thought. Translated by Albert Hofstadter. New York: Harper & Row, 1971.

The Principle of Reason. Translated by Reginald Lilly. Bloomington: Indiana University Press, 1991.

The Question concerning Technology and Other Essays. Translated by William Lovitt. New York: Harper & Row, 1977.

Schelling's Treatise on the Essence of Human Freedom. Translated by Joan Stambaugh. Athens, Ohio: Ohio University Press, 1985.

"Das 'Sein' (Ereignis)." *Heidegger Studies* 15 (1999): 9–15.

"The Self-Assertion of the German University." Translated by Karsten Harries. *Review of Metaphysics* 38 (1985): 469–80.

On Time and Being. Translated by Joan Stambaugh. Chicago: University of Chicago Press, 2002.

Vier Seminare. Frankfurt a.M.: Klostermann, 1977.

Was ist das — die Philosophie? Neske: Pfullingen, 1966.

What Is Called Thinking? Translated by J. Glenn Gray. New York: Harper & Row, 1968.

Zur Sache des Denkens. Tübingen: Max Niemeyer Verlag, 1976.

Secondary Sources

Birault, Henri et al. *L'Existence de Dieu*. Doornik: Casterman, 1961.

Braun, Hans-Jürg, ed. *Martin Heidegger und der christliche Glaube*. Zürich: Theologischer Verlag, 1990.

Brito, Emilio. "Le déracinement du vrai et la 'fuite des dieux' d'après les 'Questions fondamentales de philosophie' de Heidegger." *Revue d'Histoire et de Philosophie Religieuses* 74 (1994): 171–91.

———. "Le 'dernier Dieu' dans les 'Contributions á la philosophie' de M. Heidegger." *Église et théologie* 28 (1997): 45–75.

———. *Heidegger et l'hymne du sacré*. Leuven: Leuven University Press, 1999.

———. "Le sacré dans le cours de Heidegger sur 'La Germanie' de Hölderlin." *Science et Esprit* 47 (1995): 33–68.

———. "Le sacré dans les 'Éclaircissements' pour la poésie de Hölderlin de M. Heidegger." *Ephemerides Theologicae Lovanienses* 71 (1995): 337–69.

———. "Les Dieux, le sacré et le poète dans la conference 'Le poème' de Heidegger." *Nouvelle Revue Theologique* 117 (1995): 724–42.

———. "Les théologies de Heidegger." *Revue Théologique de Louvain* 27 (1996): 432–61.

Brkic, Pero. *Martin Heidegger und die Theologie: Ein Thema in dreifacher Fragestellung*. Mainz: Matthias Grünewald Verlag, 1994.

Buchheim, Thomas, ed. *Destruktion und Übersetzung: zu den Aufgaben von Philosophiegeschichte nach Martin Heidegger*. Weinheim: VCH, Acta Humaniora, 1989.

Bultmann, Rudolf. *Geschichte und Eschatologie*. Tübingen: Mohr, 1958.

Buren, John van. *The Young Heidegger: Rumor of the Hidden King*. Bloomington: Indiana University Press, 1994.

Caputo, John D. *Heidegger and Aquinas: Aan Essay on Overcoming Metaphysics*. New York: Fordham University Press, 1982.

———. "Heidegger's God and the Lord of History." *New Scholasticism* 57 (1983): 439–64.

Casper, Bernhard, Klaus Hemmerle, and Peter Hünermann. *Besinnung auf das Heilige*. Freiburg: Herder, 1966.

Coriando, Paola-Ludovica. *Der letzte Gott als Anfang: zur ab-gründigen Zeit-Räumlichkeit des Übergangs in Heideggers 'Beiträge zur Philosophie.'* Munich: Wilhelm Fink Verlag, 1998.

Coriando, Paola-Ludovica, ed. *Herkunft aber bleibt stets Zukunft, Martin Heidegger und die Gottesfrage.* Frankfurt a.m.: Klostermann, 1998.

Dahlstrom, Daniel O. "Heidegger's Method: Philosophical Concepts as Formal Indications." *The Review of Metaphysics* 47 (1993–94): 775–95.

Danner, Helmut. *Das Göttliche und der Gott bet Heidegger.* Meisenheim am Glan: Verlag Anton Hain, 1971.

Denker, Alfred. *Omdat filosoferen leven is, een archeologie van Martin Heideggers 'Sein und Zeit.'* Best: Damon, 1997.

Derrida, Jacques. *Psyché. Inventions de l'autre.* Paris: Galilée, 1987.

Duque, Félix. "Gegenbewegung der Zeit: die hermeneutische Verschiebung der Religion in der Phänonomenologie des jungen Heidegger." *Heidegger Studies* 15 (1999): 97–116.

Esposito, Costantino. "Die Geschichte des letzten Gottes in Heideggers *Beiträge zur Philosophie.*" *Heidegger Studies* 11 (1995): 33–59.

Fehér, István M. "Heidegger's Understanding of the Atheism of Philosophy: Philosophy, Theology, and Religion in His Early Lecture Courses Up to *Being and Time.*" *American Catholic Philosophical Quarterly* 69 (1995): 189–228.

———, ed. *Wege und Irrwege des neueren Umganges mit Heideggers Werk, Ein deutsch-ungarisches Symposium.* Berlin: Duncker & Humblot, 1991.

Feuerbach, Ludwig. *The Essence of Christianity.* Translated by George Eliot. New York: Harper & Row, 1957.

Frank, Manfred. *Der kommende Gott, Vorlesungen über die neue Mythologie.* Frankfurt a.M.: Suhrkamp Verlag, 1982.

Frithjof, Rodi, ed. *Dilthey-Jahrbuch für Philosophie und Geschichte der Geisteswissenschaften,* vol. 4, 1986–87. Göttingen: Vandenhoeck & Ruprecht, 1987.

Gadamer, Hans Georg. *Gadamer: Gesammelte Werke.* Tübingen: Mohr, 1987.

Gander, Hans-Helmuth, ed. *"Verwechselt mich vor allem nicht!" Heidegger und Nietzsche.* Frankfurt a.M.: Vittorio Klostermann, 1994.

Gethmann-Siefert, Annemarie. *Das Verhältnis von Philosophie und Theologie im Denken Martin Heideggers.* Freiburg: Karl Alber, 1974.

Gethmann-Siefert Annemarie, ed. *Philosophie und Poesie: Otto Pöggeler zum 60. Geburtstag.* Stuttgart: Frommann-Holzboog, 1988.

Gethmann-Siefert, Anne Marie and Otto Pöggeler, eds. *Heidegger und die praktische Theologie.* Frankfurt a.M.: Suhrkamp Verlag, 1988.

Greisch, Jean. "The Eschatology of Being and the God of Time in Heidegger." Translated by Dermot Moran. *International Journal of Philosophical Studies* 4, no. 1 (1996): 17–42.

Grondin, Jean. *Sources of Hermeneutics.* Albany: State University of New York Press, 1995.

Guignon, Charles. *The Cambridge Companion to Heidegger.* Cambridge: Cambridge University Press, 1993.

Haar, Michel. "Heidegger and the God of Hölderlin." *Research in Phenomenology* 19 (1989): 89–100.

————, ed. *Cahier de l'herne, Martin Heidegger.* Paris: Editions de l'herne, 1983.

Hadot, P., ed. *Historisches Wörterbuch der Philosophie.* Darmstadt: Wissenschaftliche Buchgesellschaft, 1971.

Hanley, Catriona. *Being and God in Aristotle and Heidegger: The Role of Method in Thinking the Infinite.* Lanham: Rowman & Littlefield, 2000.

Happel, M., ed. *Heidegger — neu gelesen.* Würzburg: Königshausen & Neumann, 1997.

Hatab, Lawrence. "Heidegger and Myth: A Loop in the History of Being." *Journal of the British Society for Phenomenology* 22 (1991): 45–64.

Hegel, G. W. F. *Aesthetics.* 2 vols. Translated by T. Knox. London: Oxford University Press, 1975.

————. *Lectures on the Philosophy of Religion.* 3 vols. Translated by R. F. Hodgson and J. M. Stewart. Berkeley and Los Angeles: University of California Press, 1984–87.

Helting, Holger. *Heideggers Auslegung von Hölderlins Dichtung des Heiligen, Ein Beitrag zur Grundlagenforschung des Daseinsanalyse.* Berlin: Duncker & Humblot, 1999.

Helting, Holger. *Heidegger und Meister Eckehart: Vorbereitende Überlegungen zu ihrem Gottesdenken.* Berlin: Duncker & Humblot, 1997.

Hemmerle, Klaus, Casper Bernhard, and Peter Hünermann. *Besinnung auf das Heilige.* Freiburg: Herder, 1966.

Herrmann von, Friedrich-Wilhelm. *Wege ins Ereignis, zu Heideggers 'Beiträge zur Philosophie.'* Frankfurt a.M.: Vittorio Klostermann, 1994.

Heyde, Ludwig. *The Weight of Finitude: On the Philosophical Question of God.* Translated by Alexander Harmsen and William Desmond. Albany: State University of New York Press, 1999.

————. *Het gewicht van de eindigheid, Over de filosofische vraag naar God*. Amsterdam: Boom, 1995.

Hick, John. *An Interpretation of Religion: Human Responses to the Transcendent*. London: MacMillan, 1989.

Hübner, Hans. "Martin Heideggers Götter und der christliche Gott; Theologische Besinnung über Heideggers 'Besinnung' (Band 66)." *Heidegger Studies* 15 (1999): 127–54.

Husserl, Edmund. *Formal and Transcendental Logic*. Translated by Dorion Cairns. The Hague: Nijhoff, 1969.

Jaspers, Karl. *Der philosophische Glaube angesichts der Offenbarung*. Munich: Piper, 1962.

Jaspert, Bernd. *Sachgemäße Exegese, Die Protokolle aus Rudolf Bultmann Neutestamentlichen Seminaren 1921–1951*. Marburg: N. G. Elwert Verlag, 1996.

————, ed. *Rudolf Bultmanns Werk und Wirkung*. Darmstadt: Wissenschaftliche Buchgesellschaft, 1984.

Jung, Matthias. *Das Denken des Seins und der Glaube an Gott: Zum Verhältnis von Philosophie und Theologie bei Martin Heidegger*. Würzburg: Königshausen & Neumann, 1990.

Kant, Immanuel. *Critique of Pure Reason*. Translated by Werner S. Pluhar. Indianapolis: Hackett, 1966.

————. *Werke in zehn Bänden*. Edited by W. Weischedel. Darmstadt: Wissenschaftliche Buchgesellschaft, 1975.

Kearney, Richard. "Heidegger and the Possible." *Philosophical Studies* 27 (1980): 176–95.

Kearney, R., and J. O'Leary J., eds. *Heidegger et la question de Dieu*. Paris: Bernard Grasset, 1980.

Kisiel, Theodore. *The Genesis of Heidegger's "Being and Time."* Berkeley and Los Angeles: University of California Press, 1993.

Kisiel, Theodore and John van Buren, eds. *Reading Heidegger from the Start: Essays in His Earliest Thought*. Albany: State University of New York Press, 1994.

Köchler, Hans. *Politik und Theologie bei Heidegger: Politischer Aktionismus und theologische Mystik nach 'Sein und Zeit.'* Innsbruck: Arbeitsgemeinschaft für Wissenschaft und Politik, 1991.

Kockelmans, Joseph J., ed. *A Companion to Martin Heidegger's "Being and Time."* Washington, D.C.: University Press of America, 1986.

Kovacs, George. *The Question of God in Heidegger's Phenomenology.* Evanston, Ill.: Northwestern University Press, 1990.

Krebs, Klaus Hans. *Der Strittige Rang des Seins, eine Untersuchung ze dem Problem des Heiligen in der Spatphilosophie Martin Heideggers.* Ph.D. diss, Department of Philosophy, Johannes Gutenberg-Universität zu Mainz, Bonn, 1971.

Landolt, Eduard. *Der einzige Heidegger. Eine Deutung nach dem systematischen Index.* Heidelberg: C. Winter, 1992.

Law, David R. "Negative Theology in Heidegger's *Beiträge zur Philosophie.*" *International Journal for Philosophy of Religion* 48 (2000): 139–56.

Lehmann, Karl. "Christliche Geschichtserfahrung und ontologische Frage beim jungen Heidegger." *Philosophisches Jahrbuch* 74 (1966): 126–53.

Löwith, Karl. *Heidegger — Denker in dürftiger Zeit.* Göttingen: Vandenhoeck & Ruprecht, 1965.

Luther, Martin. *Martin Luthers Werke, kritische Gesamtausgabe.* Weimar: Böhlau, 1883.

Macquarrie, John. *An Existentialist Theology: A Comparison of Heidegger and Bultmann.* Harmondworth: Penguin Books, 1973.

Marx, Karl, and Frederick Engels. *Collected Works.* London: Lawrence & Wishart, 1975.

Marx, Werner. *Gibt es auf Erden ein Maß? Grundbestimmungen einer nichtmetaphysischen Ethik.* Hamburg: Felix Meiner, 1983.

Müller, Christian. *Der Tod als Wandlungsmitte, Zur Frage nach Entscheidung, Tod und Letztem Gott in Heideggers 'Beiträge zur Philosophie.'* Berlin: Duncker & Humblot, 1999.

Nietzsche, Friedrich. *The Gay Science.* Translated by Walter Kaufmann. New York: Vintage, 1974.

———. *The Portable Nietzsche.* Edited and translated by Walter Kaufmann. New York: Vintage, 1980.

———. *Kritische Studienausgabe.* Edited by G. Colli and M. Montinari. Munich: Dt. Taschenbuch-Verlag, 1980.

Noller, Gerhard, ed. *Heidegger und die Theologie, Beginn und Fortgang der Diskussion.* Munich: Kaiser Verlag, 1967.

Ochwadt C., and E. Tecklenborg, eds. *Das Mass des Verborgenen, Heinrich Ochsner 1891–1970, zum Gedächtnis.* Hannover: Charis-Verlag, 1981.

Olivetti, Marco M., ed. *Filosofia della rivelazione.* Padova: CEDAM, 1994.

Ott, Hugo. *Martin Heidegger: Unterwegs zu seiner Biographie.* Frankfurt a.m.: Campus Verlag, 1988.

Otto, Rudolf. *The Idea of the Holy: An Inquiry into the Non-rational Factor in the Idea of the Divine and Its Relation to the Rational.* Translated by John W. Harvey. London: Oxford University Press, 1958.

Otto, W. F. *Die Gestalt und das Sein. Gesammelte Abhandlungen über den Mythos und seine Bedeutung für die Menschheit.* Darmstadt: Wiss. Buchges., 1959.

———. *Die Musen und der Göttliche Ursprung des Singens und des Sagens.* Düsseldorf: Dietrichs, 1955.

———. *Das Wort der Antike.* Stuttgart: Klett, 1962.

Papenfuß, Dietrich, and Otto Pöggeler, eds. *Zur philosophische Aktualität Heideggers.* 3 vols. Frankfurt a.M.: Vittorio Klostermann, 1990.

Pico della Mirandola. *On the Dignity of Man, On Being and the One, Heptaplus.* Translated by Charles Glenn Wallis, Paul J. W. Miller, and Douglas Carmichael. Indianapolis: Bobbs-Merill Educational Publishing, 1965.

Pöggeler, Otto. *Der Denkweg Martin Heideggers.* Pfullingen: Neske, 1963.

———. "Heideggers Begegnung mit Hölderlin." *Man and World* 10 (1977): 13–61.

———. "Martin Heidegger und die Religionsphänomenologie." *Edith Stein Jahrbuch* 2 (1996): 15–30.

———. *Martin Heidegger's Path of Thinking.* Translated by Daniel Magurshak and Sigmund Barber. Atlantic Highlands, N.J.: Humanities Press, 1995.

———. *Neue Wege mit Heidegger.* Freiburg: Karl Alber, 1992.

Pöggeler, Otto, ed. *Heidegger, Perspektiven zur Deutung seines Werkes.* Königstein: Athenäum, 1984.

Pöltner, Günther, ed. *Auf der Spur des Heiligen, Heideggers Beitrag zur Gottesfrage.* Wien: Böhlau Verlag, 1991.

Prudhomme, Jeff Owen. *God and Being: Heidegger's Relation to Theology.* Atlantic Highlands, N.J.: Humanities Press, 1997.

Ruff, Gerhard. *Am Ursprung der Zeit.* Berlin: Duncker & Humblot, 1997.

Sartre, Jean-Paul. *L'être et le néant.* Paris: Gallimard, 1943.

———. *Existentialism and Humanism,* Translated by Philip Mairet. London: Eyre Methuen, 1989.

Schaeffler, Richard. *Frömmigkeit des Denkens? Martin Heidegger und die katholische Theologie.* Darmstadt: Wissenschaftliche Buchgesellschaft, 1978.

Schleiermacher, F. D. E. *On Religion: Speeches to Its Cultured Despisers.* Edited by Richard Crouter. New York: Cambridge University Press, 1996.

Schüßler, Werner, ed. *Religionsphilosophie.* Freiburg: Karl Alber Verlag, 2000.

Schütte, Hans-Walter. *Religion und Christentum in der Theologie Rudolf Ottos.* Berlin: Verlag Walter De Gruyter, 1969.

Scott, Charles, et al., eds. *Companion to Heidegger's "Contributions to Philosophy."* Bloomington: Indiana University Press, 2001.

Sheehan, Thomas, ed. *Heidegger: The Man and the Thinker.* Chicago: Precedent Publishing, 1981.

Spaemann, Robert, and Reinhard Löw. *Die Frage Wozu? Geschichte und Wiederentdeckung des teleologischen Denkens.* Munich: Piper, 1981.

Spinoza, Baruch. *The Ethics and Selected Letters.* Translated by Samuel Shirley. Indianapolis: Hackett, 1982.

Splett, Jörg. *Die Rede vom Heiligen, über ein religionsphilosophisches Grundwort.* Freiburg: Karl Alber, 1971.

Stambaugh Joan. "The Question of God in Heidegger's Thought." *Southwestern Journal of Philosophy* 10 (1979): 127–38.

Thomä, D. *Die Zeit des Selbst und die Zeit danach. Zur Kritik der Textgeschichte Martin Heideggers 1910–1976.* Frankfurt a.M.: Suhrkamp Verlag, 1990.

Thurnher, Rainer. "Gott und Ereignis — Heideggers Gegenparadigma zur Onto-Theologie." *Heidegger Studies* 8 (1992): 81–102.

Topitsch, Ernst, ed. *Probleme der Wissenschaftstheorie: Festschrift für V. Kraft.* Wien: Springer, 1960.

Trocholepczy, Bernd. *Rechtfertigung und Seinsfrage, Anknüpfungen und Widerspruch in der Heidegger-Rezeption Bultmanns.* Herder: Freiburger theologischer Studien, 1991.

Vedder, Ben. "Heidegger's Notion of the Last God and Revelation." *Archivio de Filosofia* 62, nos. 1–3 (1994): 553–64.

————. "Die Faktizität der Hermeneutik: Ein Vorschlag." *Heidegger Studies* 12 (1996): 95–107.

————. "From the Historicality of Dasein to the Historicality of the Gods." In *Thirty-third Annual Heidegger Conference Proceedings.* Chicago: DePaul University, 1999, 1–12.

————. "Heidegger on Desire." *Continental Philosophy Review* (formerly *Man and World*) 31 (1998): 353–68.

————. "How to Trace the Notion of Desire in Heidegger's Work." In *Proceedings of Heidegger Conference Thirty-first Annual Meeting.* University Park, Pa.: The Pennsylvania State University, 1997): 1–11.

————. "Religion and Hermeneutic Philosophy." *International Journal for the Philosophy of Religion* 51 (2002): 39–54.

————. *Was ist Hermeneutik?* Stuttgart: Kohlhammer, 2000.

Vries de, Hent. *Philosophy and the Turn to Religion.* Baltimore: The Johns Hopkins University Press, 1999.

Vycinas, Vincent. *Earth and God: An Introduction to the Philosophy of Martin Heidegger.* The Hague: Martinus Nijhoff, 1961.

Index

absence of God, 4, 155, 273–74.
  See also gods
absolute foundation, 119
actualitas, 113, 271–72
actualization, 52–59, 74–75, 113, 243
actualization-sense. *See* sense-
  orientations
actual vs. the possible, 242–45
actus purus, 96, 113
"Age of the World Picture, The"
  (Heidegger), 196–97, 204
alētheia, 192–93, 209–10, 251
ambition, worldly, 63
ambitio saeculi, 63
"Anaximander Fragment"
  (Anaximander), 194
another beginning, 160, 176, 184
Anschauung, 22
anthropology, 116, 122–23, 197–99
anthropomorphic interpretation,
  206–07
Antichrist, 55
Aquinas, Thomas. *See* St. Thomas
  Aquinas
Aristotle, 6, 18, 95–109, 104–09,
  270–71
"As When on a Holiday" (Hölderlin),
  216–19
atheism, 5, 28, 189–90, 210, 266–69
attraction and withdrawal, 245
attuning, longing for, 261–62
aufheben, 83–84

Augustine. *See* St. Augustine
"Augustine and Neo-Platonism"
  (Heidegger), 59
authentic entity, 98–102. *See also*
  highest entity
authentic future, 73

Basic Problems of Phenomenology, The
  (Heidegger), 238
beata vita/beatific life, 59–65
beauty, 60
becoming, 146
being: as *actualitas,* 113, 271–72;
  Aquinas on, 114; Aristotle on,
  98–103; *brauchen* of, 194; and
  Dasein, 244–45; and divinity, 210;
  and entities, 13, 99–100, 159, 250,
  272; essence of, 60, 160; and faith,
  77; finitude of, 174; forgetfulness of,
  161–62, 169, 207–08; and God,
  193–95; of gods, 164–70; Greek
  philosophers on, 248; ground of,
  107–12; highest, 107–12, 119, 200;
  historicality of, 160, 183, 186, 213;
  history of, 166–67; and the holy, 9,
  192, 205, 276–77; and human
  subjectivity, 125; as idea, 139–40;
  and *logos,* 250; meaning of, 130–32;
  and metaphysics, 159; nearness to,
  206–11; ontic and ontological
  questions, 93–112, 103; philosophy as
  a way of, 41; and the possible,

329